SOUTHEAST ASIAN LITERATURES IN TRANSLATION

ASIAN STUDIES AT HAWAII

The Publications Committee of the Asian Studies Program will consider all manuscripts for inclusion in the series, but primary consideration will be given to the research results of graduate students and faculty at the University of Hawaii. The series includes monographs, occasional papers, translations with commentaries, and research aids.

Orders for back issues and future issues should be directed to The University Press of Hawaii, 535 Ward Avenue, Honolulu, Hawaii 96814. Present standing orders will continue to be filled without special notification.

Asian Studies at Hawaii, No. 9

SOUTHEAST ASIAN LITERATURES IN TRANSLATION:

A Preliminary Bibliography

by

Philip N. Jenner
Department of Indo-Pacific Languages
University of Hawaii

Asian Studies Program
University of Hawaii

The University Press of Hawaii
1973

The Asian Studies Program of the University of Hawaii offers
multidisciplinary course work leading to the bachelor's and
master's degrees in East Asian, Southeast Asian, and South
Asian Studies. In addition, it encourages research and
scholarly projects related to Asia. Many departments of the
University of Hawaii award advanced degrees for studies
dealing with Asia.

Library of Congress Catalog Card Number 72-619667

ISBN 0-8248-0261-6

Copyright © 1973 by The University Press of Hawaii

Manufactured in the United States of America

CONTENTS

INTRODUCTION

This bibliography, as its title indicates, is a work in progress. The response of colleagues and students to earlier versions with limited distribution made it clear that there was demand for compilation of this sort and it was felt that even in its present form the bibliography made a substantial contribution toward meeting this need.

Practical considerations have imposed two major limitations on the work. On the one hand it draws heavily on the holdings of the University of Hawaii library system, but other sources have been tapped wherever possible. Professor Jenner is continually adding to this collection and he hopes to be able to publish a more broadly based version in future. He is most grateful for suggestions from others which have aided in broadening the present collection and hopes that this volume will stimulate others to make further suggestions in the future. The second limitation is that the works are primarily in English and French and secondarily in Dutch and German, but this too reflects the limitation of library resources and time. Moreover, as the bibliography was designed originally to make Southeast Asian literature available to students here at University of Hawaii and elsewhere it was practical to concentrate on these languages initially.

Despite these limitations the work represents an impressive selection not just in terms of the total number of items included but also in the range of material presented. All the nations of Southeast Asia are represented by substantial sections, and every sort of literature from the early inscriptions and folklore to modern short stories is covered. To help guide the reader through the collection Professor Jenner has commented briefly on certain works which he considers especially important and has asterisked entries found to be of unusual interest in the classroom. In the concluding Section X the reader will find a list of books which will give the beginner a general orientation to the scholarly literature on Southeast Asia should he wish to go deeper into their cultures. Beyond these brief comments Professor Jenner has not attempted to annotate the works as he feels it is still too early to make value judgments especially as there is risk of confusing the quality of the translation with that of the original. He also does not wish to prejudice the reader, but rather to encourage him to explore the field and develop his

own tastes. Practical constraints have made it impossible
for the collection to be either exhaustive or in any way
selectively representative, but I believe that there is more
than enough here to stimulate and delight the reader. Just
perusing the titles sets one wondering. I want to know more
about "Lawyer Rabbit," and "Choo and his Melons," and what
happened in "A Harsh Frolic." What sort of man finds him-
self "Between two unfinished worlds" and how does he per-
ceive those worlds, and what was it about "Ballot No. 15"
that made it important? Recent events in Southeast Asia
have focused attention most painfully on the area, but it
is time that Westerners knew more about it than can be
learned from newspaper reports. This volume gives anyone
interested an invaluable tool which can help him toward an
understanding of the complex and varied peoples who consti-
tute Southeast Asia, not as Western scholars see them but
as they have seen themselves.

Alice G. Dewey

FOREWORD

What follows is a recasting and amplification of two
earlier bibliographies of the same title given limited distribution on 25 February 1970 and 1 September 1971 for use
in my two-semester survey of Southeast Asian literatures.
Like its predecessors, this new version is based on holdings
in the University of Hawaii Library system, primarily in
English and French, secondarily in Dutch and German. No
claim is made that it is either exhaustive or selective,
but the work now includes a good number of items obtainable
from local private collections or on interlibrary loan.

Because of its concern with literature in translation,
the bibliography may well be unique. It is not to be compared with the monumental work of Embree and Dotson (item
3369), which includes rich Literature and Folklore sections
but has a narrower geographical range and a publication date
of 1950. Apart from this, I know only of the unpublished
compilation of Mrs. Catalina A. Nemenzo, *Southeast Asian
Languages and Literature in English, 1624-1966*, which its
author informs me has 7,459 entries including, for example,
3,829 items on Philippine literature alone and 164 items on
Indonesian literature.

In a work of this modest size I have not felt it neces-
sary to discriminate translations from purely expository
works, and have accordingly mingled these two types of entry
under the most appropriate subhead. Thus Deydier's "Le Râmâyana au Laos" (item 2322), which is not a translation, is
given under Hindu-Buddhist Literature along with entries
which are translations.

My failure to annotate the bibliography more liberally
is referable to a feeling that it is too early to be making
serious value-judgments of the works cited and that qualita-
tive commentary risks confusing translations with their ori-
ginals, at least at this stage of our knowledge. I fear too
that fuller annotations might prejudice users of the bibliography for or against certain entries, which is precisely
what I wish to avoid at this time. I have sought to compen-
sate for this reticence by detailing the contents of entries
I consider especially important and by asterisking items
found to be of particular interest in the classroom.

Many friends, students as well as colleagues, have contributed to the bibliography, and to them collectively go my sincere thanks. To the Asian Studies Program and to the Graduate Research Council of the University of Hawaii I express herewith gratitude for generous grants in support of an extended sojourn in Paris during the winter of 1969-70 for collaboration on the bibliography with French and Southeast Asian colleagues and for acquisition of relevant materials. The Asian Studies Program made another grant, for which I am no less appreciative, to enable me to return to Paris in the summer of 1970 to continue the work of the previous winter.

14 July 1972   P.N.J.

A NOTE ON PERSONAL NAMES

Any system of alphabetizing personal names is bound to confuse users of a work encompassing writers from as many different backgrounds as does this. The only principle followed consistently here has been to retain the order of the various components of personal names as I have found them associated with the specific texts cited.

In general, the surname, when this exists, is given in block capitals and is used as the basis of alphabetization. For example: Maurice DURAND, J. Kasem SIBUNRUANG, Bienvenido LUMBERA.

Subordinating particles found with certain surnames (e.g., *de, van, na, bin*) are kept in lower case but, being part of the surname, are used as the basis of alphabetization. For example: Clodualdo del MUNDO, listed under *d*; R. van ECK, listed under *v*; V. na PRAMUANMARG, listed under *n*.

Because of their instability, titles and other adjuncts have been distinguished from personal names proper by being given in italics. For example: M. J. BARUCH, *Thao* Nhouy ABHAY, *Raden Adjeng* KARTINI, *Dra. Mrs* THIO, *Mom* Dusdi PARIBATRA.

Burmese names proper are given in block capitals and arranged by their first element. For example, TET TOE is listed before THAN SWE, while *U* SAUNG comes before SAW SHWE BOH. Titles occurring with Burmese names will pose a problem for users of the bibliography both because of their number and changeability and because syllables of the same shape may be names in their own right (e.g., *Maung* MAUNG, *U* KYIN U). Toponyms are treated as attributes separable from the true name and are hence given in italics: *Bhamo* NYO NWE, *Sagaing* MIN AUNG. Hybrid names are arranged according to their Burmese constituents: Pearl AUNG, Kenneth BA SEIN, Marlene KHIN GYI.

In a patently Arabic name such as Zainal Abidin bin ABDUL WAHID we have a patronymic (cf. Icelandic *Hjálmarsson*) consisting of *bin* 'son (of)' followed by a binary male personal name and listed under *b*. The name Asmah binti *Haji* OMAR is similarly a patronymic (cf. Icelandic *Hjálmarsdóttir*) consisting of *binti* 'daughter (of)' and a male personal name preceded by a religious title; it too is listed under *b*.

Other Islamic names such as Asrul SANI and Abdul MUIS, originally inseparable constructions, seem to be in the process of reanalysis, possibly under Javanese or Western influence, and developing in the direction of given name plus surname. Both with this class and with the class of unbonded names such as Yahya ISMAIL and Mohammed Taib OSMAN, the final constituent is treated as a surname and used as the basis of alphabetization.

In the case of Vietnamese names I have noted firstly the small inventory of family names (which stand first in normal order), and secondly the modern practice of identifying the individual by his given name, and have used the third syllable as the basis of arrangement (e.g., Thai van KHIEM, Doan-thi-DIEM). The same thing is done even when the intercalary particle or middle name is crowded out by a compound given name (e.g., Nguyen-chong-HUAN). I foresee objections to this practice, but point out in its defense that arrangement by surnames would be less efficient.

With Chinese names from Malaysia, Singapore and elsewhere I have had to follow the same usage because of the impossibility of knowing whether the traditional ordering of the name has been tampered with in translated materials and also because of the increasing incidence of hybrid names; hence, Lee Kok LIANG, Wong Phui NAM, Margaret LEONG, Siew Yue KILLINGLEY.

Among Chinese as well as Vietnamese names this practice has resulted in a number of departures from convention (e.g., Ho Chi MINH, Han SUYIN), which, however, should not inconvenience the reader as much as if exceptions were admitted.

Royal names and clerical names stand apart from the foregoing and have been handled on an individual basis.

A number of authors, finally, are identified with their works only by initials (e.g., E.F.D., M.K., T.M.K., V.L.). These are treated as units and arranged by their first letter even when the names for which they stand are known or can be surmised with some certainty.

ABBREVIATIONS

A   *Atlantis.*

AA   *Artibus Asiae.*

A/AQCS   *Asia: Asian Quarterly of Culture and Synthesis.*

AFS   *Asian Folklore Studies* (Society for Asian Folklore, Tokyo),
            formerly *Folklore Studies: Journal of Far Eastern Folklore*
            (S.V.D. Research Institute, Tokyo), formerly *Folklore
            Studies* (The Catholic University of Peking).

AH   *Asian Horizon.*

ALB   *The Adyar Library Bulletin.*

AM   *The Asia Magazine* (Hongkong).

AMaj   *Asia Major.*

AmAn   *American Anthropologist.*

AO   *Acta Orientalia.*

ArOr   *Archiv Orientalny.*

AS   *Asian Studies* (University of the Philippines).

B   *Burma.*

BA   *Books Abroad.*

BEFEO   *Bulletin de l'Ecole Française d'Extrême-Orient.*

BJRL   *Bulletin of the John Rylands Library* (Manchester).

BSEI   *Bulletin de la Société des Etudes Indochinoises.*

BSOAS   *Bulletin of the School of Oriental and African Studies, Univer-
            sity of London.*

BTLV   *Bijdragen tot de Taal-, Land- en Volkenkunde.*

BTLVNI   *Bijdragen tot de Taal-, Land- en Volkenkunde van Nederlandsch-
            Indië.*

EB   *Encyclopedia Britannica.*

ER	*Excursions et Reconnaissances* (Saigon).
F	*Forward* (Rangoon).
FA	*France-Asie*.
FA/A	*France-Asie / Asia*.
FEQ	*The Far Eastern Quarterly*.
G	*The Guardian* (Rangoon).
IAL	*Indian Arts and Letters*.
ITC	*Institute of Traditional Cultures* (Madras).
JA	*Journal asiatique*.
JAF	*Journal of American Folklore*.
JAOS	*The Journal of the American Oriental Society*.
JAS	*The Journal of Asian Studies*.
JBRS	*The Journal of the Burma Research Society*.
JEAS	*Journal of East Asiatic Studies* (University of the Philippines).
JH	*The Journal of History* (Manila).
JMBRAS	*Journal of the Malayan Branch of the Royal Asiatic Society*.
JOIUB	*Journal of the Oriental Institute of the University of Baroda*.
JSEAH	*Journal of Southeast Asian History*.
JSS	*Journal of the Siam Society*.
PAIBL	*Publications de l'Académie des Inscriptions et Belles-Lettres*.
RHR	*Revue de l'Histoire des Religions*.
SMJ	*Sarawak Museum Journal*.
VBQ	*Visvabharati Quarterly*.
ZB	*Zeitschrift für Buddhismus*.

SOUTHEAST ASIAN LITERATURES IN TRANSLATION

I. BURMA

GENERAL

1. Anonymous, "Burmese Palm-Leaf Books," adaptation from Burmese, in *F*, III.7 (15 November 1964): 18-20.

2. Anonymous, "Congratulations for Magwe," in *G*, XIII (1966).12: 5-6.

3. Anonymous, "Culture: Burmese Literature and Language," in *F*, II.20 (22 May 1964): 6.

4. Anonymous, "Culture: Karen Literary Contest," in *F*, VI.3 (15 September 1967): 4.

5. Anonymous, "Culture: Karen Literature," in *F*, IV.10 (1 January 1966): 3.

6. Anonymous, "Education: Literacy Campaign," in *F*, IV.16 (1 April 1966): 3.

7. Anonymous, "Education: Literacy Campaign," in *F*, V.17 (15 April 1967): 3.

8. Anonymous, "Federation of Writers and Journalists," in *G*, XV (1968). 12: 5.

9. Anonymous, "High Rate of Literacy," in *G*, XV (1968).5: 5.

10. Anonymous, "Illiteracy," in *G*, IX (1962).7: 6-7.

11. Anonymous, "In Honour of Writers of Today," in *G*, XV (1968).12: 5.

12. Anonymous, "Karen Literature," in *F*, III.9 (15 December 1964): 3.

13. Anonymous, "Kawthoolei: Karen Literature," in *F*, IV.4 (1 October 1965): 3.

14. Anonymous, "Literacy & Translation Commission," in *F*, II.3 (7 September 1963): 4.

15. Anonymous, "Literature," in *F*, II.11 (7 January 1964): 7.

16. Anonymous, "Literature: Entries for Literary Awards," in *F*, VI.1 (15 August 1967): 4.

17. Anonymous, "Literature: Prizes Awarded for Best Works of 1967," in *F*, VII.9 (15 December 1967): 4-5.

18. Anonymous, "Literature: Sarpay Beikman Awards," in *F*, III.9 (15 December 1964): 2-3.

19. Anonymous, "Literature: Sarsodaw Day Awards Presented," in *F*, VI.9 (15 December 1967): 5.

20. Anonymous, "Literature: Sarpay Beikman Board," in *F*, III.12 (1 February 1965): 2-3.

21. Anonymous, "Literature: 1964 Sarpay Beikman Prizes for Literature," in *F*, IV.9 (15 December 1965): 2-4.

22. Anonymous, "Literature for Children," in *F*, IV.4 (1 October 1965): 3.

23. Anonymous, "Mons Have Their Place," in *G*, IV (1957).3: 7.

24. Anonymous, "Power of the Pen," in *G*, XIV (1967).1: 5.

25. *Anonymous, "Printing the First Burmese Alphabet," by a Tavoyan, in *G*, IV (1957).2: 29-30.

26. Anonymous, "Samplings of Burmese Authors," translated by K., in *G*, IV (1957).8: 17-8; 10: 36-7.

27. Anonymous, "Sarpay Beikman," in *F*, II.3 (7 September 1963): 3-4.

28. Anonymous, "Sarsodaw Nay: Writers' Day," in *G*, XV (1968).12: 4.

29. Anonymous, "War Against Illiteracy," in *F*, VII.12 (1 February 1969): 1.

30. Anonymous, "Why Literacy?," in *G*, XV (1968).3: 5.

31. BA KYA and Gordon H. LUCE, "A Dictionary of Burmese Authors (translation)," in *JBRS*, 10 (1920): 137-54.

32. Anthony Herbert CHRISTIE, "Indonesia: Cultures in Historic Times," in *EB (1962)*, 12: 274a-6a.

33. *C.W. DUNN, HLA PE, and J.A. STEWART, "Country Life in Burmese Literature," in *BSOAS*, XII (1948).3-4: 703-12.

34. *Prof. U E MAUNG, "A Short Survey of Burmese Literature," in *G*, VIII (1961).9: 36.

35. *R. HALLIDAY, *The Talaings* (Rangoon: Superintendent, Government Printing, Burma, 1917), 129-46. On Mon language and literature.

36. Godfrey Eric HARVEY, "Burma: History," in *EB (1962)*, 4: 426b-9a.

37. *HLA MAUNG, "The Sociology of Burmese Literature," in *G*, IV (1957).
    4: 27-9.

38. KHIN SWE HLA, "Burmese Names," in *G*, VI (1959).10: 37-9.

39. Jordi LERMAS, "La Birmanie entr'ouvre ses trésors littéraires," in
    FA, XV (1958).143: 105-7.

40. *G.H. LUCE, "Mon Culture," in *G*, II.7 (May 1955): 27-9.

41. *Gordon H. LUCE, *Old Burma - Early Pagán*, by... assisted by Bo-Hmu
    Ba Shin, U Tin Oo, the Staff of the Burma Historical Commission,
    the Burma Archaeological Department, and Many Other Friends. Pub-
    lished for *Artibus Asiae* and The Institute of Fine Arts, New York
    University. *Artibus Asiae*..., Supplementum 25 [in 3 volumes]
    (Locust Valley, New York: J.J. Augustin, 1969-70). Definitive work
    on the archeology, architecture, and art of Pagan, with numerous
    references to Hindu-Buddhist literature.

42. *Dr* MAUNG PHYU and TAN GWAN LEONG, "Education: Bilingual or Unilin-
    gual?," in *G*, XIV (1967).5: 26-31.

43. *U NU*, "Burma's World of Letters," in *G*, IV (1957).2: 14-6.

44. NYO MYA, "The Press in Burma: A Thumb-nail Sketch," in *G*, IV (1957).
    8: 15-6.

45. *U ON PE, "Modern Burmese Literature: Its Background in the Indepen-
    dence Movement," in *Perspective of Burma* [item 48], 152-6.

46. *Maung* PE KYWE and MAUNG THEIKPA, "Exploration in the Ruins of Old
    Prome," in *F*, IV.24 (1 August 1966): 5-13.

47. *U* PE MAUNG TIN, "Some Features of the Burmese Language," in *JBRS*,
    39.2 (December 1956): 193-202.

48. *Perspective of Burma*. Supplement to *The Atlantic Monthly*, 201.2
    (February 1958). Valuable collection of articles and translations.

49. *U* SHWE MRA, "Divine Language," in *G*, XIV (1967).4: 29-32.

50. SHWAY YOE [= *Sir* James G. Scott], *The Burman: His Life and Notions*.
    With an Introduction by John K. Musgrave. The Norton Library, N212
    (New York: W.W. Norton, 1963), Chapter LXI, "Selections from the
    Literature," 566-76.

51. TET TOE, "Burmese Is Difficult," in *F*, II.3 (7 September 1963): 21.

52. *TET TOE, "The Renaissance of the Thirties," in *F*, I.21 (7 June 1963): 21-2.

53. *TET TOE, "Post-war Burmese Writing: Fiction," in *F*, I.23 (7 July 1963): 15-6.

54. TET TOE, "Post-war Burmese Writing: Non-fiction," in *F*, I.24 (22 July 1963): 19-20.

55. *U THEIN HAN, "A Study of the Rise of [the] Burmese Novel," in *G*, XV (1968).3: 45. Summary of an address.

56. Hugh TINKER, "A Short Survey of Burmese History," in *G*, VIII (1961). 12: 44.

57. *VUM KO HAU, "The First Printed Burmese Book," in *G*, VIII (1961).2: 17-9.

58. *Ma YI YI*, "Burmese Sources for the History of the Konbaung Period, 1752-1885," in *JSEAH*, 6 (1965).1: 48-66.

FOLK LITERATURE

59. Anonymous, "A Burmese Love Song," in *Indian Antiquary*, 23 (1894): 262-3. Burmese text with translation.

60. Anonymous, "Tunes from the Past: Songs of Oolay," in *G*, VII (May 1960): 8-9.

61. Pearl AUNG, "Competing with Rich Neighbours," a Burmese folk tale retold by..., in *F*, VI.7 (15 November 1967): 11.

62. Pearl AUNG, "The Selfish Hunter," a Kachin folk tale retold by..., in *F*, VI.10 (1 January 1968): 11.

63. Pearl AUNG, "Maung Peak Kyaing," a Burmese folk tale retold by..., in *G*, XV (1968).9: 10-1.

64. Pearl AUNG, "The Snake Princess," Burmese folk tales retold by..., in *G*, XV (1968).10: 24-5.

65. Pearl AUNG, "The Prince of Thihapura," Burmese folk tales retold by..., in *G*, XV (1968).11: 26-7.

66. Pearl AUNG, "Ngamoyeik the Crocodile," Burmese folk tales retold by..., in *G*, XV (1968).12: 24-5.

67. Pearl AUNG, "Four Deaf People," Burmese folk tales retold by...,
     in *G*, XVI (1969).1: 38-9.

68. Pearl AUNG, "Four Foolish Friends," Burmese folk tales retold by..
     . , in *G*, XVI (1969).2: 25-6.

69. Pearl AUNG, "The Food Fit for Kings," Burmese folk tales retold by
     ..., in *G*, XVI (1969).3: 25-6.

70. Kenneth BA SEIN, "Popular Rhymes," selected Burmese folk songs,
     translated by..., in *G*, IX (1962).2: 24.

71. Kenneth BA SEIN, "Nursery Songs," selected Burmese folk songs,
     translated by..., in *G*, IX (1962).3: 15.

72. Kenneth BA SEIN, "Miscellaneous Folk Songs," translated by..., in
     G, IX (1962).4: 40.

73. Kenneth BA SEIN, "Rural Life," translated by..., in *F*, II.17 (7 Ap-
     ril 1964): 19.

74. Kenneth BA SEIN, "A Rural Rhapsody," translated by..., in *F*, IV.3
     (15 September 1965): 22.

75. Kenneth BA SEIN, "Burmese Proverbs and Parables," in *G*, XII (1965).
     8: 34.

76. Kenneth BA SEIN, "Burmese Proverbs and Parables," in *G*, XIII (1966).
     5: 34.

77. Kenneth BA SEIN, "Rural Drum Songs," translated by..., in *F*, IV.10
     (1 January 1966): 16.

78. Kenneth BA SEIN, "An Old *Aing* Song," translated by..., in *F*, V.9
     (15 December 1966): 23.

79. Kenneth BA SEIN, "The Parrots She Has Bred," a 16th-century nursery
     rhyme, translated by..., in *G*, XIV (1967).1: 31.

80. Kenneth BA SEIN, "The Matchless Maiden," a 19th-century *lungyin*,
     translated by..., in *F*, VI.4 (1 October 1967): 11.

81. H. BHOLST, "The Tale of Master Head," a Burmese tale, in *G*, IV
     (1957).11: 24.

82. Eleanor BROCKETT, *Burmese and Thai Fairy Tales*, Retold by... (Lon-
     don: Frederick Muller, 1965).

83. H. CALTHROP, *Burmese Tales and Sketches*, No. 1 (Calcutta: Thacker,
     1895).

84. Harold FIELDING-HALL, *Palace Tales* (London: Harper, 1899).

85. John S. FURNIVALL, "Three Songs," in *JBRS*, 3 (1913): 34-9. Burmese text with translation.

86. H. GO SUAN NANG, "Leng Tong Moih," a Chin legend, very much abridged, in *G*, IX (1962).3: 46-7.

87. H. GO SUAN NANG, "The Little Chicken's Revenge," a Chin folk tale, in *G*, IX (1962).6: 42.

88. G.E.R. GRANT-BROWN, "Translation of Burmese Songs," in *JBRS*, 1 (1911): 99-102.

89. Rao Bahadur GUPTE, "Some Burmese Proverbs," in *Indian Antiquary*, 51 (1922): 227-8.

90. *Ludu U* HLA, "Bo Hein," a Chin folk tale, translated by E., in *F*, V. 15 (15 March 1967): 11.

91. *Ludu U* HLA, "Double Fatigue for Tongue-wagging," an Inle folk tale, translated by K., in *F*, V.16 (1 April 1967): 18.

92. *Ludu U* HLA, "Two Stubborn Jungle Cocks," a Somra Naga folk tale, translated by K., in *F*, V.18 (1 May 1967): 22.

93. *Ludu U* HLA, "True Love," a Taung-yo folk tale, translated by K., in *F*, VII.4 (1 October 1968): 10.

94. *Ludu U* HLA, "The Cock, the Bullocks and the Buffaloes," a Palaung folk tale, translated by K., in *F*, VII.6 (1 November 1968): 17.

95. *Ludu U* HLA, "Rich in Wisdom Too," a Burmese folk tale, translated by K., in *F*, VII.7 (15 November 1968): 17.

96. *Ludu U* HLA, "U Pan Hmway's Method," an East Karen folk tale, translated by K., in *F*, VII.11 (15 January 1969): 11.

97. *U HLA PE, *Burmese Proverbs*. Wisdom of the East series. UNESCO Collection of Representative Works, Burmese Series (London: John Murray, [c 1962]). Best available work on the subject.

98. *Maung HTIN AUNG, "Burmese Crocodile Tales," in *Folk-Lore*, 42 (1931): 79-82.

99. *Maung HTIN AUNG, *Burmese Folk-Tales* (Calcutta: Oxford University Press, 1948).

100. *Maung HTIN AUNG, *Burmese Law Tales: The Legal Element in Burmese Folklore* (London: Oxford University Press, 1962).

101. *Dr* HTIN AUNG, *Burmese Folk Tales*. Magnetic tape recording (27 minutes). Asia Society Presents series.

102. *Maung* HTIN AUNG and Helen G. TRAGER, *A Kingdom Lost for a Drop of Honey, and Other Burmese Folktales*. Illustrated by Paw Oo Thet (New York: Parents' Magazine Press, [c 1968]).

103. K., "Rice Pounding Songs," translated by..., in *G*, II.6 (April 1955): 44.

104. K., "Rice Pounding Songs," translated by..., in *G*, II.8 (June 1955): 42.

105. K., "Rice Pounding Songs," translated by..., in *F*, IV.8 (1 December 1965): 22.

106. K., "Ahsha," a Palaung folk tale, translated by..., in *F*, VI.6 (1 November 1967): 22.

107. K., *"Ozi* Songs," translated by..., in *F*, III.1 (15 August 1964): 22; III.2 (1 September 1964): 22.

108. K., "Old 'Waiting' Songs," translated by..., in *F*, III.6 (1 November 1964): 22.

109. K., "Boat Songs," translated by..., in *F*, III.7 (15 November 1964): 21.

110. K., "Karen-Aw Songs," translated by..., in *F*, III.8 (1 December 1964): 22.

111. K., "Mon Songs," translated by..., in *F*, III.9 (15 December 1964): 23.

112. K., *"Dohpat* Songs," translated by..., in *F*, III.11 (15 January 1965): 23.

113. K., "An Old Ballad," translated by..., in *F*, III.12 (1 February 1965): 21.

114. K., "Royal Drum Songs," translated by..., in *F*, III.19 (15 May 1965): 26.

115. K., *"Aing* Song (Bathetic)," translated by..., in *F*, IV.2 (1 September 1965): 22.

116. K., *"Byaw*-drum Songs," translated by..., in *F*, IV.5 (15 October 1965): 22.

117. K., *"Aing* Song (Ironic)," translated by..., in *F*, IV.7 (15 November 1965): 11.

118. K., "Old *Aing* Song," translated by..., in *F*, IV.9 (15 December 1965): 17.

119. K., "An Old *Aing* Song," translated by..., in *F*, V.2 (1 September 1966): 22.

120. K., "*Bongyi* Songs," translated by..., in *F*, V.7 (15 November 1966): 22.

121. K., "Farmer-Figure Vaunting Song," translated by..., in *F*, V.12 (1 February 1967): 19.

122. K., "Songs of the Shwebo Drums," translated by..., in *F*, V.14 (1 March 1967): 22.

123. K. and G.H.L., "Folk Songs," translated by..., in *G*, II.2 (December 1954): 40.

124. *U* KHIN ZAW, "Rice Pounding Songs," collected and translated by..., in *Perspective of Burma* [item 48], 125.

125. *U* KHIN ZAW, "A Folk-song Collector's Letter," in *F*, I.17 (7 April 1963): 20-2; I.13 (7 February 1963): 19-20; I.12 [*sic*] (22 January 1963 [*sic*]): 29-30.

126. *KIN MAUNG LAT, "Burmese Proverbs: A Supplement to Existing Collections," in *BSOAS*, X (1940-42).1: 31-51.

127. KYI MAY KAUNG, "Beatitude," translated by Min Shin, in Garnett [item 3294], 165-7.

128. LU GALE, "Paddy Planting Songs in Burmese and English," in *JBRS*, 21 (1931): 15-25.

129. *U* LU GALE, "Paddy Planting Songs," recorded by..., translated by K. and J.A.S., in *F*, I.5 (7 October 1962): 20-1. Reprinted from *JBRS*, 21 (1931): 15-25.

130. Gordon H. LUCE, "Leik Kam pha ma Wuttu or The Story of the Turtle," in *JBRS*, 11 (1921): 19-28.

131. F.V. LUSTIG, "Paddy Planting Song," translated by..., in *F*, VII.2 (1 September 1968): 11.

132. M.B.K., "The Legend of Shwekyundaw Reserve," in *G*, VIII (1961).2: 23-4.

133. *Major* Anthony Gilchrist McCALL, "Folk-lore," in his *Lushai Chrysalis* (London: Luzac, 1949), 74-94. Thirteen folk tales.

134. MINTHUWUN, "Min Shwe Ni, the Archer," a Burmese folk tale, in *G*, IV (1957).10: 38-9.

135. MU MU WAIN, "Burmese Folk Tales with Proverbs: The Judge Who Cheated," in *G*, XV (1968).6: 29.

136. PO BYU, "Burmese Proverbs and Sayings," in *JBRS*, 6 (1916): 131-7.

137. *U* PO LATT, "The Jungle," "The Rains," "The Hunter," and "The Fisherman," from *Anthology of Folk Songs* compiled by..., translated by Kenneth Ba Sein, in *F*, I.8 (22 November 1962): 20.

138. *U* PO LATT, "The Weaver," "The Butterfly," and "The Moon and the Stars," from *Anthology of Folk Songs* compiled by..., translated by Kenneth Ba Sein, in *F*, I.10 (22 December 1962): 22.

139. *U* PO LATT, "The Ploughman" and "The Peasant Girl," from *Anthology of Folk Songs* compiled by..., translated by Kenneth Ba Sein, in *F*, I.12 (22 January 1963): 31.

140. *U* PO LATT, "The Peasants Sing," from *Anthology of Folk Songs* compiled by..., translated by Kenneth Ba Sein, in *F*, I.17 (7 April 1963): 23.

141. *U* PO LATT, "[Untitled poem]," from *Anthology of Folk Songs* compiled by..., translated by Kenneth Ba Sein, in *F*, II.8 (22 November 1963): 21.

142. *U* PO THAN, "Out of the Past: Poems from the Burmese," in *G*, XIII (1966).2: 9-10.

143. Maurice RUSSELL, "Mahawthada the Wise," in Garnett [item 3294], 168-74.

144. SAN SHWE BU, "Leik-Kam-Pha-Ma-Wuttu, or The Story of the Turtle (verse)," in *JBRS*, 11 (1921): 19-28.

145. Francis SANG CIN, "Rul Rel, the Lazy Boy," a Chin folk tale, in *G*, VI (1959).9: 43.

146. Francis SANG CIN, "The Golden Princess," a Chin folk tale, in *G*, VIII (1961).3: 46-7.

147. *Sir* J.G. SCOTT, *Burma: A Handbook of Practical Information*. Third Edition, revised (London: Daniel O'Connor, 1921). General remarks on Burmese literature, 426-44; "The History of Tagaung Tanyap," 444-52; specimens of poetry, 452-9.

148. *Prof* Ashraf SIDDIQI, "Folklore in Burma, India and Pakistan," in *G*, IX (1962).8: 33-4.

149. Melford E. SPIRO, *Burmese Supernaturalism: A Study in the Explanation and Reduction of Suffering.* Prentice-Hall College Anthropology Series (Englewood Cliffs, New Jersey: Prentice-Hall, [c 1967]), notably Chapters II, III, and IV.

150. Francis STORY, "Myth and Magic in Burma," in *G,* VIII (1961).1: 21-2. Reprinted from *Eastern World* (1960).

151. *Maung* THAN SEIN and Alan DUNDES, "Twenty-three Riddles from Central Burma," in *JAF,* 77.303 (January–March 1964): 69-75.

152. *U* WI, "Some Burmese Riddle Verses," translated by..., in *Perspective of Burma* [item 48], 121.

153. M. Allan WILLIAMS, "The Snake Prince and the Youngest of Seven Sisters," a Burmese folk tale [in verse], in *G,* XII (1965).11: 19-20.

154. M. Allan WILLIAMS, "The Lazy Man," a Burmese folk tale [in verse], in *G,* XIII (1966).1: 34-5.

155. M. Allan WILLIAMS, "The Eclipse of the Moon," a Burmese folk tale [in verse], in *G,* XIII (1966).2: 22-3.

156. [M. Allan WILLIAMS,] "How the Crocodile Lost Its Tongue," a Burmese folk tale [in verse], in *G,* XIII (1966).3: 30-1.

157. M. Allan WILLIAMS, "Master Thumb," a Burmese folk tale [in verse], in *G,* XIII (1966).5: 14-5.

158. M. Allan WILLIAMS, "Maung Pauk Kyaing," a Burmese folk tale [in verse], in *G,* XIII (1966).6: 28-9.

159. M. Allan WILLIAMS, "Daywaw," a Burmese folk tale [in verse], in *G,* XIII (1966).8: 18-9.

160. *M. Allan WILLIAMS, "Lawyer Rabbit," a Mindat Chin folk tale [in verse], in *G,* XIII (1966).9: 16.

161. M. Allan WILLIAMS, "Three Precious Sentences," a Shan and Padaung folk tale [in verse], in *G,* XIII (1966).10: 14-5.

162. M. Allan WILLIAMS, "Po Seik and Mai Kha," a Burmese folk tale [in verse], in *G,* XIII (1966).11: 20-1.

163. M. Allan WILLIAMS, "The Kingdom of the Deaf," a Burmese folk tale [in verse], in *G,* XIV (1967).2: 34.

164. M. Allan WILLIAMS, "If Dreams Come True," a Burmese folk tale [in verse], in *G,* XIV (1967).3: 27.

165. M. Allan WILLIAMS, "Chain Reaction," a Burmese folk tale [in verse], in *G*, XIV (1967).4: 21.

166. M. Allan WILLIAMS, "Maung Po and the Tiger," a Burmese folk tale [in verse], in *G*, XIV (1967).5: 24-5.

167. *M. Allan WILLIAMS, "The Rabbit and the Tiger," a Burmese folk tale [in verse], in *G*, XIV (1967).6: 28.

168. M. Allan WILLIAMS, "A Guide to Gossips," a Mon folk tale [in verse], in *G*, XIV (1967).7: 46.

169. M. Allan WILLIAMS, "An Unheard of Tale," a Karen folk tale [in verse], in *G*, XIV (1967).8: 22.

170. M. Allan WILLIAMS, "Mister Courageous," a Kachin folk tale [in verse], in *G*, XIV (1967).10: 26-8.

171. M. Allan WILLIAMS, "Why the Bat Goes About Only at Night," a Lushai folk tale [in verse], in *G*, XIV (1967).12: 45.

172. M. Allan WILLIAMS, "The Frog Maiden," a Burmese folk tale [in verse], in *G*, XV (1968).1: 32-3.

173. M. Allan WILLIAMS, "The Bamboo Pitcher," a Karen folk tale [in verse], in *G*, XV (1968).2: 42-3.

174. M. Allan WILLIAMS, "Hkun Sak," an Arakanese-Shan-Padaung folk tale [in verse], in *G*, XV (1968).4: 26-8.

175. M. Allan WILLIAMS, "The Magic Tongs of Pagan," a Burmese folk tale [in verse], in *G*, XV (1968).7: 42.

176. M. Allan WILLIAMS, "An Itching Palm and an Aching Back," a Burmese folk tale [in verse], in *G*, XV (1968).8: 32.

177. M. Allan WILLIAMS, "A Lay-Brother's Trespass," a Burmese folk tale [in verse], in *G*, XV (1968).8: 47.

178. M. Allan WILLIAMS, "Rubies, Tigers and Crocodiles," a Burmese folk tale [in verse], in *G*, XV (1968).11: 48.

179. M. Allan WILLIAMS, "Mai Htway and the Big Tortoise," a Burmese folk tale [in verse], in *G*, XV (1968).12: 38-40.

180. M. Allan WILLIAMS, "The Eleven Brothers and One Sister," a Shan folk tale [in verse], in *G*, XVI (1969).1: 26-7.

181. M. Allan WILLIAMS, "Princess Mwaynoon and Prince Nanda," a Mon folk tale [in verse], in *G*, XVI (1969).3: 34-7.

BUDDHIST LITERATURE

182. Vivian BA, "A Burmese Painting of the *Nimi-Jātaka* 1869 by Saya Ko
      Kya Nyun in the Musée Guimet of Paris (a Description and Commen-
      tary)," in *G*, XIII (1966).2: 33-43.

183. *Mabel Haynes BODE, *The Pali Literature of Burma* (London: Royal
      Asiatic Society of Great Britain and Ireland, 1966).

184. Marguerite-Marie DENECK, "Un manuscrit birman au Musée Guimet: Le
      Nimi-Jātaka," in *BSEI*, Nouvelle Série, XXVII (1952).1: 63-78.

185. *Pierre DUPONT, *La version mône du Nārada-jātaka*. Publications de
      l'Ecole Française d'Extrême-Orient, Volume XXXVI (Saigon: Ecole
      Française d'Extrême-Orient, 1954).

186. *Charles DUROISELLE, "Upagutta et Mara," in *BEFEO*, 4 (1904): 414-28.
      Critical presentation of a Buddhist legend.

187. James GRAY, *Ancient Proverbs and Maxims from Burmese Sources; or,
      The Niti Literature of Burma* (London: Trubner, 1886).

188. G.H. LUCE, "The 550 *jātakas* in old Burma," in *AA*, XIX (1956).3-4:
      291-307.

189. *U* SEIN TU, miscellaneous verses from *The Lokanīti*, translated by...,
      in *G*, XII (1965).2: 28 ("On the Sage," viii, ix); 3: 13 ("On the
      Sage," x, xi, xii); 4: 16 ("On the Sage," xiii, xiv, xv); 5: 17
      ("On the Sage," xvi, xvii, xviii); 7: 30 ("On the Sage," xxiii,
      xxiv, xxv, xxvi); 8: 25 ("On the Sage," xxvii, xxviii, xxix, xxx);
      9: 25 ("On the Sage," xxxi, xxxii, xxxiii); 10: 31 ("On the Sage,"
      xxxiv, xxxv, xxxvi, xxxvii, xxxviii); 12: 15 ("On the Good Man,"
      i, ii, iii, ix); *G*, XIII (1966).9: 12 ("On the Foolish Base Man,"
      vii, viii, ix, x, xi); 11: 12 ("On the Friend," i, ii, iii, iv).

190. *U* SHWE MRA, "Some Aspects of Pali Literature," in *G*, XIV (1967).7:
      40-3.

191. Robert F. SPENCER, "Ethical Expression in a Burmese *Jātaka*," in *JAF*,
      79.311 (January-March 1966): 278-301.

192. *Ludwik STERNBACH, "The Pāli *Lokanīti* and the Burmese *Nīti kyan* and
      their sources," in *BSOAS*, XXVI (1963).2: 329-45.

INSCRIPTIONS

193. *C.O. BLAGDEN, "Mon Inscriptions. Section II - The Medieval Mon Records. Nos XIII - XVIII," in *Epigraphica Birmanica*, being lithic and other inscriptions of Burma. Edited by U Mya. Volume IV, Parts I and II (Rangoon: Superintendent, Government Printing and Stationery, 1936).

194. *Chas. DUROISELLE, "The Talaing Plaques on the Ananda Plates," reprinted in *Epigraphica Birmanica*, being Lithic and Other Inscriptions of Burma. Archaeological Survey of Burma, Volume II[,] Parts I and II. Edited by... (Rangoon: Superintendent, Government Printing and Stationery, 1961-1962).

195. *Chas. DUROISELLE, *Epigraphica Birmanica*, being Lithic and Other Inscriptions of Burma. Archaeological Survey of Burma. Volume I[,] Part II, Edited by... (Rangoon: Superintendent, Government Printing and Stationery, Union of Burma, 1960).

196. E.H. JOHNSTON, "Some Sanskrit Inscriptions of Arakan," in *BSOAS*, XI (1944).2: 357-85 + plates.

197. *Gordon H. LUCE, "The Shwegugyi Pagoda Inscription," translated by ..., in *JBRS*, X (1920): 72-4.

198. *Gordon H. LUCE, "Theravada Kingship in Pagan," translation of the Shwegugyi Pagoda Inscription by..., reprinted from *JBRS*, X (1920): 72-4, in Harry J. Benda and John A. Larkin, *The World of Southeast Asia: Selected Historical Documents* (New York: Harper & Row, [c 1967]), 34-7.

199. J.A. STEWART, "Burmese Dedicatory Inscription of A.D. 1683," in *BSOAS*, VII (1933-35).3: 541-4.

200. Ma YI YI, "Burmese Sources for the History of the Konbaung Period, 1752-1885" [item 58].

CHRONICLES

201. *PE MAUNG TIN and G.H. LUCE, *The Glass Palace Chronicle*. Translated by... (Oxford: at the Clarendon Press, 1923).

202. *PE MAUNG TIN and G.H. LUCE, *The Glass Palace Chronicle*. Translated by... (Rangoon: Rangoon University Press, 1960).

203. *Sir* James George SCOTT, "Hsenwi State Chronicle," in *G*, XIV (1967). 1: 27-31.

204. *Ma* YI YI, "Burmese Sources for the History of the Konbaung Period, 1752-1885" [item 58].

PRE-MODERN PROSE AND POETRY

205. *Thiri Pyana U* AUNG THAN, "Padethayaza: Poet of the Peasants," in *F*, II.2 (22 August 1963): 12-3.

206. BA HAN, "Shin Uttamagyaw and His Tawla: a Nature Poem (trans.)," in *JBRS*, 7 (1917): 172-3, 261-2; 8 (1918): 29-31, 150-1, 261-2; 9 (1919): 25-6, 107-8, 149-50; 10 (1920): 14.

207. BA HAN, "Seindakyawthu: Man and Poet," in *JBRS*, 8 (1918): 107-11.

208. BA HAN, "Letwethondara's Poem," in *JBRS*, 12 (1922): 34.

209. Kenneth BA SEIN, "Her Anxiety," translated by..., in *F*, IV.19 (15 May 1966): 22. Composed in the late Konbaung period.

210. Kenneth BA SEIN, "Shwebo *Bongyi* Song (Konbaung Period)," translated by..., in *F*, V.16 (1 April 1967): 22.

211. Kenneth BA SEIN, "The Shwemaing Lass," translated by..., in *F*, V. 11 (15 January 1967): 15. A *hangyin* of the Konbaung period.

212. *J.P. CONNOR, "The Ramayana in Burma," in *JBRS*, XV (1925): 80-1.

213. D., C., "Burmese Prosody," in *JBRS*, 2 (1912): 93-4.

214. HLA PE, "Dawn Songs," in *BSOAS*, XX (1957): 343-50.

215. HLA PE, "Burmese," in Hatto [item 3296], 181-5.

216. *U* HTIN AUNG, *Epistles Written on the Eve of the Anglo-Burman War.* Translated and Annotated by Maung Htin Aung (The Hague: M. Nijhoff, 1968).

217. K., "Samplings from Burmese Classics: Shin Ottamakyaw and Nawaday Gyi," translated by..., in *F*, II.7 (7 November 1963): 20.

218. KHIN MYO CHIT and WIN PE, "Natshinnaung," in *G*, VI (1959).3: 21-2. On an early poet.

219. *U* KYEE [*d.* 1886], "Rural Life," translated by Kenneth Ba Sein, in *F*, II.15 (7 March 1964): 22. From his *Anthology of Folk Songs*.

220. *U* KYEE, "Bucolic Songs of U Kyee," translated by K., in *F*, III.16
      (1 April 1965): 22; III.21 (15 June 1965): 22; III.22 (1 July
      1965): 21.

221. *U* KYEE, "Come to Our Village Once," translated by Kenneth Ba Sein,
      in *F*, IV.6 (1 November 1965): 22. A rural rhapsody.

222. *U* KYEE, "As Usual During the Rains," translated by Kenneth Ba Sein,
      in *F*, IV.14 (1 March 1966): 22. Composed about 1860.

223. **U* KYEE, "Graceful Is the Country Girl," translated by Kenneth Ba
      Sein, in *F*, V.3 (15 September 1966): 9. A rural song.

224. *U* KYEE, "Welcome to Our Village," translated by M. Allan Williams,
      in *F*, V.4 (1 October 1966): 22.

225. *U* KYEE, "A Sardonic Smile," translated by Kenneth Ba Sein, in *F*, V.
      5 (15 October 1966): 22.

226. **U* KYEE, "Graceful Is the Rural Lass," translated by Kenneth Ba Sein,
      in *G*, XIV (1967).12: 47.

227. *U* KYEE, "The Toddy Tapper (*Luan-gyin*)," translated by Kenneth Ba
      Sein, in *G*, XV (1968).2: 32.

228. KYIN HAN, "Letwethondara's Poem," in *JBRS*, 12 (1922): 35-8, 152.

229. Gordon H. LUCE, "English Poetical Translations of the *Yadus* of the
      Let-we-thondara," in *JBRS*, 6 (1916): 13-7.

230. *Shin* MAHARATTHASARA [1468-1530], "My Absent Love," translated by M.
      Allan Williams, in *G*, XII (1965).3: 26.

231. *Shin* MAHARATTHASARA, "Fair Maid of Ava," translated by M. Allan
      Williams, in *G*, XII (1965).8: 17.

232. *Shin* MAHARATTHASARA, "A Selection from *Gambhisara*," translated by
      Kyaiklat Ohn, in *F*, IV.21 (15 June 1966): 22.

233. *Maha Atula* MINGYI, "*Tagu*," translated by Kenneth Ba Sein, in *G*, XII
      (1965).4: 8. Ode to April.

234. *Maha Atula* MINGYI, "*Tabaung*," translated by Kenneth Ba Sein, in *F*,
      IV.15 (15 March 1966): 22. Ode to March, composed in 1820.

235. *Maha Atula* MINGYI, "*Tagu*," translated by Kenneth Ba Sein, in *F*, V.
      17 (15 April 1967): 22. Ode to April.

236. *Maha Atula* MINGYI, "The Month of *Tabaing* [*sic*]," translated by Maung
      Moe Thant, in *G*, XVI (1969).3: 15. Ode to March.

237. [*Queen*] *Ma* MYA LAY, "Farewell to the Past, My Lord," translated by
      Kenneth Ba Sein, in *F*, IV.20 (1 June 1966): 22. An early 19th-
      century *tedat*.

238. *U* MYAT SAN [*ca*. 1728-1799], "To the Rains of September," translated
      by M. Allan Williams, in *G*, XII (1965).9: 46.

239. *Maung* MYITTA, "Two *Kabyam*'s," in *G*, XV (1968).1: 44.

240. *Letwe* NAWRAHTA, "The Song of the *Bo*-tree Leaves," translated by K.,
      in *F*, IV.24 (1 August 1966): 22. Composed in 1770.

241. [*Lady*] *Shin* NYEIN MAI [*of Taungdwin*], "Do You Want Me, My Love?,"
      translated by Kenneth Ba Sein, in *F*, IV.4 (1 October 1965): 22. A
      17th-century lyric.

242. *Taungdwin Shin* NYEIN MAI, "Dilemma," translated by Kenneth Ba Sein,
      in *G*, XII (1965).10: 12. Composed during the Nyaungyan dynasty.

243. *Lady Shin* NYEIN MAI *of Taungdwin*, "Alas, These Tolls and Taxes!,"
      translated by Kenneth Ba Sein, in *G*, XIII (1966).6: 23. A 16th-
      century [*sic*] *aing-gyin*.

244. *Wungyi* PADAYTHA YAZA [= Padesaraja], "The Ploughman," translated
      freely by M. Allan Williams, in *G*, IX (1962).11: 36. A *tya* song
      composed in the 18th century. See item 245.

245. *Wungyi* PADEṢARAJA [= Padaytha Yaza], "The Peasant," translated by
      K., in *F*, III.24 (1 August 1965): 20. Closer rendering of item 244.

246. *Achoktan Saya* PE [early 19th century], "My Troth," translated by
      M. Allan Williams, in *G*, XII (1965).2: 15.

247. PO BYU, "A Study of Letwe-thondara's Poem Written During His Exile,"
      in *JBRS*, 7 (1917): 45-54.

248. PO BYU, "Shin Uttamagyaw and His *Tawla*: a Nature Poem," in *JBRS*, 7
      (1927): 159-71, 255-61; 8 (1928): 21-9, 143-50, 255-61; 9 (1929):
      15-25, 103-7, 145-9; 10 (1930): 13-4.

249. *Sale U* PONNYA [1812-1867], "Rural Ways," translated by Kenneth Ba
      Sein, in *F*, I.24 (22 July 1963): 22.

250. *U* PONNYA, "Inle Lake," translated by Kenneth Ba Sein, in *F*, IV.11
      (15 January 1966): 22.

251. *U* PONNYA, "Paragon of Beauty," translated by Kenneth Ba Sein, in *F*,
      IV.23 (15 July 1966): 22.

252. *U* PONNYA, "Hide-and-Seek," translated by Kenneth Ba Sein, in *G*, XIV
      (1967).10: 35. A *te-tut* composed during the reign of King Mindon.

253. SAN SHWE BU, "Tase-hna-ra-thi *Ratu* by Ugga Byan (text)," in *JBRS*,
      13 (1923): 232-5.

254. SHWE ZAN AUNG, "The Probable Origin of Burmese Poetry," in *JBRS*, 8
      (1918): 9-14.

255. SHWE ZAN AUNG, "*Ratu*s or Lyrical Poems of Letwethondara," in *JBRS*,
      11 (1921): 98-102.

256. SHWE ZAN AUNG, "Letwethondara's Poem," in *JBRS*, 12 (1922): 153-4.

257. *Theippan* SOE YIN, "Romances of U Ponnya," in *G*, XV (1968).10: 21-2.

258. *J.A. STEWART, "The Song of the Three Mons," in *BSOAS*, IX (1937-39).
      1: 33-9.

259. *Letwe* THONDARA [18th century], "Meza *Ratu* (Ode to the Foothills of
      Meza)," translated by K., in *F*, II.1 (7 August 1963): 12-3.

260. UGGA BYAN [late 16th century], "*Pyatho*," translated from the Arakan-
      ese by M.S. Collis, in *G*, VIII (1961).1: 25. Ode to January.

261. UGGA BYAN, "*Tabodwe*," translated from the Arakanese by M.S. Collis,
      in *G*, VIII (1961).2: 19. Ode to February.

262. UGGA BYAN, "*Tabaung*," translated from the Arakanese by M.S. Collis,
      in *G*, VIII (1961).3: 18. Ode to March.

263. UGGA BYAN, "*Tagu*," translated [from the Arakanese] by M.S. Collis,
      in *G*, XII (1965).9: 13. Ode to April.

264. *U* YAR [18th century], "*Tagu* (April)," translated by Tin U, in *G*, VI
      (1959).4: 11.

MODERN SHORT STORIES

265. Donny AUNG, "Man in a Hurry," in *G*, XII (1965).8: 9-10.

266. Donny AUNG, "The Night of the Storm," in *G*, XIII (1966).3: 40-2, 44.

267. Donny AUNG, "Up in the Clouds," in *G*, XIII (1966).7: 20-5.

268. Donny AUNG, "Powerful Stuff," in *G*, XIII (1966).9: 13-6.

269. Donny AUNG, "The House Across the Street," in *G*, XIV (1967).7: 21-3.

270. Donny AUNG, " The Flaming Skies," in *G*, XV (1968).6: 23-5.

271. Donny AUNG, "The Tree," in *G*, XV (1968).7: 17-20, 22.

272. Donny AUNG, "The Watch," in *G*, XV (1968).8: 38-9.

273. Donny AUNG, "The Collector," in *G*, XV (1968).9: 33-7.

274. Donny AUNG, "The Ghost of Pinewoods," in *G*, XV (1968).12: 41-8.

275. P. AUNG KHIN, "The Rage of the Storm," in *G*, VIII (1961).3: 33-7.

276. P. AUNG KHIN, "Thirteen Black Cats," in *G*, VIII (1961).4: 33-7.

277. P. AUNG KHIN, "Taken In, Taken Out," in *G*, VIII (1961).5: 29-32.

278. P. AUNG KHIN, "A Handful of Roses," in *G*, VIII (1961).9: 39-42.

279. P. AUNG KHIN, "Faith, Hope and Calamity," in *G*, VIII (1961).10: 42-5.

280. P. AUNG KHIN, "The Nimble Fingers," in *G*, VIII (1961).12: 33-6.

281. P. AUNG KHIN, "Love on Second Sight," in *G*, IX (1962).4: 47-8.

282. P. AUNG KHIN, "The Victims of the *Nats*," in *G*, IX (1962).8: 42-3.

283. P. AUNG KHIN, "The Proposal," in *G*, IX (1962).12: 41-4.

284. AUNG BALA, "The Wallet," in *G*, VIII (1961).10: 46.

285. Katherine BA THIKE, "Love and Understanding," in *G*, XIII (1966).8: 39-41.

286. E.T.G., "The Chief," in *G*, XIV (1967).12: 18-21.

287. E.T.G., "Star of Hope," in *G*, XV (1968).3: 12-5.

288. E.T.G., "Gift of the Gods," in *G*, XV (1968).9: 18-20.

289. GAYATNI, "A Real Beauty," translated by T., in *F*, V.18 (1 May 1967): 15-7.

290. *Ko* GYI ZAW, "The Night and the Difference," in *G*, VI (1959).5: 28-30.

291. *Saya* HLA MYINT, "K'wan Chi and a Bottle of Rum," translated by Hal Henti, in *G*, XIII (1966).4: 41-4.

292. HLA YEE YEE, "Return to Me," in *G*, XII (1965).2: 34-5.

293. HTILAR KYIN, "Ma Ma Molly - Mingadaw," in *G*, VIII (1961).7: 43-4; 8: 37-9; 9: 37-8.

294. HTIN FATT, "A Reminiscence," in *G*, XIV (1967).3: 37-8.

295. HTIN LIN, "An Idyll," in *G*, VIII (1961).1: 23-5.

296. K., "Po Thein: Prophet," in *G*, IV (1957).4: 41-5.

297. K., "The Gloom of God," in *G*, IV (1957).5: 9-11.

298. KHIN KHIN SAW, "Friendship in a Garden of Roses," in *G*, XII (1965).
      11: 23-5.

299. KHIN KHIN SAW, "The Night of Errors," in *G*, XIII (1966).3: 15-8; 4:
      21-4.

300. KHIN KHIN SAW, "I Remember When," in *G*, XIII (1966).8: 12-7.

301. KHIN KHIN SAW, "Poor Me! Poor Me! Said the Bachelor," in *G*, XIV
      (1967).6: 18-21.

302. KHIN KHIN SAW, "The Other Ma Pu," in *G*, XIV (1967).8: 20-1.

303. KHIN KHIN SAW, "Till Then, My Darling, Wait for Me," in *G*, XV
      (1968).1: 21-5.

304. KHIN LAT, "Let Not a Dead Tiger Live!," translated by Maung Maung
      Pye, in *G*, XII (1965).4: 14-6.

305. *KHIN MYO CHIT, "The 13-carat Diamond," in *G*, II.11 (September 1955):
      15-9.

306. KHIN MYO CHIT, "The Golden Princess," in *G*, IV (1957).7: 21-2.

307. *Daw KHIN MYO CHIT, "The 13-carat Diamond," in *Perspective of Burma*
      [item 48], 113-6.

308. KHIN MYO CHIT, "A Buddhist Childhood," in *C*, VIII (1961).1: 17-20.
      A chapter from her autobiography.

309. KHIN MYO CHIT, "*Shin Pyu*," in *G*, VIII (1961).4: 19-20. A chapter
      from her autobiography.

310. KHIN MYO CHIT, "The Ruse," in *F*, II.3 (7 September 1963): 22-4.

311. *Daw KHIN MYO CHIT, "The 13-carat Diamond," in Hanrahan [item 3295],
      457-65.

312. KHIN MYO CHIT and HTIN LIN, "*Aye-Yeik-Tha*: Cool and Pleasant Shade,"
      in *G*, VIII (1961).7: 25-7; 8: 25-6. Autobiographical reminiscences.

313. KHIN SWE HLA, "Mu Mu and the Oysters," in *G*, VI (1959).8: 23.

314. *Maung* KO, "Chums," in *G*, IX (1962).10: 45-6.

315. *Maung* KO YU, "The Paradise," translated by [U] Bar Bar, in *G*, XII (1965).5: 27-8.

316. KYAW HTUN, "Ma Moe Wants to be a Crocodile," in *G*, XIV (1967).11: 36-7.

317. KYAW HTUN, "The Card," in *G*, XV (1968).1: 29-30.

318. KYI MA, "Reunion," translated by Maung Lwin Tun, in *G*, XII (1965). 7: 24.

319. KYI MAY KAUNG, "Not Every Needy Poor a Thief Nor Every Hag a Witch," in *G*, IV (1957).1: 37-8.

320. KYI MAY KAUNG, "A Soul in a Soul's Stead," in *G*, IV (1957).9: 32-4.

321. LIN YON NI, "The Thief," translated by U Bar Bar, in *G*, IX (1962). 2: 43-4.

322. LIN YON NI, "Mi Aye," translated by Maung Ko, in *G*, IX (1962).6: 39-40. Reprinted from *Shumawa*, February 1961.

323. M.M., "Stranger Than Fiction," in *G*, XIV (1967).3: 28-9.

324. M.N., "Reminiscences of an Old Rangoon Collegian," in *G*, XIII (1966). 10: 21-5.

325. MA MA LAY, "Irony of Fate," in *G*, VI (1959).7: 33-6; 8: 13-7.

326. *U* MAY AUNG, "Her Belief," translated by J.F. Jackson, in *G*, VI (1959).11: 28-32.

327. *Daw MI MI KHAING, "A Sawbwa Dies," in José [item 3297], 202-12.

328. *Daw* MI MI KHAING, *Burmese Family*. Illustrated by G.N. Kinch (Bloomington: Indiana University Press, [c 1962]).

329. *Sagaing* MIN AUNG, "The Profit," translated by S.K.G., in *F*, V.20 (1 June 1967): 17.

330. MIN SHIN, "Back from the Wars," translated by K., in *F*, I.11 (7 January 1963): 25-7.

331. MIN SHIN, "A Slip of the Hand," translated by Kyi May Kaung, in *F*, II.9 (7 December 1963): 21-2.

332. MIN SHIN, "Beatitude," translated by Kyi May Kaung, in *F*, II.12 (22 January 1964): 21.

333. MIN SHIN, "Village Maiden," translated by Kyi May Kaung, in *G*, IV
      (1957).11: 37-40.

334. MIN SHIN, "Village Maiden," translated by Kyi May Kaung, in *F*, II.
      16 (22 March 1964): 19-21.

335. NYEIN GYAN, "The Stray," in *G*, IX (1962).1: 40-1.

336. *Maung* NYEIN GYAN, "Ma Paun," in *G*, IX (1962).7: 38-40.

337. *Tekkatho* NYO MAY, "The Parting: A Resistance Story," in *G*, II.5
      (March 1955): 20-4.

338. P. MONIN, "Retribution," translated by Ko Ko Aye, in *G*, VIII (1961).
      2: 2.

339. P. MONIN, "Debts," translated by Ko Ko Aye, in *G*, VIII (1961).6:
      39-40.

340. PE THAN, "The Gong Man," in *G*, XIV (1967).9: 20.

341. *Sao* SHIN MUN, "A Cherry Flower from the Land of the Shans," transla-
      ted by Hal Henti, in *G*, XIII (1966).6: 35-6.

342. SEIN TA LAY, "The Hidden Hand," in *G*, IX (1962).3: 38-40.

343. *Dagon* SHWE HMYAR, "The Prince of the Prison," translated by H. Conar,
      in *Perspective of Burma* [item 48], 147-51.

344. *Dagon* SHWE HMYAR, "The Prince of the Prison," translated by H. Conar,
      in Hanrahan [item 3295], 446-57.

345. *Theippan* SOE YIN, "Hla Khin," in *G*, II.1 (November 1954): 42-5.

346. *Theippan* SOE YIN, "Ko Nyo, the Wise Mentor," in *G*, IV (1957).11: 25-
      7.

347. C.A. SOORMA, "The Spy," in *G*, XIV (1967).4: 17-20; 5: 33-8.

348. *Thawda* SWE, "May They Return," translated by K., in *G*, VI (1959).9:
      23-5.

349. *Thawda* SWE, "The *Nat* and I," translated by Khin Myo Chit, in *F*, I.4
      (22 September 1962): 22-3.

350. *Thawda* SWE, "*Nats* and Men," translated by Khin Myo Chit, in *F*, I.6
      (22 October 1962): 20-2.

351. *Thawda* SWE, "Cataracts," translated by Khin Myo Chit, in *F*, I.10 (22
      December 1962): 20-1.

352. *Dagon* TAYA, "Two Lives," translated by U Bar Bar, in *G*, VI (1959). 5: 23-6.

353. *Dagon* TAYA, "The Silken Curtain," translated by U Bar Bar, in *G*, IX (1962).9: 36-8.

354. TET TOE, "The Smile," in *F*, II.4 (22 September 1963): 21-2.

355. TET TOE, "Loving Kindness," in *F*, II.11 (7 January 1964): 28-30.

356. THAN SWE, "A Hardened Heart," translated by Ko Ko Aye, in *G*, VIII (1961).11: 39-41.

357. THAYNLIN YAN NAUNG, "Haven For Me," translated by T., in *F*, V.19 (15 May 1967): 21-3.

358. THEOPHILUS, "Ai Hpun's Sapphire," in *G*, IV (1957).12: 37-9.

359. THU KHA, "Five *Kyat*s," translated [? by U Bar Bar], in *G*, IV (1957). 7: 37.

360. THU KHA, "The Fisherman," translated by U Bar Bar, in *G*, IV (1957). 10: 51-2.

361. TIN SWE, "Mother, Son, Cousins and War," in *G*, XII (1965).3: 30-3.

362. TIN SWE, "Asia for Asians Only," in *G*, XII (1965).12: 21-4.

363. TIN SWE, "His Wallet," in *G*, XIII (1966).9: 47-8.

364. TIN SWE, "Anatomy of Love," in *G*, XIII (1966).12: 24-7.

365. ULAY, "A Grandfather's Love," in *G*, XIV (1967).10: 41.

366. D.R. WEERA, "The Dream," in *F*, I.20 (22 May 1963): 18-21.

367. D.R. WEERA, "The Least He Could Do," in *F*, II.10 (22 December 1963): 12-5.

368. *WIN PE, "The Enlightenment of Koyin Thila," in *G*, IV (1957).10: 27-30.

369. *U WIN PE, "Prelude to Glory," in José [item 3297], 30-42.

370. *U WIN PE, "Prelude to Glory," in *Of Love and Hope* [item 3291], 61-76.

371. *ZAWGYI [= U Thein Han], "His Spouse," translated by Win Pe, in *G*, II. 10 (August 1955): 31-3.

372. *ZAWGYI, "Pagan Market," translated by Kyaw Htun, in *G*, IV (1957).3: 13-5.

373. *ZAWGYI, "His Spouse," translated by Win Pe, in Wigmore [item 3300], 22-8.

374. *ZAWGYI, "His Spouse," translated by Win Pe, in Milton and Clifford [item 3298], 138-43.

375. *ZAWGYI, "His Spouse," translated by U Win Pe, in Shimer [item 3299], 346-51.

376. ZEYA, "The Rose of Youth," translated by Ba Moe, in *G*, XIV (1967).8: 27-8.

THE NOVEL

377. TET TOE, "The Burmese Novel," in *F*, II.7 (7 November 1963): 21-2.

378. TET TOE, "Modern Burmese Novel," in *F*, II.8 (22 November 1963): 22; II.10 (22 December 1963): 21-2.

379. THAN TUN, "Burmese Novel," in *G*, XIV (1967).9: 28-30.

380. TIN SWE, "Burma's First Novel," in *G*, XIII (1966).2: 45-7.

MODERN POETRY

381. AH NWE, "The Firefly," translated by Kenneth Ba Sein, in *G*, XV (1968).1: 12.

382. ANANDA, "All in a Day," in *G*, XV (1968).11: 27.

383. ANANDA THURIYA, "The Law of Nature," translated by Kenneth Ba Sein, in *G*, VIII (1961).1: 50.

384. ANANDA THURIYA, "Poem," rendered into blank verse by M. A[llan]. Williams, in *G*, IX (1962).2: 16.

385. Anonymous, "Observant Little One," in *G*, VIII (1961).4: 24. Reprinted from *The Burma Translation Society Monthly Pamphlet*, April 1952.

386. Anonymous, "In Memoriam," in *G*, XII (1965).7: 42.

387. ANYARTHA, "Taunggyi Town," in *G*, XV (1968).3: 28.

388. ANYARTHA, "Taunggyi Town," in *G*, XV (1968).9: 48 [*sic*].

389. AUNG DUN, "Prize Poetry," in *JBRS*, 7 (1917): 111-4. Prize-winning
      poem in competition sponsored by Burma Research Society; Burmese
      text with translation.

390. AUNG KHAING, "Let's Roam the Beach," in *G*, XIV (1967).7: 48.

391. AUNG SHWE, "The Globate Beau," in *G*, IX (1962).3: 42.

392. AUNG SOE, "Dream Poems," translated by Aung Htut, in *G*, IX (1962).
      4: 13.

393. AUNG THAN TUN, "Day and Life," in *G*, XV (1968).8: 25.

394. *Maung* AUNG TUN, "O River!," in *G*, IX (1962).7: 34.

395. AYE KYI SEIN, "Oh, Monsoon, the New Season," translated by Yangon
      Hla Thein, in *G*, XIII (1966).6: 34.

396. BA MOE, "Our Independence," in *G*, XV (1968).1: 15.

397. BA MOE, "The Undaunted Burman: A Marching Song," translated by...,
      in *G*, XV (1968).5: 42.

398. Kenneth BA SEIN, "The Martyr," in *G*, VI (1959).5: 36.

399. Kenneth BA SEIN, "Poems," in *G*, VI (1959).8: 34-5.

400. Kenneth BA SEIN, "The Pebble," in *G*, VI (1959).11: 35.

401. Kenneth BA SEIN, "Freedom," in *G*, VIII (1961).1: 16.

402. Kenneth BA SEIN, "For the Cause," in *G*, VIII (1961).2: 43.

403. Kenneth BA SEIN, "The Symphony-Bird," in *G*, VIII (1961).3: 31.

404. Kenneth BA SEIN, "Dagon Mail or Dragon-Trail?," in *G*, VIII (1961).4:
      44.

405. Kenneth BA SEIN, "Mutation," in *G*, VIII (1961).5: 37.

406. Kenneth BA SEIN, "Out of the Elements," in *G*, VIII (1961).5: 37.

407. Kenneth BA SEIN, "Pearl Lake," in *G*, VIII (1961).6: 36.

408. Kenneth BA SEIN, "The Three Types," in *G*, VIII (1961).7: 16.

409. Kenneth BA SEIN, "Infidelity," in *G*, VIII (1961).9: 38.

410. Kenneth BA SEIN, "The Master," in *G*, VIII (1961).10: 21.

411. Kenneth BA SEIN, "Two Pagan Cities," in *G*, IX (1962).1: 39.

412. Kenneth BA SEIN, *"Wazo,"* translated by..., in *F*, III.23 (15 July 1965): 21. Ode to July.

413. Kenneth BA SEIN, "The Long Journey," in *G*, XII (1965).2: 30-1.

414. Kenneth BA SEIN, "The Golden Gong," in *G*, XII (1965).3: 42.

415. Kenneth BA SEIN, "The Transgressor," in *G*, XII (1965).7: 11.

416. Kenneth BA SEIN, "Independence," in *G*, XIII (1966).1: 18.

417. Kenneth BA SEIN, *"Tagu,"* translated by..., in *G*, XIII (1966).4: 40. Ode to April.

418. Kenneth BA SEIN, "The Conceited One," translated by..., in *F*, V.1 (15 August 1966): 11. From *Pyithu Tay-than*, edited by U Maung Maung Tin.

419. Kenneth BA SEIN, "A Pilgrim's Prayer," in *G*, XIII (1966).7: 19.

420. Kenneth BA SEIN, "Love and the Intellect," in *G*, XIII (1966).8: 31.

421. Kenneth BA SEIN, "Like the Ivy," in *G*, XIII (1966).10: 36.

422. Kenneth BA SEIN, "Guard This Freedom," in *G*, XIV (1967).1: 26.

423. Kenneth BA SEIN, "The Bonfire," in *G*, XIV (1967).3: 36.

424. Kenneth BA SEIN, "His Guardian," in *G*, XIV (1967).4: 28.

425. Kenneth BA SEIN, "A *Thinggyan* Gift," in *G*, XIV (1967).4: 38.

426. Kenneth BA SEIN, "The Flame That Never Fails," in *G*, XIV (1967).5: 14.

427. Kenneth BA SEIN, "The Little Bird," translated by..., in *G*, XIV (1967).5: 38.

428. Kenneth BA SEIN, "Shan-land Cherries," in *G*, XIV (1967).6: 14.

429. Kenneth BA SEIN, "The Hammer Strikes," in *G*, XIV (1967).6: 21.

430. Kenneth BA SEIN, "Ask Every Shrine," in *G*, XIV (1967).8: 30.

431. Kenneth BA SEIN, "Limbs of Life," in *G*, XIV (1967).11: 30.

432. Kenneth BA SEIN, "Neither Guns Nor Gold," in *G*, XV (1968).2: 38.

433. Kenneth BA SEIN, "I Saw Her Pass," in *G*, XV (1968).3: 39.

434. Kenneth BA SEIN, "Good Deeds Will Last," in *G*, XV (1968).4: 42.

435. Kenneth BA SEIN, "His Hamlet," translated by..., in *F*, VI.15 (15 March 1968): 15.

436. Kenneth BA SEIN, "Fruits of Freedom," in *G*, XVI (1969).1: 15.

437. BA THAN, "On Discovery of Art," in *G*, XII (1965).4: 13.

438. BA THAN, "Definition of a Genius," in *G*, XII (1965).5: 8.

439. BA THAN, "The Earth[l]y Trinity (*Tisarana Lokiya*)," in *G*, XIV (1967).12: 32.

440. BA THAN, "Two Moods on Two Trends of Civilisation," in *G*, XV (1968). 8: 36-7.

441. BA THAN, "The Garden of My Heart," in *G*, XV (1968).11: 24-5.

442. Katherine BA THIKE, "*Thingyan* Is Here!," in *G*, XIII (1966).4: 24.

443. Katherine BA THIKE, "Magical May," in *G*, XIII (1966).5: 44.

444. Katherine BA THIKE, "Nineteenth July," in *G*, XIII (1966).7: 45.

445. Katherine BA THIKE, "O Wonderful Rain!," in *G*, XIV (1967).9: 39.

446. *U* BA YIN, "Little Things Become Larger," translated by..., in *G*, IX (1962).6: 36.

447. BU'TALIN CHITLAY, "So Says the Mother Star," translated by Kenneth Ba Sein, in *G*, XIII (1966).2: 20.

448. BU'TALIN CHITLAY, "Aristocratic Etiquette," translated by Kenneth Ba Sein, in *G*, XIII (1966).3: 14.

449. BU'TALIN CHITLAY, "The Hand That Interposed," translated by Kenneth Ba Sein, in *G*, XIII (1966).4: 39.

450. BU'TALIN CHITLAY, "The Jasmine Refutes," translated by Kenneth Ba Sein, in *G*, XIII (1966).6: 43.

451. BU'TALIN CHITLAY, "I Wish I Couldn't Love," translated by Kenneth Ba Sein, in *G*, XIII (1966).7: 32.

452. BU'TALIN CHITLAY, "Good-will," translated by Kenneth Ba Sein, in *G*, XIII (1966).11: 35.

453. *U* CHAN THA, "Oxford," in *G*, IV (1957).2: 31.

454. CHIN GALAY, "Wan Winmanaw," in *G*, VIII (1961).4: 32.

455. CHIN GALAY, "Ma Sein Aye of Mesai," in *G*, VIII (1961).5: 23.

456. CHIN GALAY, *"Ramwong,"* in *G*, VIII (1961).7: 13.

457. CHIN GALAY, "Ism," in *G*, VIII (1961).9: 23.

458. CHIN GALAY, "M.P.," in *G*, VIII (1961).12: 20.

459. *Maung* CHO PYONE, "Freedom Land," in *G*, VIII (1961).10: 41.

460. E.F.D., "The Land of Pagodas," in *G*, IX (1962).10: 14.

461. E.F.D., "There's a Calling," in *G*, IX (1962).10: 16.

462. E.F.D., "There's a Word," in *G*, IX (1962).11: 18.

463. E.F.D., "The Drunkard's Lament," in *G*, IX (1962).12: 44.

464. G.H.L., "Drum and Pterocarp," translated by..., in *F*, II.16 (22 March 1964): 18.

465. Patricia GARLAN, *"Pongyi,"* in *G*, IX (1962).2: 27.

466. Kenneth C. GODDEN, "My Meiktila," in *G*, IX (1962).5: 35.

467. Hal HENTI, *"Karma,"* in *G*, XIII (1966).1: 20.

468. HLA PE, "Lament," translated by..., in *G*, XII (1965).3: 33.

469. HLA YEE YEE, "If I Die," in *G*, XII (1965).2: 35.

470. HLA YEE YEE, "A Mother's Reveries," in *G*, XIII (1966).6: 17.

471. HLA YEE YEE, "The Tale of a TB Patient," in *G*, XV (1968).8: 44.

472. HLA YEE YEE, "To the Koel," in *G*, XVI (1969).3: 33.

473. HLINE PWINT, "Image of the 'Mirage'," in *G*, XIV (1967).11: 37.

474. HLINE PWINT, "Ingratitude," in *G*, XV (1968).3: 15.

475. HLINE PWINT, "Human Gems," in *G*, XV (1968).10: 9.

476. HLINE PWINT, "Love and Compassion," in *G*, XV (1968).12: 23.

477. HNIN NGWE YI, "A Plea to Death," translated by Moe Thant, in *G*, XIV (1967).6: 48.

478. HNIN NGWE YI, "O, Mother Date!," translated by Maung Moe Thant, in *G*, XV (1968).2: 44.

479. *Popa* HNIN WAY WAY, "Kyet Mauk Nan," translated by F. Lustig, in *G*, XV (1968).6: 30-1.

480. HTILA SITTHU, "O yellow leaf floating down the Mekong," translated by Moe Swe, in *G*, IX (1962).10: 20.

481. HTILA SITTHU, "O yellow leaf floating down the Mekong," translated by Moe Swe, in *G*, IX (1962).11: 22 [*sic*].

482. HTILA SITTHU, "Maw's Summer," translated by K., in *F*, I.20 (22 May 1963): 22.

483. HTILA SITTHU, "Artist's Anxiety," translated by K., in *F*, I.21 (7 June 1963): 20.

484. HTILA SITTHU, "Love's Downstream and Upstream," translated by K., in *F*, II.2 (22 August 1963): 21.

485. *Maung* HTWE AUNG, "The Creator," in *G*, XV (1968).9: 17.

486. *Maung* HTWE AUNG, "Never Say Die," in *G*, XVI (1969).1: 45.

487. *J.A.S., "*Gya E* - The Endless Song," translated by..., in *G*, VIII (1961).5: 25. Reprinted from *Burma Research Society, Fiftieth Anniversary Publications No. 2*.

488. Dorothy M. JORDAN, "Nothing Can Happen in Burma," in *G*, VIII (1961). 3: 23.

489. K., "Roses," translated by..., in *G*, II.1 (November 1954): 14.

490. K., "Said She," translated by..., in *G*, II.11 (September 1955): 38.

491. K., "The Domestic Duck," translated by..., in *G*, II.12 (October 1955): 33.

492. K., "Forward," translated by..., in *F*, III.10 (1 January 1965): 28.

493. K., "Locked Out," translated by..., in *F*, III.15 (15 March 1965): 22.

494. K., "Prayer from Afar," translated by..., in *G*, XIII (1966).1: 42.

495. K., "Dilemma," translated by..., in *F*, IV.12 (1 February 1966): 22.

496. K., "Panglong," translated by..., in *F*, IV.13 (15 February 1966): 22.

497. K., "Ode to *Thingyan*," translated by..., in *F*, IV.17 (15 April 1966): 22.

498. K., "National Anthem (Chorus)," translated by..., in *F*, V.13 (15 February 1967): 22.

499. K., "The Peasant," translated by..., in *F*, V.15 (15 March 1967): 17.

500. K., "Marching Off," translated by..., in *F*, V.20 (1 June 1967): 9.

501. K., "The Burman (The Peoples of the Union of Burma)," translated by..., in *F*, V.23 (15 July 1967): 22.

502. K., "*Pyatho* (the Tenth Burmese Month)," translated by..., in *F*, VI. 11 (15 January 1968): 22. Ode to January.

503. K., "*Wazo* (the fourth month of the Burmese calendar)," translated by..., in *F*, VI.22 (1 July 1968): 6. Ode to July.

504. K.B.T., "Martyr's Day," in *G*, XV (1968).8: 20.

505. KAMRUD DEAN, "Two Mirrors," in *G*, XIV (1967).7: 10.

506. KAMRUD DEAN, "Rise and Fall," in *G*, XIV (1967).8: 9.

507. KAMRUD DEAN, "The Mirror and the Image," in *G*, XV (1968).7: 11.

508. Marlene KHIN GYI, "The Kingdom of the Irrawaddy," in *G*, IX (1962). 5: 43.

509. KHIN KHIN SAW, "Where Art Thou, Little One?," in *G*, XV (1968).10: 30.

510. KHIN MAUNG HTAY, "A Journey, a Yearning," in *G*, IX (1962).10: 29.

511. KHIN MAUNG HTAY, "The Incompatibles," in *G*, XIV (1967).9: 35.

512. KHIN THAN YI, "Mother," in *G*, IX (1962).2: 38.

513. Albert KHIN ZAW, "The Enshrined Voice," in *G*, VI (1959).3: 27.

514. KO KO GYI, "Last Words of a Hero," in *G*, IV (1957).6: 19.

515. Surinder KUMAR, "The Rain Drops," in *G*, XII (1965).7: 47.

516. KYAW SHIN, "The Rural Pagoda," in *G*, XV (1968).3: 20.

517. KYAW WIN, "Naughty Lyrics," in *G*, IX (1962).6: 28.

518. KYI AUNG, "The Girl With the Snake Tattoo," translated by Kenneth

Ba Sein, in *G*, XII (1965).3: 21. From his *A Hundred Moons*.

519. KYI AUNG, "The Painting of *The World by Day*," translated by Kenneth Ba Sein, in *G*, XII (1965).7: 35. From his *A Hundred Moons*.

520. *U* KYIN U, *"Tagu,"* translated by Kenneth Ba Sein, in *G*, IX (1962). 4: 30. Ode to April.

521. *U* KYIN U, "Sea-shells," translated by Kenneth Ba Sein, in *F*, II. 21 (15 June 1964): 16.

522. *U* KYIN U, *"Tabaung,"* translated by M. Allan Williams, in *G*, XII (1965).4: 28. Ode to March.

523. *U* KYIN U, *"Kason,"* translated by Kenneth Ba Sein, in *F*, V.19 (15 May 1967): 17. A *lei-gyo* ode to May.

524. L., "Understanding," in *G*, VIII (1961).12: 23.

525. *Maung* LU PAIN, "The League," in *G*, IV (1957).2: 36.

526. *Maung* LU PAIN, "The Three Sisters," in *G*, IV (1957).3: 35.

527. *Maung* LU PAIN, *"Thingyan* in Retrospect," in *G*, IV (1957).6: 28.

528. *Maung* LU PAIN, "Yeiktha and Kwetthit," in *G*, IV (1957).12: 36.

529. *Maung* LU PAIN, "Cockroach in an Office," in *G*, VI (1959).1: 31.

530. *Maung* LU PAIN, "Four Pieces," in *G*, VI (1959).2: 35.

531. *Maung* LU PAIN, "More Pieces," in *G*, VI (1959).3: 34.

532. *Maung* LU PAIN, "Parodies," in *G*, VI (1959).4: 12.

533. *Maung* LU PAIN, "Poems," in *G*, VI (1959).12: 26-7.

534. *Maung* LU PAIN, "And You, Soldier," in *G*, VIII (1961).1: 26-7.

535. *Maung* LU PAIN, "I Can Do No Wrong," in *G*, VIII (1961).5: 26-7.

536. *Maung* LU PAIN, "The Immaturity of the Mirror," in *G*, VIII (1961). 10: 26-7.

537. *Maung* LU PAIN, "Answering a Peasant," in *G*, IX (1962).1: 18-9.

538. *Maung* LU PAIN, "Let Us Evolve With Honour," in *G*, IX (1962).2: 30.

539. *Maung* LU PAIN, "Man In Our Time," in *G*, IX (1962).5: 26-7.

540. *Maung* LU PAIN, "The Kiss of Death?," in *G*, IX (1962).7: 12.

541. *Maung* LU PAIN, "Brave New Century," in *G*, IX (1962).8: 24.

542. *Maung* LU PAIN, "On Understanding Our Renaissance," in *G*, IX (1962). 9: 16.

543. *Maung* LU PAIN, "Nuclear Determinism," in *G*, IX (1962).10: 26-7.

544. *Maung* LU PAIN, "Half Our Elite Are Phony," in *G*, IX (1962).11: 26-7.

545. *Maung* LU PAIN, "Three Poems," in *G*, IX (1962).12: 26-7.

546. *Maung* LU PAIN, "Let Us Proceed," in *G*, XII (1965).3: 22-3.

547. *Maung* LU PAIN, "I Have Risen," in *G*, XII (1965).4: 26-7.

548. *Maung* LU PAIN, "On Political Detention," in *G*, XII (1965).5: 18-9.

549. *Maung* LU PAIN, "Pygmies In an Age of Giants?," in *G*, XII (1965).8: 18-9.

550. *Maung* LU PAIN, "The Process of Poetry," in *G*, XII (1965).9: 38-9.

551. *Maung* LU PAIN, "The Great Struggle Within," in *G*, XII (1965).10: 26-8.

552. *Maung* LU PAIN, "The Sorrows of Young United Nations," in *G*, XII (1965).11: 26-7.

553. *Maung* LU PAIN, "A New Burma Is Our Business," in *G*, XIII (1966).1: 22-3.

554. *Maung* LU PAIN, "On Revolution," in *G*, XIII (1966).3: 38-9.

555. *Maung* LU PAIN, "Writings on Our Century's Wall: *On Aggreooion* and *On the So-called Nuclear Non-proliferation*," in *G*, XIII (1966).4: 26-7.

556. *Maung* LU PAIN, "Remember the Four Great Absentees," in *G*, XIII (1966).7: 26-8.

557. *Maung* LU PAIN, "A Tremendous Trifle?," in *G*, XIII (1966).8: 26-7.

558. *Maung* LU PAIN, "The Value of Printed Knowledge," in *G*, XIII (1966). 10: 26-7.

559. *Maung* LU PAIN, "An Obscure Old Woman," in *G*, XIII (1966).11: 30-1.

560. *Maung* LU PAIN, "A Presence of Mind," in *G*, XIII (1966).12: 22-3.

561. *Maung* LU PAIN, "The Outcast," in *G*, XIV (1967).1: 18-21.

562. *Maung* LU PAIN, "The Price of Dignity," in *G*, XIV (1967).2: 30-1.

563. *Maung* LU PAIN, "Revelation by an Air-raid," in *G*, XIV (1967).3: 22-3.

564. *Maung* LU PAIN, "Personal and Sentimental," in *G*, XIV (1967).4: 14-6.

565. *Maung* LU PAIN, "Home-coming and Re-appreciation," in *G*, XIV (1967). 6: 40-1.

566. *Maung* LU PAIN, "Yesterday, Today and Tomorrow," in *G*, XIV (1967).7: 26-7.

567. *Maung* LU PAIN, "The World at Midnight," in *G*, XIV (1967).9: 18-9.

568. *Maung* LU PAIN, "An Important Change and Corresponding Counter-Action," in *G*, XIV (1967).9: 26.

569. *Maung* LU PAIN, "Lessons from Aung San," in *G*, XIV (1967).9: 27.

570. *Maung* LU PAIN, "Tribute to Bo Maung Gale," in *G*, XIV (1967).10: 36.

571. *Maung* LU PAIN, "Overheard in an Hotel Lounge," in *G*, XIV (1967).10: 44-5.

572. *Maung* LU PAIN, "Ambition Aflame," in *G*, XIV (1967).12: 22-5.

573. *Maung* LU PAIN, "An Improved National Economy Ahead?," in *G*, XIV (1967).12: 36.

574. *Maung* LU PAIN, "Kite-Flying," in *G*, XV (1968).1: 26-8.

575. *Maung* LU PAIN, "Dilemma and the Way Out," in *G*, XV (1968).1: 38.

576. *Maung* LU PAIN, "National Self-Criticism," in *G*, XV (1968).2: 39.

577. *Maung* LU PAIN, "The View from Kaba Aye Pagoda," in *G*, XV (1968).5: 40.

578. *Maung* LU PAIN, "Looking Back While Going Forward," in *G*, XV (1968). 6: 26-7.

579. *Maung* LU PAIN, "Time and a Time-keeper," in *G*, XV (1968).7: 28.

580. *Maung* LU PAIN, "Socialist Thoughts for Martyr's Day," in *G*, XV (1968).8: 26-8.

581. *Maung* LU SOE, "An Epitaph," in *G*, VI (1959).5: 36.

582. *Maung* LU SOE, "The Prisoner," in *G*, VI (1959).7: 28.

583. Friedrich V. LUSTIG, "An Appraisal of Modern Burmese Poets," in *G*, XIV (1967).10: 9–12.

584. LWIN, "A Respite," in *G*, XIII (1966).9: 33.

585. LWIN, "Life-saver," in *G*, XIV (1967).6: 36.

586. LWIN, "Misfits," in *G*, XIV (1967).7: 30.

587. LWIN, "The Greatest Wall," in *G*, XIV (1967).8: 28.

588. M.K., "Vostok II, the Spaceship," in *G*, VIII (1961).10: 14.

589. M.M.T., "In Memoriam," in *G*, XIV (1967).7: 39.

590. M.M.T., "Advice," in *G*, XV (1968).11: 28.

591. M.M.T., "The Lament of the Princess Myin-Saing," rendered in[to] English by..., in *G*, XV (1968).10: 45.

592. *Mingyi* MAHADAMIKA YAZA, "Burmese Cheroot," translated by Kyaw Win, in *F*, IV.22 (1 July 1966): 22.

593. MAI KHWE, "My Gift Cheroot," rendered into heroic couplet by M. A[1-lan]. Williams, in *G*, IX (1962).4: 27.

594. MAN MYAING, "Martyr's Day," in *G*, XIV (1967).9: 12.

595. Marilyn MAN-THU, "The Flute," in *G*, VI (1959).6: 20.

596. Marilyn MAN-THU, "Nanda and Mwe-lun," in *G*, IX (1962).6: 12.

597. MANLAY, "Time Does Not Wait," in *G*, VIII (1961).12: 26.

598. *U* MAUNG GALE, "*Wazo*," translated by K., in *F*, II.24 (1 August 1964): 20. Ode to July.

599. MAUNG MAUNG, "The Archway of Love," in *G*, IX (1962).2: 40.

600. MAUNG MAUNG, "To a Fallen Leaf," in *G*, IX (1962).4: 32.

601. MAUNG MAUNG GHOSE, "Irrawaddy," in *G*, IX (1962).7: 36.

602. MAUNG MAUNG THAIK, "A Harsh Frolic," in *G*, VI (1959).4: 18.

603. MAUNG MAUNG THAIK, "No Birds Sing," in *G*, VI (1959).5: 17.

604. MAUNG MAUNG THAIK, "Songs," in *G*, VI (1959).9: 20.

605.   MAUNG MAUNG THAIK, "On the Bank of Hlaing," in *G*, VIII (1961).4: 16.

606.   *Kanbe* MAUNG YANKIN, "This Day (to May Day)," translated by K., in *F*, VI.18 (1 May 1968): 11.

607.   MAY, "In the Twilight," in *G*, XVI (1969).2: 11.

608.   MAY AUNG, "The Dying Nation," in *G*, IV (1957).1: 32.

609.   MAY AUNG, "A Cry in the Wilderness," in *G*, VI (1959).1: 27.

610.   MAY MAY KYAING, "Hope of the Night," in *G*, XIV (1967).12: 35.

611.   MAY MAY KYAING, "In Search of a Pastoral Under the Sun," in *G*, XV (1968).1: 41.

612.   MAY MAY KYAING, "Plea to Mankind," in *G*, XV (1968).3: 40.

613.   MAY MAY KYAING, "Nostalgia," in *G*, XV (1968).6: 42-3.

614.   MI MI KHAING, "Sunset," in *G*, XII (1965).2: 48.

615.   MI MI KHAING, "Sunset," in *G*, XII (1965).5: 47 [*sic*].

616.   *Phothudaw U* MIN, "A Fateful Year," translated by Tin Oo, in *G*, IX (1962).7: 22.

617.   *Phothudaw U* MIN, "*Tazaungmon*," translated by Kenneth Ba Sein, in *F*, V.8 (1 December 1966): 11. Ode to November.

618.   *Phothudaw U* MIN, "*Nayon* (the Third Burmese Month)," translated by K., in *F*, V.21 (15 June 1967): 17. Ode to June.

619.   *Phothudaw U* MIN, "*Wagaung* (the Fifth Burmese Month)," translated by K., in *F*, VI.2 (1 September 1967): 17. Ode to August.

620.   *Phothudaw U* MIN, "*Nattaw* (the Ninth Burmese Month)," translated by K., in *F*, VI.9 (15 December 1967): 11. Ode to December.

621.   *Phothudaw U* MIN, "*Tabodwe* (the Eleventh Burmese Month)," translated by K., in *F*, VI.13 (15 February 1968): 22. Ode to February.

622.   *Phothudaw U* MIN, "*Tawthalin* (the Sixth Burmese Month)," translated by Q., in *F*, VII.4 (1 October 1968): 11. Ode to September.

623.   MIN THU WUN, "Po Maing Comes," translated by Win Pe, in *F*, II.5 (7 October 1963): 22. Ballad reprinted from *Myawadi Magazine*.

624.   MIN THU WUN, "His Message," translated by Win Pe, in *F*, II.14 (22 February 1964): 21.

625. MIN THU WUN, "Courage!," translated by K., in *F*, VI.10 (1 January 1968): 5.

626. MIN THU WUN, "To *Ashin Maha* Rahthasara," translated by K., in *F*, VII.9 (15 December 1968): 18.

627. MIN YU WAY, "Unity," translated by M. Tin Aung, in *G*, VIII (1961). 12: 36.

628. MIN YU WAY, "A Paddy Field's Interlude," translated by Yangon Hla Thein, in *G*, XIII (1966).1: 17.

629. MIN YU WAY, "Union Festival," translated by K., in *F*, VII.13 (15 February 1969): 11.

630. *Maung* MOE THANT, "The Truth," in *G*, XIV (1967).8: 48.

631. *Maung* MOE THANT, "The Eternal *Frondosa*," in *G*, XIV (1967).11: 35.

632. *Maung* MOE THANT, "Bards of Burma," in *G*, XIV (1967).12: 17.

633. *Maung* MOE THANT, "Civilisation in the Wilderness," in *G*, XV (1968). 4: 36.

634. *Maung* MOE THANT, "When Peace Descends on Earth," in *G*, XV (1968).6: 15.

635. *Maung* MOE THANT, "That Day Was Night," in *G*, XV (1968).8: 16.

636. *Maung* MOE THANT, "*Tabodwe*," translated by..., in *G*, XVI (1969).2: 9. Ode to February.

637. Ken J. MONISSE, "The Jeweler," in *G*, VIII (1961).1: 44.

638. Ken J. MONISSE, "The First Shower," in *G*, VIII (1961).6: 31.

639. Ken J. MONISSE, "Night and the River," in *G*, IX (1962).5: 12.

640. Ken J. MONISSE, "Nostalgia," in *G*, IX (1962).11: 38.

641. Bela MUKERJI, "The Truth," in *G*, IX (1962).4: 16.

642. Marlene MUNRO, "The Pagoda," in *G*, IX (1962).1: 41.

643. Marlene MUNRO, "The Telephone," in *G*, IX (1962).2: 47.

644. Marlene MUNRO, "Love Is a Woman," in *G*, IX (1962).3: 17.

645. Marlene MUNRO, "Anger Is a Man," in *G*, IX (1962).4: 44.

646.   Marlene MUNRO, "The Cool Drink," in *G*, IX (1962).5: 30.

647.   Marlene MUNRO, "The Fan," in *G*, IX (1962).12: 12.

648.   MYA YI THANT, "Aspirations," translated by Kenneth Ba Sein, in *G*,
       XII (1965).4: 32.

649.   MYA YI THANT, "The Flower's Lament," translated by Maung Moe Thant,
       in *G*, XII (1965).12: 39.

650.   MYA YI THANT, "Alienation," translated by Maung Moe Thant, in *G*,
       XIII (1965).5: 20.

651.   MYA YI THANT, "Un-withering Flowers," translated by Kenneth Ba Sein,
       in *G*, XIII (1966).7: 13.

652.   MYA YI THANT, "Our Teacher," translated by Kenneth Ba Sein, in *G*,
       XIII (1966).10: 12.

653.   MYAT MUN, "Feverish Dream," in *G*, IV (1957).2: 39.

654.   MYAT MUN, "Together We'll Strive," translated by Kenneth Ba Sein,
       in *G*, XIV (1967).4: 13.

655.   MYAT MUN, "This Happy Day," translated by Kenneth Ba Sein, in *G*,
       XIV (1967).4: 32.

656.   MYAT MUN, "The Annual Lament," translated by Maung Moe Thant, in *G*,
       XIV (1967).8: 47.

657.   MYAT MUN, "The Oath of 'Freedom'," translated by Maung Moe Thant,
       in *G*, XV (1968).2: 13.

658.   MYAT MUN, "The Glorious Day," translated by Maung Moe Thant, in *G*,
       XV (1968).3: 41.

659.   MYAT MUN, "The Benefactors," translated by Kenneth Ba Sein, in *G*,
       XV (1968).8: 9.

660.   MYAT MUN, "March On With the Flag," translated by Maung Moe Thant,
       in *G*, XVI (1969).1: 13.

661.   MYAT MUN, "The Delightful Day," translated by Maung Moe Thant, in
       G, XVI (1969).3: 9.

662.   *Kyan-mar-yay-hmu* MYINT OO, "Come to the Naga Hills," in *G*, XVI (1969).
       3: 12.

663.   *Pyinmana* MYINT HLAING, "Martyr's Day," translated by K., in *F*, IV.23
       (15 July 1966): 5.

664. MYINT MYINT THU, "The Gardener and the Flower," translated by Yin
      Yin Thein, in *G*, XIV (1967).7: 32.

665. MYO SWE, "Look Not in Anger," in *G*, XV (1968).8: 48.

666. N.N., "Boredom in Evacuation Camp, 1943," in *G*, II.2 (December
      1954): 37.

667. N.N., "National Anthem (Chorus)," translated by..., in *G*, II.3
      (January 1955): 9.

668. N.N., "A Dirge (For a Cock Killed in Bali by a Tourist Taxi)," in
      G, II.4 (February 1955): 21.

669. N.N., "At Old Borobudur," in *G*, II.5 (March 1955): 37.

670. N.N., "The Yearning Cloud," in *G*, II.6 (April 1955): 42.

671. N.N., "The Voice of Bandung," in *G*, II.9 (July 1955): 21.

672. N.N., "Points of View," in *G*, II.11 (September 1955): 11.

673. N.N., "Shan Lake," in *G*, II.12 (October 1955): 15.

674. N.N., "Mandalay Revisited," in *G*, IV (1957).9: 24.

675. N.N., "One Afternoon in 1970," in *G*, VI (1959).2: 24.

676. N.N., "Poems on Kuala Lumpur," in *G*, VI (1959).11: 26-7.

677. N.N., "A Moment of Truth," in *G*, VIII (1961).9: 33.

678. N.N., "The Nineteenth of July," in *G*, XII (1965).7: 36.

679. N.N., "Delayed Solution to a Puzzle," in *G*, XIII (1966).6: 18-20.

680. N.N., *"Sein Choo Kyar Nyaung* or A Lament of the Consort of Crown
      Prince Kanaung," in *G*, XIII (1966).8: 11.

681. *U* NAY WIN, "Song of Welcome to the Britain-Burma Society," transla-
      ted by Dr Hla Pe, in *G*, IX (1962).9: 38.

682. *Maung* NE WIN, "The *Padauk*'s Prayer," translated by Kenneth Ba Sein,
      in *F*, VI.17 (15 April 1968): 19.

683. NGWE TA YI, "The Horizon," translated by M. Tin Aung, in *G*, IX
      (1962).8: 32.

684. NGWE TARYAR, "The May Day Ray," translated by K., in *F*, IV.18 (1
      May 1966): 22.

685. NUTHAZIN, "Life's Prisoner," adapted by M. Swe from a poem in *Mya-waddi Magazine*, August 1962, in *G*, IX (1962).12: 19.

686. NU YIN, "A Farmer's Invitation," translated by T., in *F*, II.4 (22 September 1963): 20.

687. NU YIN, "Mere Boy," translated by T., in *F*, II.6 (22 October 1963): 21.

688. NU YIN, "Knowledge and Wisdom," translated by T., in *F*, II.12 (22 January 1964): 22.

689. NU YIN, "Let's Work Hard, Brother and Sister," translated by T., in *F*, II.19 (7 March 1964): 22.

690. NU YIN, "The Auspicious Nineteenth," translated by K., in *F*, V.10 (1 January 1967): 17.

691. NU YIN, "Six Shimmering Stars," translated by T., in *F*, V.13 (15 February 1967): 4.

692. NU YIN, "Unified Resistance," translated by T., in *F*, V.16 (1 April 1967): 11.

693. NU YIN, "Toward the Portal," translated by T., in *F*, V.18 (1 May 1967): 5.

694. NU YIN, "The Union Day, 1968," translated by T., in *F*, VI.13 (15 February 1968): 11.

695. NU YIN, "Inle," translated by F.V. Lustig, in *F*, VI.21 (15 June 1968): 11.

696. NU YIN, "Hero Born," translated by K., in *F*, VI.23 (15 July 1968): 21.

697. *Myoma U Ba* NYEIN, "Just You and I," translated by M. Allan Williams, in *G*, XII (1965).5: 24. Popular song.

698. *Myoma [U Ba]* NYEIN, "The Mandarin Duck," translated by Kenneth Ba Sein, in *G*, XII (1965).12: 16. Song.

699. *Myoma [U Ba]* NYEIN, "Good, Efficient People," translated by Kenneth Ba Sein, in *G*, XIII (1966).5: 45. Song.

700. *Bhamo* NYO NWE, "The Village Raw Tea Party," translated by Shan Swe, in *G*, XV (1968).12: 37.

701. NYUNT WEI, "The Visitor," in *G*, IV (1957).12: 28.

702. NYUNT WEI, "Reverie at Two A.M.," in *G*, IX (1962).5: 20.

703. *Maung* PAN HMWE, "The Foolish Bird," translated by One-Not-Too-Wise, in *G*, XIV (1967).5: 23.

704. *Maung* PAN HMWE, "Literature and the People," translated by Kenneth Ba Sein, in *G*, XIV (1967).9: 15.

705. *Maung* PAN HMWE, "The Apparition," translated by Maung Moe Thant, in *G*, XIV (1967).10: 19.

706. *U* PYAN [PYONE] CHO, "*Waso*," translated by Kenneth Ba Sein, in *F*, V.22 (1 July 1967): 17. Ode to July.

707. *U* PYONE [PYAN] CHO, "The Month of *Tazaungmon*," translated by Kenneth Ba Sein, in *F*, VI.6 (1 November 1967): 11. Ode to November.

708. *Myawaddi Mingyi U* SA, "Rain God," translated by Kenneth Ba Sein, in *F*, V.24 (1 August 1967): 11.

709. SAMARI, "Oblivion," in *G*, VIII (1961).12: 32.

710. *Maung* SAN THU, "The Call of Duty," translated by T., in *F*, IV.1 (15 August 1965): 7.

711. *U* SAUNG, "Rural Life," translated by Kenneth Ba Sein, in *F*, II.22 (1 July 1964): 21.

712. SAW SHWE BOH, "Peasant Poet *Kyabin Saya* Hpee," adapted into English by K.H., in *F*, VII.7 (15 November 1968): 20-4.

713. SHAN SWE, "To a Friend: Dream of an Ardent Golfer," in *G*, XIII (1966).10: 20.

714. SHWEMAN ZEYA, "Along the Moat," in *G*, VI (1959).7: 28.

715. R. Gin Khai SUAN, "All these I owe to my angel Mother," in *G*, IX (1962).10: 44.

716. Robert Gin Khai SUAN, "Beauty Is the Youngster's Pride," in *G*, XV (1968).6: 22.

717. SUAN [SWAN] YI, "Mi Byaing, the Hawker," translated by Kenneth Ba Sein, in *F*, II.10 (22 December 1963): 20.

718. *Maung* SWAN [SUAN] YI, "This Is Her Way," translated by M. Tin Aung, in *G*, VIII (1961).8: 19. Reprinted from *Ngwe Ta Yi Magazine*, May 1961.

719. *Maung* SWAN YI, "The End of a Flower," translated by M. Tin Aung, in *G*, IX (1962).4: 48.

720. T.M.K., *"Pan Pwint Tha Nat,"* in *G*, VI (1959).8: 24.

721. TET TOE, "Post-war Burmese Writing: Poetry," in *F*, II.1 (7 August 1963): 21-2.

722. THA NU, "May Day - Labour Day," in *G*, XIV (1967).6: 16-7.

723. THA NU, "Twenty-One Years Have Passed," in *G*, XVI (1969).2: 40.

724. *Ashin* THAW-BITASARA, "'Tis high time to start," rendered into verse by Ashin Khina-tawa, in *G*, XIV (1967).10: 40.

725. *Maung* THI OO, "Past and Present," translated by M. Tin Aung, in *G*, VIII (1961).11: 43. Reprinted from *Ngwe Ta Yi Magazine*, February 1961.

726. *Thandwe Maung* THIN MON, "The *Tabaung* [March] Resistance," translated by Kyaiklat Ohn, in *F*, IV.16 (1 April 1966): 22.

727. TIN MO [MOE], "Mother," translated by Kenneth Ba Sein, in *G*, VI (1959).6: 20. From his *Phan-Mi-Ein Kabyah-Myah*.

728. TIN MOE [MO], "The Glass Lamp," translated by Kenneth Ba Sein, in *G*, VIII (1961).11: 31. From his *Lantern-lite Lyrics*.

729. TIN MOE, "The Alma Mater," translated by Kenneth Ba Sein, in *G*, VIII (1961).12: 27. From his *Lantern-lite Lyrics*.

730. TIN MOE, "A Lover's Reverie," translated by Kenneth Ba Sein, in *G*, IX (1962).1: 26. From his *Lantern-lite Lyrics*.

731. TIN MOE, "Verse on Youth," translated by Kenneth Ba Sein, in *G*, IX (1962).2: 28. From his *Lantern-lite Lyrics*.

732. TIN MOE, "Mother," translated by Kenneth Ba Sein, in *G*, IX (1962). 3: 37. From his *Lantern-lite Lyrics*.

733. TIN MOE, "The Little Boat" and "The Great Guest," translated by Kenneth Ba Sein, in *G*, IX (1962).4: 28. From his *Lantern-lite Lyrics*.

734. TIN MOE, "From a Dream to a Verse," translated by Kenneth Ba Sein, in *G*, IX (1962).5: 36. From his *Lantern-lite Lyrics*.

735. TIN MOE, "The Little Flower Boat," translated by Kenneth Ba Sein, in *G*, IX (1962).6: 13. From his *Lantern-lite Lyrics*.

736. TIN MOE, "The Thief" and "Habitat," translated by Kenneth Ba Sein, in *G*, IX (1962).8: 28. From his *Lantern-lite Lyrics*.

737. TIN MOE, "So Let It Be," translated by Kenneth Ba Sein, in *G*, IX (1962).9: 27. From his *Lantern-lite Lyrics*.

738. TIN MOE, "The Unopen'd Bud," translated by Kenneth Ba Sein, in *G*, XII (1965).8: 41.

739. TIN MOE, "The Village Fair," translated by Kenneth Ba Sein, in *G*, XII (1965).10: 16.

740. TIN MOE, "Face to Face with Love," translated by Kenneth Ba Sein, in *G*, XII (1965).10: 38.

741. TIN MOE, "December Thoughts," translated by Kenneth Ba Sein, in *G*, XII (1965).12: 28.

742. TIN MOE, "On the First Day of the New Year," translated by Kenneth Ba Sein, in *G*, XIII (1966).1: 25.

743. TIN MOE, "Coconut Palm Beach," translated by Kenneth Ba Sein, in *G*, XIII (1966).8: 23.

744. TIN MOE, "The Hamlet on the War-path," translated by Kenneth Ba Sein, in *G*, XIII (1966).8: 38.

745. TIN MOE, "Dad's Book Shelf," translated by Kenneth Ba Sein, in *G*, XIV (1967).1: 17.

746. TIN MOE, "Good Gifts," translated by Kenneth Ba Sein, in *G*, XIV (1967).2: 33.

747. TIN MOE, "Each One With Its Own Beauty," translated by Maung Moe Thant, in *G*, XV (1968).9: 15.

748. TIN MOE, "Arches of Years," translated by Shan Swe, in *G*, XVI (1969).1: 39.

749. TIN MOH [MOE], "The Perfidious Lotus," translated by Kenneth Ba Sein, in *G*, VI (1959).12: 16. From his *Phan-Mi-Ein Kabya-Myah*.

750. TIN OO LAY, "A Soldier's Plea," in *G*, VIII (1961).7: 24.

751. TIN OO LAY, "The Cult of the Gun," in *G*, VIII (1961).10: 32.

752. TIN OO LAY, "Healer," in *G*, VIII (1961).12: 14.

753. TIN OO LAY, "Pwa Khin," in *G*, IX (1962).1: 24.

754. TIN OO LAY, "Died Not In Vain," in *G*, IX (1962).1: 48.

755. TIN OO LAY, "Less the Label," in *G*, IX (1962).11: 21.

756. TIN U, "Lyrics to the Twelve Months: *Kason* (May)," translated by.. . , in *G*, VI (1959).5: 12.

757.   TIN U, "Lyrics to the Twelve Months: *Nayon* (June)," translated by
       ..., in *G*, VI (1959).6: 12.

758.   TIN U, "Lyrics to the Twelve Months: *Wazo* (July)," translated by
       ..., in *G*, VI (1959).7: 12.

759.   TIN U, "Lyrics to the Twelve Months: *Wagaung* (August)," translated
       by..., in *G*, VI (1959).8: 12.

760.   TIN U: "Lyrics to the Twelve Months: *Tawthalin* (September)," trans-
       lated by..., in *G*, VI (1959).9: 12.

761.   TIN U, "Lyrics to the Twelve Months: *Tazaungmon* (November) and *Nadaw*
       (December)," translated by..., in *G*, VI (1959).12: 12-3.

762.   THURIYAKANTI, "Independence Day," in *F*, II.11 (7 January 1964): 8.

763.   *Tekkatho* TOE AUNG, "Towards Right Existence," translated by K., in
       F, VI.14 (1 March 1968): 11.

764.   *Banmauk* TUN NYO, "The Legend of a Title," in *G*, VIII (1961).9: 21.

765.   *Banmauk* TUN NYO, "*Thakin* San-Ma-Tu Goes to Town," in *G*, IX (1962).
       4: 24.

766.   M. Allan WILLIAMS, "Lullaby," translated freely by..., in *G*, IX
       (1962).8: 16.

767.   M. Allan WILLIAMS, "Lullaby," translated by..., in *G*, XII (1965).8:
       46. Composed around the 19th century.

768.   M. Allan WILLIAMS, "Translating Burmese Poetry," in *G*, XII (1965).
       12: 30-2.

769.   Gladys WIN MYINT, "A Golfer's Plight," in *G*, IX (1962).7: 19.

770.   WIN NYUNT AUNG, "The Nightmare," translated by M. Tin Aung, in *G*,
       VIII (1961).9: 25.

771.   WIN PE, "My Prayer," in *G*, II.1 (November 1954): 20.

772.   *WIN PE, "Twante Canal," in *G*, II.2 (December 1954): 24.

773.   *WIN PE, "Unarm, Eros," in *G*, II.3 (January 1955): 42.

774.   *WIN PE, "Now As the *Padauk*," in *G*, II.6 (April 1955): 9.

775.   WIN PE, "Zen," in *G*, II.12 (October 1955): 26.

776.   *WIN PE, "Poem," in *G*, IV (1957).3: 37.

777. WIN PE, "Things," in *G*, IV (1957).4: 12.

778. *WIN PE, "Poem," in *G*, IV (1957).7: 37.

779. WIN PE, "To M.," in *G*, IV (1957).8: 18.

780. *WIN PE, "Tavoy Evening," in *Perspective of Burma* [item 48], 156.

781. WIN PE, "To Paw Paw (a Karen Headman)," in *G*, VI (1959).1: 44.

782. *WIN PE, "Four Poems," in *G*, VI (1959).5: 32.

783. *WIN PE, "Three Poems on Pain," in *G*, VI (1959).6: 47.

784. *WIN PE, "Two Poems of Recollection," in *G*, VI (1959).8: 38.

785. *WIN PE, "A Time to Go," in *G*, VI (1959).9: 33.

786. Rangoon, the Capital City," in *G*, VIII (1961).1: 12-4.

787. WIN PE, "I Don't Complain," in *G*, VIII (1961).3: 43-4.

788. *WIN PE, "The Farmer," translated by..., in *F*, II.18 (22 April 1964):
     15.

789. WIN PE, "Not Knowing," in *G*, XIII (1966).6: 44.

790. *WIN PE, "Ripeness Is All," in *G*, XIII (1966).7: 33.

791. WIN PE, "I Am Not an Anyathian," in *G*, XIV (1967).7: 20.

792. *WIN PE, "Ploughing," in *G*, XIV (1967).8: 26.

793. *WIN PE, "Washing Plates," in *G*, XIV (1967).9: 33.

794. WIN PE, "Living in Rangoon," in *G*, XIV (1967).10: 43.

795. WIN PE, "Island in Inya Lake," in *G*, XIV (1967).12: 10.

796. *WIN PE, "Poem," in *G*, XV (1968).6: 44.

797. WIN PE, "this poem," in *G*, XV (1968).12: 32.

798. *U* WUN, "The Burman and His Songs," in *G*, VIII (1961).11: 47.

799. Yaaseen YAAZA, "Mosquitoes," in *G*, XV (1968).4: 45.

800. YE AUNG, "The Message," translated by Kenneth Ba Sein, in *G*, XIII
     (1966).12: 35.

801. YE AUNG, "Alushka," translated by Kenneth Ba Sein, in *G*, XIV (1967).
     1: 32.

802. YE AUNG, "Message: the Reply," translated by Kenneth Ba Sein, in *G*, XIV (1967).3: 34.

803. *Bhamo* YE MYINT, "Independence Day Slogans - Echoes," translated by K., in *F*, VII.10 (1 January 1969): 11.

804. *Tetkatho* YU MUN, "The Flower That Isn't," translated by Khin Maung Win, in *G*, IX (1962).10: 12.

805. ZAWGYI [= U Thein Han], "War and Youth," in *G*, IV (1957).4: 11.

806. ZAWGYI, "To the *Shwe-byon Nat* Festival," translated by K., in *G*, IV (1957).9: 30-1.

807. *ZAWGYI, "The *Beda* Flower," freely adapted from the Burmese original, in *Perspective of Burma* [item 48], 112.

808. *ZAWGYI, "The *Beda* Flower," in Wigmore [item 3300], 28.

809. ZAWGYI, "The Sky-lark," translated by Kenneth Ba Sein, in *G*, XII (1965).5: 28.

810. ZAWGYI, "Your House," translated by K., in *F*, VII.12 (1 February 1969): 11.

DRAMA

811. Anonymous, "Burmese Dance and Drama," in *ITC*, I (1959): 163-7.

812. Anonymous, "Burmese Drama: Old Type and New Type," in *G*, XVI (1969). 2: 5-6.

813. Anonymous, "A New Look for Burmese Dramatic Arts," in *F*, I.8 (22 November 1962): 10-4.

814. ANT MAUNG, "U Kyin U and U Pon Nya," in *G*, IV (1957).2: 33.

815. P. AUNG KHIN, "The Crossroads: A Radio Play," in *G*, XII (1965).10: 42-9.

816. P. AUNG KHIN, "The Avenger: A Radio Play," in *G*, XIII (1966).4: 9-18.

817. P. AUNG KHIN, "The House Across the Street: A Radio Play," in *G*, XV (1968).10: 33-8.

818. *U* BA CHO DERDOKE, "The Burmese Marionette Stage," in *AH*, I (1948): 51-8.

819. *U* BA CHO DERDOKE, "The Burmese Marionette Stage," in *G*, I (January 1954): 15-7.

820. BA HAN, "U Ponnya's *Wizaya* (an estimate)," in *JBRS*, 6 (1916): 139-43.

821. BA HAN, "U Ponnya's *Paduma* (a criticism)," in *JBRS*, 7 (1917): 137-41.

822. *Dr* BA HAN, "The Evolution of Burmese Dramatic Performance and Festal Occasions," in *G*, XIII (1966).9: 18-24. Summary of a lecture.

823. G.E.R. GRANT-BROWN, "The Burmese Drama," in *ZB*, VI (1924-25): 160-4.

824. Archibald Ross COLQUHOUN, *Amongst the Shans* (New York: Scribner and Welford, 1885), Chapter 11.

825. J.A.M. GYI, "At the Play in Burma," in *BM*, CLXXI (April 1902): 562-71.

826. HLA PE, *Konmara Pya Zat: An Example of Popular Burmese Drama* (London: Luzac, 1952).

827. *Maung* HTIN AUNG, *Burmese Drama: A Study, with Translations, of Burmese Plays* (London: Oxford University Press, 1957). Includes full translation of four dramas, partial translation of eight.

828. *Maung* HTIN AUNG, "Tragedy and the Burmese Drama," in *JBRS*, XXIX (1939): 157-65.

829. *U* HTIN AUNG, "Tragedy and the Burmese Drama," in *B*, II (April 1952): 33-8.

830. Martin HÜRLIMANN, "Burmanisches Puppenspiel," in *A*, VII (1935): 73-7 + illustrations.

831. KHIN MYO CHIT and WIN PE, "The Quest," in *G*, IX (1962).8: 30-2. A play.

832. *U* LU PE WIN, "Some Aspects of Burmese Culture," in *JBRS*, XLI (December 1958): 32-3.

833. E. MAUNG, "The Burmese Drama," in *JBRS*, VIII (1918): 33-8.

834. *U* NU, *The People Win Through: A Play*. With a biographical introduction by Edward Hunter (New York: Taplinger, 1957).

835. NYUNT WEI, "Press Conference," in *G*, IV (June 1957): 41-3. A one-act sketch.

836. *U* OHN KHIN, "The 'Great Po Sein' I Knew," in *G*, IV (1957).1: 42-3.

837. PE THAN, "Burmese Comedians," in *G*, XII (1965).3: 46.

838. PE THAN, "Address to the Orchestra," in *G*, XIII (1966).10: 25. On song in the theater.

839. PE THAN, *"Ngo Chin,"* in *G*, XIV (1967).10: 25. Song in the dance-drama.

840. C. Harcourt ROBERTS, *Burmese Vignettes* (London: Luzac, 1949), Chapter VII.

841. SAW SHWE BOH, "Abaya Kumar," adapted into English by S.K.G., in *F*, VII.11 (15 January 1969): 12-6.

842. *Lt Col* Edward SLADEN and *Col* SPARKS, "The Silver Hill," a Burmese drama, translated by..., in *G*, IV (1957).4: 36-40; 5: 17-24. Reprinted from the translation of 1856.

843. John A. STEWART, "The Burmese Drama," in *JBRS*, 2 (1912): 30-7.

844. M. Allan WILLIAMS, "The Burmese Dramatists' Dramatist," in *G*, XII (1965).4: 28.

845. WIN PE, "Razadarit and Minrekyawawa," in *G*, VI (1959).7: 39-41. A one-act play.

846. WIN PE, "A Nameless Monk," in *G*, VI (1959).10: 34-6. A play.

847. WIN PE, "The Sea and the Stream," in *G*, VIII (1961).2: 29-31. A play.

848. WIN PE, "Kuttumbiyaputta Tissa Thera," in *G*, VIII (1961).5: 46-8. A play.

849. WIN PE, "Heartsickness," in *G*, VIII (1961).6: 35-6. A play.

850. WIN PE, "Intent to Rob," in *G*, VIII (1961).11: 37-8. A play.

851. WIN PE, "Rangoon, 1972," in *G*, IX (1962).2: 41-2. A play.

852. WIN PE, "Upaka and Cava," in *G*, IX (1962).7: 26-8. A play.

853. WIN PE, "The Pearl King," in *G*, IX (1962).10: 33-5. A play.

854. WIN PE, "The Third Man," in *G*, IX (1962).9: 33-5. A radio play.

855. J.A. WITHEY, "The Burmese *Pwe* Through Western Eyes," in *G*, VIII (1961).3: 39-40.

II. CAMBODIA

GENERAL

856. Etienne AYMONIER, "La littérature," in his *Le Cambodge. I: Le royaume actuel* (Paris: Ernest Leroux, 1900), 43-4.

857. Etienne AYMONIER, *The Literature of Cambodia*. Translated [by PNJ] from his "La littérature" [item 856]. Mimeographed.

858. *Jacques BARUCH, *Bibliographie des traductions françaises des littératures du Viêt-Nam et du Cambodge*. Etudes Orientales, N° 3 (Bruxelles: Thanh Long, 1968).

859. Solange BERNARD-THIERRY, "Le Cambodge à travers sa littérature," in *Présence du Cambodge* [item 871], 440-50.

860. Solange BERNARD-THIERRY, "Le roi dans la littérature cambodgienne," in *Présence du Cambodge* [item 871], 456-9.

861. Pierre BITARD, "La littérature cambodgienne moderne," in *Présence du Cambodge* [item 871], 467-79.

862. George COEDÈS, "Littérature cambodgienne," in *Indochine*. Ouvrage publié sous la direction de M. Sylvain Lévi. Exposition Coloniale Internationale de Paris, Commissariat Général (Paris: Société d'Editions Géographiques, Maritimes et Coloniales, 1931), I: 180-92.

863. George COEDÈS, *The Literature of Cambodia*. Translated [by PNJ] from his "Littérature cambodgienne" [item 862]. Mimeographed.

864. Jeanne CUISINIER, "The Gestures in the Cambodian Ballet: Their Traditional and Symbolic Significance," translated from the author's French MS., in *IAL*, New Series, I (1927).2: 93-103.

865. Hubert DESCHAMPS, "Cambodia: History," in *EB (1962)*, 4: 640b-1b.

866. *Judith JACOB, "Some Features of Khmer Versification," in Charles Ernest Bazell et al., *In Memory of J.R. Firth* (London: Longmans, 1966), 227-41. Outstanding description of Khmer metrics, with specimens of chanting.

867. Adhémard LECLÈRE, "Le mariage cambodgien," extrait de [son] *Cambodge: Fêtes civiles et religieuses*. Annales du Musée Guimet. Bibliothèque de Vulgarisation, tome 42: 535-51. Published as appendix to Martini et Bernard [item 895], 275-89.

868. Georges MASPERO, "Littérature khmere," in *Un empire colonial français: l'Indochine.* Ouvrage publié sous la direction de M. Georges Maspero (Paris et Bruxelles: G. Van OEst, 1929), I: 297-305.

869. Georges MASPERO, *The Literature of Cambodia.* Translated [by PNJ] from his "Littérature khmere" [item 868]. Mimeographed.

870. *Guy PORÉE, "Personnages comiques des contes populaires," in *Présence du Cambodge* [item 871], 460-6.

871. *Présence du Cambodge.* Numéro spécial de *FA*, XII.114-115 (Novembre-Décembre 1955).

872. Christopher PYM, "Literary Taste," in his *The Ancient Civilization of Angkor.* A Mentor Book, MT858 (New York: The New American Library, 1968), 103-9. Good, imaginative reconstruction of the role of letters in the Angkorian period.

873. *J. ROESKÉ, "Métrique khmère, *Bat* et *Kalabat*," in *Anthropos*, VIII (1913).4-5: 670-87; 6: 1026-43. Useful compendium of metrics, complemented by item 866.

874. Solange THIERRY, "La légende apprivoisée," in her *Les Khmers.* Collection "Le Temps Qui Court," 33 (Paris: Editions du Seuil, 1964), 161-75.

FOLK LITERATURE

875. Anonymous, "Histoire de l'ours et de l'arbre *banra*," in *Présence du Cambodge* [item 871], 535.

876. Dr BARADAT, "Sras Banh Dang et sa légende," in *BSEI*, Nouvelle Série, XIV (1939).1-2: 101-17. Chong tale from western Pursat province.

877. Solange BERNARD, "Quelques aspects de la chance dans les contes populaires du Cambodge," in *BSEI*, Nouvelle Série, XXVII (1952).3: 251-60.

878. Solange BERNARD-THIERRY, "Notes de littérature populaire comparée. II. -Conte siamois et conte cambodgien," in *BSEI*, Nouvelle Série, XXVIII (1953).1: 22-4.

879. Solange BERNARD-THIERRY, "Poèmes populaires," traduits par..., in *Présence du Cambodge* [item 871], 517-22.

880. Solange BERNARD-THIERRY, "Histoire de la marmite longue et de l'anguille longue," traduction de..., in *Présence du Cambodge* [item

871], 538.

881. Solange BERNARD-THIERRY, "La naissance des moustiques," traduction de..., in *Présence du Cambodge* [item 871], 528-30.

882. Solange BERNARD-THIERRY, "La naissance des serpents, ou l'histoire du serpent Ken Kan," traduction de..., in *Présence du Cambodge* [item 871], 531-4.

883. Solange BERNARD-THIERRY, "Histoire des quatre chauves (épisode des cheveux)," traduction de..., in *Présence du Cambodge* [item 871], 541-2.

884. Solange BERNARD-THIERRY, "Le trompeur trompé (légende khmère)," in *FA*, XIV (1957).138-139: 395-8.

885. Pierre BITARD, "La légende de Mathakut, génie protecteur du village de Vœunsai," in *BSEI*, Nouvelle Série, XXVII (1952).4: 449-52.

886. *George COEDÈS, "Etudes cambodgiennes. I. -La légende de la Nāgī," in *BEFEO*, XI (1911).3-4: 391-3. Analysis of one of the few extant origin myths.

887. *L. FINOT, "Sur quelques traditions indochinoises," in *Bulletin de la Commission Archéologique de l'Indochine*, 1911: 20-37.

888. W. Leslie GARNETT, "Barcarolle," translated [from the French] by....., in Garnett [item 3294], 146-7.

889. W. Leslie GARNETT, "Legend of the Thunder," translated [from the French] by..., in Garnett [item 3294], 143-5. See item 902.

890. M̃e GERNY MARCHAL, "Les quatre pattes du chat (Conte cambodgien)," in *BSEI*, 2e Semestre, 1913: 43-6. To be compared with version of same tale in Leclère [item 895], 182-4.

891. Mme M. GERNY-MARCHAL, "Contes cambodgiens et laotiens," in *Revue indochinoise*, Nouvelle Série, XXXII (1919).7-8: 71-7. Contains "Le pari: Conte cambodgien" (71-2), in verse.

892. Philip N. JENNER, *Tales of the Hare*. Translated by..., from the Khmer text collected by P. Midan [item 908, 49-116]. Close translation of all twenty-eight tales. Typescript.

893. Pierre-Jean LASPEYRES, "Petites chansons khmères pour une guitare," traduction de..., in *FA*, XV (1958).143: 108-14.

894. *Adhémard LECLÈRE, *Cambodge: Contes et légendes*, recueillis et publiés en français par... Avec introduction par Léon Feer (Paris: Emile Bouillon, 1895). Outstanding anthology of traditional literature.

895. *Adhémard LECLÈRE, "Contes," in his *Cambodge* [item 894], Troisième Partie, 53-159. Comprises "Le Perroquet et la Merle" (53-69), collected partly in Kampot in 1889, partly in Sambaur in 1891; "Néang Kantoc" (70-90), a Khmer version of the Cinderella tale, followed by a Vietnamese analogue [item 3085] collected by Landes (91-8); "Néang Chhouk" (99-111); "Néang Soc Kraaup" (112-43); "Mono-Véan" (144-59).

896. *Adhémard LECLÈRE, "Contes judiciaires," in his *Cambodge* [item 894], Quatrième Partie, 161-200. Comprises "L'étudiant Tissab-Moc" (161-5); "La statue vivifiée" (166-9); "Néang Montéa-Vatdey" (170-4); "Tête à tête" (175); "Le marchand et les trois passagers" (176-8); "Les trois frères (1)" (179-80), "Les trois frères (2)" (181); "Les quatre pattes du chat" (182-4), to be compared with Gerny Marchal [item 890]; "Les quatre aveugles" (185-8); "Le voleur et les quatre femmes" (189-91); "Les quatre hommes vertueux" (192-9), followed by a Note (200) by Léon Feer calling attention to an analogue in the Sanskrit *Vetālapañcaviṃśati*

897. *Adhémard LECLÈRE, "Contes malais," in his *Cambodge* [item 894], Sixième Partie, 295-306. Comprises "Le combat du buffle et du bufflon" (295-300), "Arrivée des Malais à Kampot" (301-5), followed by an unattributed Note (306).

898. *Adhémard LECLÈRE, "Histoire locale," in his *Cambodge* [item 894], Deuxième Partie, 39-52. Comprises only "Le déchou Kraham-Ka et le déchou Yat" (39-52).

899. *Adhémard LECLÈRE, "Légendes bouddhiques," in his *Cambodge* [item 894], Première Partie, 1-38. Comprises "Le satra du roi Chéa-Ly" (1-35), "La graine de moutarde" (36-8).

900. *L. MALLERET, "Traditions légendaires des Cambodgiens de Cochinchine relevant d'une interprétation ethno-sociologique," in *Institut Indochinois pour l'Etude de l'Homme, Bulletins et Travaux*, 4 (1941). 1-2: 169-80.

901. François MARTINI, "Les quatre compagnons," in *FA*, III (1948).28: 849-51.

902. François MARTINI, "Légende de la Foudre," traduction de..., in *Présence du Cambodge* [item 871], 526-7. See item 889.

903. *François MARTINI et Solange BERNARD, *Contes populaires inédits du Cambodge*. Traduits par... Préface de M. Jean Przyluski. Collection Documentaire de Folklore de Tous les Pays, Tome II (Paris: G.P. Maisonneuve, [c 1946]). Best available collection of folktales in translation. Comprises "L'ami et la femme adultère" (258-64), "La Bonne Fortune et la Malchance" (116-23), "Comment un voleur fut révélé par un parfum" (171-5), "Une contestation d'enfant" (179-80),

"Histoire des deux amis qui voulaient tarir la mer" (127-33), "Les
deux frères et le coq chasseur" (17-32), "Histoire des deux hommes
et du parapluie" (181-2), "L'enfant qui tua sa grand'mère" (150-1),
"Histoire de l'Homme au couteau" (33-71), "Histoire de l'Homme au
crottin de cheval" (155-60), "Histoire du Jeune homme à la noix de
coco" (194-202), "Histoire du lièvre et deux compagnons" (228-31),
"Maître Pang et Dame Ti, ou l'Homme qui épousa un fantôme" (271-4),
"Histoire du paresseux à l'épouse vertueuse" (161-5), "Histoire des
quatre chauves" (186-93), "Histoire des quatre compères qui se par-
tageaient de l'or" (183-4), "Histoire de Sok le Doux et de Sok le
Méchant" (134-49), "L'homme aux trente sapèques" (265-70), "L'homme
qui déterrit les crabes" (106-15), "Le sieur Croûte de riz" (72-
105), "Conte du sorcier, du vieux et de la vieille" (166-8), "La
légende du tigre" (215-8), "Histoire du tigre, du singe et du
lièvre" (219-27), "La tortue et le singe" (232-3), "Histoire d'un
vol de bœuf" (176-8), "Histoire du Voleur au bon cœur" (203-12),
"Histoire de la vraie mère, du vrai père et de la vraie femme"
(237-57).

904. François MARTINI et Solange BERNARD-THIERRY, "Conte du sorcier, du
      vieux et de la vieille," traduction de..., in *Présence du Cambodge*
      [item 871], 536-7. Reprinted from item 903 (166-8).

905. François MARTINI et Solange BERNARD-THIERRY, "Légende du tigre,"
      in *Présence du Cambodge* [item 871], 524-5. Reprinted from item 903
      (215-8).

906. François MARTINI et Solange BERNARD-THIERRY, "Histoire des trois
      Setthi," traduction de..., in *Présence du Cambodge* [item 871],
      539-40.

907. *P. MIDAN, "Le roman cambodgien du lièvre," légendes recueillies
      par... et illustrées par l'artiste khmer Mao, in *Extrême-Asie / Re-
      vue indochinoise*, VIII (1927).8: 276-92; 9: 315-34; 10: 365-82.
      See item 908.

908. *P. MIDAN, "Histoires du Juge Lièvre," recueil de contes cambodgiens
      traduits et annotés par..., in *BSEI*, Nouvelle Série, VIII (1933).
      4: 1-116. Best available collection of tales of the trickster hare,
      even more useful than item 907. Comprises introduction (iii-vi),
      translation (1-39), Notes (41-8), followed by Khmer text ((ii) +
      49-116). See item 892.

909. G.-H. MONOD, "Le Sophea Lièvre (Sophea Tonsai)," Conte khmèr tra-
      duit par..., in *La revue du Pacifique*, 2 (1923).6: 691-709. More
      tales of the trickster hare.

910. *G.-H. MONOD, "Folk-lore du Cambodge. Thmenh-Chey: Légende cambo-
      dgienne," in *Extrême-Asie*, Nouvelle Série, VI (1932).62: 452-7,
      467-72. Best available selection of tales from *Dhanañjaya* cycle.

911.   N. ONN, "La légende du Phnom Srey et du Phnom Pros," un conte in-
       édit khmèr recueilli et traduit par... [Avec des] dessins origi-
       naux de S. Suzuki, in *Cambodge: Revue Illustrée Khmère*, Editée par
       l'Association Samdach Sutharot, Phnom-Penh, Nº 1 (1ᵉʳ janvier
       1953): 29-32. See item 921.

912.   N. ONN, *Phnom Srey and Phnom Pros: a Khmer Legend*. Translated by
       Arthur S. Recchi [from item 911]. Typescript. See item 921.

913.   NOUTH-ONN, "La jeune fille aux cheveux dénoués: La légende du
       Phnom-Sampeou ou Légende de Néang Ramsay-Sâk," racontée par... Il-
       lustrée par des compositions inédites de P. Rabassi, in *Cambodge:
       Revue Illustrée Khmère*, Editée par l'Association Samdach Sutharot,
       Phnom-Penh, Nº 2 (1 avril 1953): 45-52. Sequel in item 914.

914.   NOUTH-ONN, "Les rivales: une légende khmère inédite," racontée par
       ... Illustrée par des compositions inédites de M. Rabassi, in *Cam-
       bodge: Revue Illustrée Khmère*, Editée par l'Association Samdach
       Sutharot, Phnom-Penh, Nº 3 (juillet 1953): 44-51. Continuation of
       item 913.

915.   NOUTH-ONN, *The Story of Néang Ramsay-Sâk*, retold by... Translated
       [by PNJ from items 913 and 914]. Mimeographed.

916.   *Dʳ A. PANNETIER, "Sentences et proverbes cambodgiens," in *BEFEO*,
       XV (1915).3: 47-71. Scholarly compendium of proverb literature in
       romanized Khmer with translation and sparse commentary. Best col-
       lection available.

917.   Dr A. PANNETIER, "Proverbes cambodgiens," in *Présence du Cambodge*
       [item 871], 515-6. Brief extract from item 916.

918.   *F. POULICHET, "Douze fables cambodgiennes," in *Revue indochinoise*,
       Juillet 1913: 75-87. Contains "Le roi khmer" (75-6), "Le *hangsa* et
       la tortue" (76-7), "Comment l'éléphant docile devint furieux" (77-
       9), "Le serpent et la tortue" (79-80), "Le cheval boiteux" (80-1),
       "Le crocodile et le lièvre" (81-2), "Le gros éléphant et le petit
       Thiep" (82-3), "Le cerf, l'aigle et la tortue" (83-4), "Le singe
       et le *kleng klong*" (84), "Le bonze et le chasseur" (85), "L'ours
       et le figuier sauvage" (85-6), "La vieille femme et le chat" (87).
       Representative selection of fables, with human as well as animal
       protagonists.

919.   *F. POULICHET, *Twelve Cambodian Fables*. Translated [by PNJ from item
       918]. Typescript.

920.   Solange THIERRY, "Essai sur les proverbes cambodgiens," in *Revue
       de Psychologie des peuples*, 13 (1958): 431-43.

921.   Christian VELDER, "His Hill, Her Mountain," a folk tale adapted

from Cambodian by... English version by Sumalee Viravaidya, in *Bangkok World: Standard Bangkok Magazine*, Saturday 15 May 1971: 11. See items 911 and 912.

922. Christian VELDER, "The Ruse That Worked Too Well," a Khmer folk tale adapted by... Translated by Sumalee Viravaidya, in *Bangkok World: Standard Bangkok Magazine*, Saturday 25 September 1971: 13.

923. *Princesse* Pingpeang YUKANTHOR, "Folklore cambodgien: Sentences cambodgiennes - Adages et dictons," in *FA*, 16 (Août 1947): 812-3.

HINDU-BUDDHIST LITERATURE

924. Solange BERNARD-THIERRY, "Le sens du merveilleux et l'héroïsme dans le *Rāmāyana* cambodgien," in *Présence du Cambodge* [item 871], 451-5.

925. *Pierre BITARD, "Cinq jātakas cambodgiens," in *BSEI*, Nouvelle Série, XXX (1955).2: 121-33. Comprises "Histoire de la jeune esclave Thūna" (125-7), "Histoire de la jeune fille malheureuse" (127-8), "Histoire du jeune Guttila" (128-30), "Histoire de la vieille femme Chandali" (131), "Histoire de la jeune fille Kesakārī" (132-3).

926. V. GOLOUBEW, "Mélanges sur le Cambodge ancien. I. -Les légendes de la Nāgī et de l'Apsaras," in *BEFEO*, 24 (1924): 501-10.

927. Padmanabh S. JAINI, "*Mahādibbamanta*: a *Paritta* Manuscript from Cambodia," in *BSOAS*, XXVIII (1965).1: 61-80.

928. Suzanne KARPELÈS, "The Influence of Indian Civilization in Further India (The Expression of the *Rāmāyana* in the Cambodian Version)," in *IAL*, New Series, I (1927).1: 30-9.

929. Adhémard LECLÈRE, "Le roi Sédathnou et la reine Sépya. Buddhisme et Brahmanisme: Trois petits livres," Traduit du Cambodgien en Français, in *BSEI*, 1er Semestre, 1912: 35-8.

930. *François MARTINI, "En marge du *Rāmāyana* cambodgien," in *JA*, 238.1 (1950): 81-90.

931. François MARTINI, "*Rāmakerti* (Extraits)," in *Présence du Cambodge* [item 871], 505-9. Selected passages from the Khmer adaptation of the *Rāma* story.

932. Jules-Adrien MARX, "Les premières larmes du Bouddha. Légende cambodgienne," in *BSEI*, 54 (1908).1: 157-9.

933. J. TAUPIN, "Une douzaine d'équitables jugements des Bodisattwa,"
      traduits du cambodgien par... Tiré [*sic*] des textes Khmêrs re-
      cueillis par M. Aymonier, in *BSEI*, 2e Semestre, 1886: 15-31.

                              INSCRIPTIONS

934. Lawrence Palmer BRIGGS, "The Oath of Allegiance," in his *The An-
      cient Khmer Empire*. Published as *Transactions of the American Phil-
      osophical Society*, New Series, 41 (1951).1 (Philadelphia: The Amer-
      ican Philosophical Society, February 1951), 151a. Translation from
      the French of George Cœdès, "Etudes cambodgiennes. IX. -Le serment
      des fonctionnaires de Sūryavarman I," in *BEFEO*, XIII (1913).6: 11-
      7. See K.292 in *Inscriptions du Cambodge* [item 937], III: 205-16.

935. Lawrence Palmer BRIGGS, "The Oath of Allegiance to a Khmer Sove-
      reign," translated by..., in Harry J. Benda and John A. Larkin, *The
      World of Southeast Asia: Selected Historical Documents* (New York:
      Harper & Row, [c 1967]), 33-4.

936. G. COEDÈS, "Inventaire des inscriptions du Champa et du Cambodge,"
      in *BEFEO*, VIII (1908).1-2: 37-92.

937. *G. COEDÈS, *Inscriptions du Cambodge* [in eight volumes], éditéees
      et traduites par... Ecole Française d'Extrême-Orient, Collection
      de Textes et Documents sur l'Indochine, III (Paris / Hanoi: Ecole
      Française d'Extrême-Orient, 1937-66). Monumental work encompassing
      principal epigraphical remains in Khmer, Sanskrit and Pāli, with
      romanized texts followed by translation and accompanied by copious
      philological notes.

938. *G. COEDÈS, "Connaissance d'Angkor par l'épigraphie," in *BSEI*, Nou-
      velle Série, XXVII (1952).2: 137-49.

939. G. COEDÈS, "La stèle de Tûol Rolom Tim: essai d'interprétation par
      la langue bahnar d'un texte juridique khmèr du xe siècle," in *JA*,
      242 (1954): 49-67. Valuable as illustrating the problems of paleo-
      graphy and the range of Khmer epigraphy.

940. G. COEDÈS, "Documents épigraphiques provenant de Tenasserim," in
      *Felicitation Volumes of Southeast Asian Studies presented to His
      Highness Prince Dhaninivat*... (Bangkok: The Siam Society, 1965),
      II: 203-9. Khmer epigraphical texts from Burma.

941. G. COEDÈS et Henri PARMENTIER, *Listes générales des inscriptions
      et des monuments du Champa et du Cambodge* (Hanoi: Ecole Française
      d'Extrême-Orient, 1923).

942. Jean FILLIOZAT, "Une inscription cambodgienne en pāli et en khmer

de 1566 (K.82, Vatt Nagar)," in *Comptes Rendus de l'Académie des Inscriptions et Belles-Lettres*, 1969: 93-106 + 2 plates.

943. Emile GASPARDONE, "L'histoire et la philologie indochinoises," in *Revue historique*, 198.71 (1947): 1-15.

944. *Saveros LEWITZ, "Textes en kmer moyen: Inscriptions modernes d'Angkor 2 et 3," in *BEFEO*, LVII (1970): 55-82. First of a series of exhaustive studies of forty inscriptions from the Middle Khmer period by the *doyenne* of Khmer studies; romanized texts, translation, and detailed notes.

945. *Saveros LEWITZ, "L'inscription de Phimeanakas (K.484) (Etude linguistique)," in *BEFEO*, LVIII (1971): 91-103. Brilliant reinterpretation of a remarkable 12th-century bilingual text.

946. *Saveros LEWITZ, "Inscriptions modernes d'Angkor 4, 5, 6 et 7," in *BEFEO*, LVIII (1971): 105-23. Continuation of item 944, of special interest as reflecting the mentality of the times.

947. *Saveros LEWITZ, "Inscriptions modernes d'Angkor 1, 8 et 9," in *BEFEO*, LIX (1972). Continuation of item 946, not yet distributed.

948. *Saveros LEWITZ, "Inscriptions modernes d'Angkor 10, 11, 12, 13, 14, 15, 16a, 16b et 16c," in *BEFEO*, LIX (1972). Continuation of item 947.

949. Auguste PAVIE, *Recherches sur l'histoire du Cambodge, du Laos et du Siam*. Mission Pavie Indo-Chine, 1879-1895. Etudes diverses, II (Paris: Ernest Leroux, 1898), 203-24.

CHRONICLES

950. *Francis GARNIER, "Chronique royale du Cambodge," in *JA*, Série 6, XVIII (Octobre-Novembre-Décembre 1871): 336-85; XX (Août-Septembre 1872): 112-44.

951. Milton OSBORNE and David K. WYATT, "The Abridged Cambodian Chronicle: a Thai Version of Cambodian History," in *FA/A*, N⁰ 193, XXII (1968).2: 189-203.

PRE-MODERN PROSE AND POETRY

952. Solange BERNARD-THIERRY, "Sagesse du Cambodge," in *Présence du Cambodge* [item 871], 436-9. On the codes of conduct.

953. *Pierre BITARD, "Etudes Cambodgiennes," in *BSEI*, Nouvelle Série, XXIX (1954).1: 51-79. Contains translations from several prophetic texts, 64-7.

954. *Pierre BITARD, "Etudes khmères: Le manuscrit 145 du fonds khmèr de la Bibliothèque Nationale de Paris," in *BSEI*, Nouvelle Série, XXXI (1956).4: 309-24. Translation with commentary of early 19th-century treatise on interpretation of dreams, cawing of crows, bodily *frissons*, moles; valuable as index of certain folk beliefs and of premodern documentary style.

955. L. FEER, "Etudes cambodgiennes. La collection Hennecart de la Bibliothèque Nationale," in *JA*, Septième Série, IX (1877): 161-234. Contains detailed synopsis of Dr Hennecart's manuscript translation of metrical romance of *Lakṣaṇavong* (188-202), extract from *Traiphum* (202-15), two prophetic almanacs for 1865 and 1866 (215-21).

956. L. FINOT, "Proverbes cambodgiennes," in *Revue indochinois*, Janvier 1904: 71-3. Translation of one recension of *Cpā'pa bākya cā'sa* or 'Code of Old Sayings', short metrical compilation of ethical and related aphorisms.

957. J. GUESDON, "Réach Kol: Analyse et critique du poème khmèr," in *Anthropos*, I (1906): 804-17.

958. Philip N. JENNER, *The Khmer Code of Conduct for Young Men*. Introduction, romanized text, translation, notes to the *Cpā'pa prusa* of *paṇḍita* Mai; typescript.

959. Suzanne KARPELÈS, "Histoire du Prince *Préas Sang* dit *Ngos*," d'après la traduction de..., in *Danses cambodgiennes* [item 984], 91-5. Khmer version of the Thai dramatization of the *Sang Thong* story, based on the *Suvaṇṇasaṅkhajātaka* and cognate with the *Saṅkhasilpajāya* romance.

960. *Adhémard LECLÈRE, "Jataka du Bouddha," in his *Cambodge* [item 894], Cinquième Partie, 201-93. Comprises "Préa-Sang-Sêl-Chey" (201-43), "Le Satra de Préa-Sang-Sêl-Chey" (244-93), collected partly in Veal Renh in 1888, partly in Kompong Thom in 1893.

961. *Adhémard LECLÈRE, *Préaḥ Sangsèlchey*. Translated [by PNJ from item 960, 201-43]. Typescript.

962. *Saveros LEWITZ, *Le traité sur le patrimoine*. Close but lucid translation, with full notes, of *Cpā'pa kerti kāla*; typescript.

963. François MARTINI, "Pour réussir dans la vie: *Chbàp Ker-Kal* (Extraits)," in *Présence du Cambodge* [item 871], 510-1.

964. François MARTINI, "*Néang* Phim (conte khmèr)," inspiré du conte cambodgien intitulé *La femme rusée*, in *FA*, XIII.128 (1957): 531-5.

965. Auguste PAVIE, "Les douze jeunes filles," in his *Recherches sur la littérature du Cambodge, du Laos et du Siam*. Mission Pavie Indo-Chine, 1879-1895. Etudes diverses, I (Paris: Ernest Leroux, 1898), 27-52.

966. Auguste PAVIE, "*Néang* Kakey," in his *Recherches sur la littérature* ... [item 965], 155-68.

967. Auguste PAVIE, "*Néang* Roum-Say-Sock," in his *Recherches sur la littérature*... [item 965], 1-26.

968. *Auguste PAVIE, *Sanselkey (Conte cambodgien)* (Paris: Bossard, 1921). One version of the *Sankhasilpajāya* romance. See items 959-61.

969. *Auguste PAVIE, *Sanselkey: a Khmer Romance*. Translated [by PNJ from item 968]. Mimeographed.

970. *Auguste PAVIE, "Vorvong et Saurivong," in his *Recherches sur la littérature*... [item 965], 53-154. One version, in considerable detail, of a favorite metrical romance.

971. Auguste PAVIE, "Vorvong et Saurivong (Extrait)," in *FA*, 37-38 (Printemps 1949): 953-8. Excerpt from item 970.

972. *Loka uka ñā* SUTTANTA PRĪJĀ INDA, *La morale aux jeunes filles*. Collection "Culture et Civilisation Khmères," N° 9 (Phnom-Penh: Université Bouddhique Preah Sihanouk Raj, n.d. [*ca* 1965]). Translation of *Cpā'pa srī* or 'Code of Conduct for Young Women '.

973. *J. TAUPIN, "Etudes sur la littérature khmère: *Néath Outtami*, poème cambodgien," in *BSEI*, I (1886): 23-47. Summary of old metrical romance, valuable for its reference to a number of familiar motifs.

974. *J. TAUPIN, "Prophéties khmères (Traduction d'anciens textes cambodgiens)," in *BSEI*, 2e Semestre, 1887: 5-22. Illustrates nature and rôle of prophesy during pre-modern period.

975. *Solange THIERRY, "La place des textes de sagesse dans la littérature cambodgienne traditionnelle," in *Revue de l'Ecole Nationale des Langues Orientales*, V (1968): 163-84. On the codes of conduct.

MODERN SHORT STORIES

976. *LY NGAN, "Le père," in *Réalités cambodgiennes*, N° 676 (14ème année), Vendredi 5 décembre 1969: 18-22. Landmark in development of a modern literature, written originally in French.

977. *LY NGAN, *The Father (Le Père)*. Translated [by PNJ from item 976]. Mimeographed.

MODERN POETRY

978. *S.A.R. le Prince* SISOWATH Monireth, "Le chant du sampanier," Un poème inédit de..., in *Cambodge: Revue Illustrée Khmère*, Editée par l'Association Samdach Sutharot, Phnom-Penh, N° 2 (1 avril 1953): 27-30. Contemporary only in date.

979. *H.R.H. Prince* SISOWATH Monireth, *Song of the Boatman*. Translated [by PNJ from item 978].

DRAMA

980. D., "*Nang Talung*," in *JSS*, XLVII (1959).2: 181.

981. Henri MARCHAL, "Note sur un théâtre d'ombres à Siemréap," in *BSEI*, Nouvelle Série, XXXIII (1958).3: 251-60.

982. R.L., "Le théâtre d'ombres et la musique traditionnelle khmère à Kuala Lumpur," in *Réalités cambodgiennes*, N° 653 (13ème année), Vendredi 27 juin 1969: 10-1.

983. *Dato Haji* Mubin SHEPPARD, "The Khmer Shadow Play and Its Links With Ancient India: A possible source of the Malay shadow play of Kelantan and Trengganu," in *JMBRAS*, XLI (1968).1: 199-204 + plate.

984. *Samdach Chaufea* THIOUNN, *Danses cambodgiennes*, d'après la version originale du..., revue et augmentée par Jeanne Cuisinier. Illustrations de Sappho Marchal. Préface par P. Pasquier. Deuxième Edition (Phnom-Penh: Institut Bouddhique, 1956).

III. CHAMPA

GENERAL

985. *E. AYMONIER, "Les Tchames et leurs religions," in *RHR*, XXIV (1891): 7-111.

986. *E. AYMONIER, *Les Tchames et leurs religions*. Extrait du tome XXIV de la *Revue de l'Histoire des Religions* (Paris: Ernest Leroux, 1891).

987. Antoine CABATON, "Les Chams de l'Indochine," Extrait de la *Revue coloniale* [no publication data], 321-34.

988. Anthony Herbert CHRISTIE, "Indonesia: Cultures in Historic Times," in *EB (1962)*, 12: 274a-6a.

989. E.-M. DURAND, "Notes sur les Chams. VI. -Les Basêḥ," in *BEFEO*, VII (1907).3-4: 313-21. On sacerdotal "caste" of brahmanist Cham.

990. *Georges MASPERO, *Le royaume de Champa* (Paris et Bruxelles: G. Van OEst, 1928). Classic history of Cham kingdom, outdated but not yet superseded.

991. *Paul MUS, "Littérature chame," in *Indochine*. Ouvrage publié sous la direction de M. Sylvain Lévi. Exposition Coloniale Internationale de Paris, Commissariat Général (Paris: Société d'Editions Géographiques, Maritimes et Coloniales, 1931), I: 193-200. Brief but reliable synopsis of literature as so far known.

992. *Paul MUS, *The Literature of Champa*. Translated [by PNJ from item 991]. Mimeographed.

993. *Dr A. SALLET*, "Les souvenirs chams dans le lok-lore et les coyances annamites du Quang-Nam," in *Bulletin des Amis du Vieux Hué*, 2 (Avril-Juin 1923): 201-28.

FOLK LITERATURE

994. E.-M. DURAND, "Notes sur les Chams. II. -Légendes historiques de Po Çah Inö," in *BEFEO*, V (1905).3-4: 373-7.

995. *E.-M. DURAND, "Notes sur les Chams. XII. -La Cendrillon chame,"

in *BEFEO*, XII (1912).4: 1-35. Cham analogue of the Cinderella tale.

996. *Edouard HUBER, "Etudes indochinoises. I. -La légende du *Rāmāyaṇa* en Annam," in *BEFEO*, V (1905).1-2: 168. Illustrating development of literary epic into folk tradition.

997. *Edouard HUBER, "Etudes indochinoises. V. -Le jardinier régicide qui devint roi," in *BEFEO*, V (1905).1-2: 176-84. Cham version of well-known tale-type.

998. Thai-Van-KIEM, "Thiên-Y-A-Na or the Legend of Poh Nagar (Cham legend)," in *A/AQCS*, IV (1954).15: 406-13.

999. *A. LANDES, "Contes tjames," traduits et annotés par..., in *ER*, 29 (1887): 51-130. Comprises "Noix de Coco" (53-73), "Kadôp et Kadœk" (73-4), "Tabong le paresseux" (74-9), "Kadœk gendre" (79-83), "Les ruses du lièvre" (83-91), "Halwëi sauvé par le lièvre" (92-3), "Lutte du tigre et du vautour" (93-6), "Le Fort" (96-103), "L'homme amoureux de la fille du roi" (103-4), "Histoire de Kajong et de Halœk" (105-16), "Histoire des deux frères pauvres" (116-8), "Le niais" (118-9), "Prédestination" (119-21), "Le gendre aveugle" (121-6), "Histoire d'un gardeur de buffles" (127-8), "Histoire du seigneur Klong Garay" (128-30), "Chanson d'enfants" (130). Sixteen tales of markedly authentic flavor collected by Landes from a Cham informant in Saigon in the 1880's; best collection available.

1000. *A. LANDES, *The Wiles of the Hare*. Translated [by PNJ from item 999, 83-91]. Typescript. Nine tales of the hare told as one.

1001. *A. LANDES, *Some Cham Tales. I: Coconut*. Translated [by PNJ from item 999, 53-73]. Typescript.

1002. *A. LANDES, *Three Cham Tales. II: Kadôp and Kadoek, III: Lazy Tabong, IV: Son-in-law Kadoek*. Translated [by PNJ from item 999, 73-4, 74-9, 79-83]. Typescript.

1003. *Paul MUS, "Etudes indiennes et indochinoises. IV. -Deux légendes chames," in *BEFEO*, XXXI (1931).1-2: 39-101 + plates of the manuscript of "Légende du roi Tabai. Texte cham (p. 75-79)."

INSCRIPTIONS

1004. E. AYMONIER, "Première étude sur les inscriptions tchames," in *JA*, janvier-février 1891.

1005. A. BERGAIGNE, "Inscriptions de Campā. Notices et extraits des

manuscrits de la Bibliothèque Nationale et autres bibliothèques,"
in *PAIBL*, XXVII (1893).2.

1006. G. COEDÈS, "Inventaire des inscriptions du Champa et du Cambodge"
       [item 936].

1007. G. COEDÈS et Henri PARMENTIER, *Listes générales des inscriptions
       et des monuments du Champa et du Cambodge* [item 941].

1008. Louis FINOT, "Notes d'épigraphie. XII. -Nouvelles inscriptions de
       Pō Klaun̈ Garai," in *BEFEO*, IX (1909).2: 205-9.

1009. Edouard HUBER, "Etudes indochinoises. VIII. -La stèle de Hué," in
       BEFEO, XI (1911).3-4: 259-60.

1010. Edouard HUBER, "Etudes indochinoises. IX. -Trois nouvelles inscrip-
       tions du roi Prakāçadharma du Campā," in *BEFEO*, XI (1911).3-4:
       260-4.

1011. Edouard HUBER, "Etudes indochinoises. X. -L'épigraphie du grand
       temple de Mī-Son," in *BEFEO*, XI (1911).3-4: 264-7.

1012. Edouard HUBER, "Etudes indochinoises. XI. -L'inscription bouddhi-
       que de Rôn (Quang-Binh)," in *BEFEO*, XI (1911).3-4: 207.

1013. Edouard HUBER, "Etudes indochinoises. XII. -L'épigraphie de la
       dynastie de Đồng-duong," in *BEFEO*, XI (1911).3-4: 268-311.

1014. *R.C. MAJUMDAR, *Ancient Indian Colonies in the Far East*. Vol. I:
       Champa. Greater India Society Publications No. 1 (Lahore: The Pun-
       jab Sanskrit Book Depot, 1927), Book III, "The Inscriptions of
       Champa."

1015. Paul MUS, "L'inscription à Valmiki de Prakaçadharma (Tra-kiêu),"
       in *BEFEO*, XXVIII (1928).1-2: 147-52.

                                CHRONICLES

1016. *Etienne AYMONIER, "XXIV. Traduction de la Chronique royale," 87-
       92 in his "Grammaire de la langue chame," in *ER*, 31 (1889): 5-92.
       Preceded by "XXII. Transcription de la Chronique royale" (77-81)
       and "XXIII. Lexique de la Chronique royale" (82-7).

1017. Etienne AYMONIER, "Légendes historiques des Chames," in *ER*, 32
       (1890): 145-206.

1018. *E.-M. DURAND, "Notes sur les Chams. III. -La chronique royale," in *BEFEO*, V (1905).3-4: 377-82.

1019. E.-M. DURAND, "Notes sur les Chams. VIII. -La chronique de Pō Nagar," in *BEFEO*, VII (1907).3-4: 339-45. Cham text with translation.

1020. E.-M. DURAND, "Notes sur les Chams. XI. -Les archives des derniers rois chams," in *BEFEO*, VII (1907).3-4: 353-5.

PRE-MODERN PROSE AND POETRY

1021. *Antoine CABATON, "Textes," in his *Nouvelles recherches sur les Chams*. Publications de l'Ecole Française d'Extrême-Orient, Volume II (Paris: Ernest Leroux, 1901), 97-184. Cham text with translation of numerous hymns, prayers, chants.

1022. E.-M. DURAND, "Notes sur les Chams. VII. -Le livre d'Anouchirvân," in *BEFEO*, VII (1907).3-4: 321-39. Brahmanic cosmological text with translation and commentary.

IV. INDONESIA

GENERAL

1023. S Takdir ALISJAHBANA, *Indonesian Language and Literature: Two Essays*. Cultural Report Series, No. 11 (New Haven: Southeast Asia Studies, Yale University, 1962).

1024. A.J. ARBERRY, "Khargūshi's Manual of Sufism," in *BSOAS*, IX (1937-39).2: 345-9.

1025. Adriaan J. BARNOUW, "Cross Currents of Culture in Indonesia," in *FEQ*, V (1946).2: 143-51.

1026. *C.C. BERG, "Bijdragen tot de kennis der Panji-verhalen," in *BTLV*, 110 (1954).3: 189-216; 4: 305-34.

1027. Asmah binti *Haji* OMAR, "Towards the Unification of *Bahasa Melayu* and *Bahasa Indonesia*: An account of efforts to standardise the spelling systems of Malay in Malaysia and Indonesia," in *Tenggara*, I (1967): 112-5.

1028. John F. CADY, *Southeast Asia: Its Historical Development* (New York: McGraw-Hill, [c 1964]), Chapter 8, "Muslim Malacca...."

1029. Anthony Herbert CHRISTIE, "Indonesia: Cultures in Historic Times," in *EB (1962)*, 12: 274a-6a.

1030. L.M. COSTER-WIJSMAN, "Illustrations in a Javanese Manuscript," in *BTLV*, 109 (1953).2: 153-63.

1031. Jeanne CUISINIER, "Kartini, 'mère des Indonésiennes' (1879-1904)," in *FA/A*, XVII (1961).169: 2475-8.

1032. *Prof Dr* J.P.B. de JOSSELIN de JONG, "Oost-Indonesische Poëzie," in *BTLVNI*, 100 (1941): 235-54.

1033. *John M. ECHOLS, *Indonesian Writing in Translation*. Compiled and edited, with an introduction, by... Translation Series, Modern Indonesia Project (Ithaca, New York: Southeast Asia Program, Department of Far Eastern Studies, Cornell University, [c 1956]). Outstanding anthology of modern prose and poetry, regrettably out of print.

1034. *Alberta Joy FREIDUS, *Sumatran Contributions to the Development of Indonesian Literature, 1920-1942*. A Thesis Submitted to the

Graduate Division of the University of Hawaii in partial fulfill-
ment of the requirements for the degree of Master of Arts in Asian
Studies, June 1969. Well-researched study devoted largely to the
impact of Minangkabau writers.

1035. Clifford GEERTZ, *The Religion of Java* (Glencoe, Illinois: The Free
       Press of Glencoe, [c 1960]).

1036. H.A.R. GIBB, *Mohammedanism: An Historical Survey*. Second Edition.
       The Home University Library of Modern Knowledge, No. 197 (London:
       Oxford University Press, 1953).

1037. *Sir* Hamilton A.R. GIBB, *Mohammedanism: An Historical Survey*. A Men-
       tor Book, M136 (New York: The New American Library, 1955).

1038. Alfred GUILLAUME, *Islam*. Pelican Books, A 311 (Harmondsworth,
       Middlesex: Penguin Books, 1954).

1039. D.G.E. HALL, *A History of South-East Asia* (London: Macmillan,
       1955), Chapter 10, "Malacca and the Spread of Islam."

1040. Tom HARRISON, review of *Der Totenkult der Ngadju Dayak in Süd-
       Borneo* by Hans Schärer [item 1058], in *SMJ*, New Series, XV (1967).
       30-31: 456. Reprinted from *Pacific Affairs*, 1967.

1041. James S. HOLMES, "A Quarter Century of Indonesian Literature," in
       BA, 29 (1955).1: 31-5.

1042. C. HOOYKAAS, "Books made in Bali," in *BTLV*, 119 (1963).4: 371-86.

1043. *Dr* Jacoba HOOYKAAS, "The Rainbow in ancient Indonesian religion,"
       in *BTLV*, 112 (1956).3: 291-322.

1044. Kingsley Garland JAYNE, Charles HOSE, Edward SALMON, and Gerrit
       Willem OVERDIJKINK, "Malay Archipelago: History," in *EB (1962)*,
       14: 720a-1b.

1045. *A. JOHNS, "The Novel as a Guide to Indonesian Social History," in
       BTLV, 115 (1959).3: 232-48.

1046. *A.H. JOHNS, "Sufism as a Category in Indonesian Literature and
       History," in *JSEAH*, 2 (1961).2: 10-23.

1047. *Anthony H. JOHNS, "Genesis of a Modern Literature," in *Indonesia*.
       Ruth T. McVey, Editor. Survey of World Cultures [No. 12] (New
       Haven: South East Asia Studies, Yale University, by arrangement
       with HRAF Press, [c 1963]), 410-37.

1048. Armand KAHN, *La littérature arabe*. Avec un Essai sur La Civilisa-
       tion arabe par Charles Simond. Anthologie des Chefs-d'œuvre clas-

siques de toutes les époques et de tous les pays (Prosateurs et
Poètes). Encyclopédie Littéraire Illustrée (Paris: Louis-Michaud,
n.d. [ca 1930]).

1049. M.B., "Modern Literature of Indonesia," in *A/AQCS*, I (1952).4:
512-6.

1050. *Perspective of Indonesia*. Supplement to *The Atlantic Monthly*,
199.6 (June 1956). Valuable collection of articles and translations.

1051. Th.G.Th. PIGEAUD, *Literature of Java*. Catalog raisonné of Javanese
manuscripts in the University of Leiden and other public collections in the Netherlands (The Hague & Leiden: M. Nyhoff, 1967-70).
In three volumes.

1052. Burton RAFFEL, "Indonesia and the Nobel Prize," in *BA*, 41 (1967).
1: 42-3.

1053. *Dr W.H. RASSERS, Pañji, the Culture Hero*. A Structural Study of
Religion in Java. Koninklijk Instituut voor Taal-, Land- en
Volkenkunde, Translation Series 3 (The Hague: Martinus Nijhoff,
1959). Collection of penetrating essays, of unusual value in de-
fining the basis of literary esthetics and subliterary themes.

1054. Anton SAAL, "Javanische Literatur und Sprache," in *Asien*, II (Mai
1903): 117-20.

1055. Asrul SANI, "The Literary Movement: A Mirror of Social Development," translated by John M. Echols, in *Perspective of Indonesia*
[item 1050], 137-41.

1056. Hans SCHÄRER, *Die Gottesidee der Ngadju Dajak in Süd-Borneo* (Leiden: E.J. Brill, 1946).

1057. Hans SCHÄRER, *Ngadju Religion: The Conception of God among a South
Borneo People*. Translated by Rodney Needham. With a preface by P.
O. de Josselin de Jong. Koninklijk Instituut voor Taal-, Land- en
Volkenkunde, Translation Series 6 (The Hague: M. Nijhoff, 1963).

1058. Hans SCHÄRER, *Der Totenkult der Ngadju Dajak in Süd-Borneo: Mythen
zum Totenkult und die Texte zum Tantolak Matei* [in two volumes].
Koninklijk Instituut voor Taal-, Land- en Volkenkunde. Verhande-
lingen, Deel 51, 1 en 2 ('S-Gravenshage: M. Nijhoff, 1966).

1059. Idris SHAH, *The Sufis*. Introduction by Robert Graves (Garden City,
New York: Doubleday, 1964).

1060. Idries SHAH, *Tales of the Dervishes: Teaching-stories of the Sufi
Masters over the past thousand years*. Selected from the Sufi classics, from oral tradition, from unpublished manuscripts and schools

of Sufi teaching in many countries. A Dutton Paperback, D 262 (New York: E.P. Dutton, 1970).

1061. Wilfred Cantwell SMITH, *Islam in Modern History*. A Mentor Book, MD 268 (New York: The New American Library, 1959).

1062. A.L. SÖTEMANN, *De structuur van Max Havelaar: Bijdrage tot het onderzoek naar de interpretatie en evaluatie van de roman*. Doctoral dissertation, Rijksuniversiteit te Utrecht, 1966.

1063. John A. SUBHAN, *Sufism: Its Saints and Shrines*. An Introduction to the Study of Sufism with Special Reference to India and Pakistan. Revised Edition (Lucknow: The Lucknow Publishing House, 1960).

1064. Kusumowidagdo SUWITO and anonymous, "Indonesia: History," in *EB (1962)*, 12: 268a-70a.

1065. A. TEEUW, "Iets over de jongste Indonesische letterkunde: Het werk van Sitor Situmorang," in *BTLV*, 112 (1956).1: 41-54.

1066. A. TEEUW, *Modern Indonesian Literature*. Koninklijk Instituut voor Taal-, Land- en Volkenkunde, Translation Series 10 (The Hague: Martinus Nijhoff, 1967).

1067. A. TEEUW, "Modern Indonesian Literature Abroad," in *BTLV*, 127 (1971).2: 256-63.

1068. *Dr* P. VOORHOEVE, "Batak Bark Books," in *BJRL*, 33 (1951).1: 283-98.

1069. P. VOORHOEVE, "Indonesische handschriften in de Universiteitsbibliotheek te Leiden," in *BTLV*, 108 (1952).3: 209-19.

1070. *Dr* P. VOORHOEVE, *The Chester Beatty Library: A Catalogue of the Batak Manuscripts*, including two Javanese Manuscripts and a Balinese Painting... with 10 plates, 1 in colour, and numerous figures (Dublin: Hodges Figgis, 1961).

1071. C.W. WATSON, "Some Preliminary Remarks on the Antecedents of Modern Indonesian Literature," in *BTLV*, 127 (1971).2: 417-33.

1072. John Alden WILLIAMS, *Islam*. Edited by... Great Religions of Modern Man. Richard A. Gard, General Editor. A Washington Square Press Book, W 803 (New York: Washington Square Press, 1963).

1073. H.B. YASSIN, "The Emergence of a New Generation," translated by Adibah Amin, in *Tenggara*, 4 (1969): 73-88.

1074. *V.A. ZHUKOVSKY, "Persian Ṣūfiism," translated from the Russian [by E.D.R.], in *BSOAS*, V (1928-30).3: 475-88.

1075. *V. ZHUKOVSKY, "The Idea of Man and Knowledge in the Conception of Persian Mystics," translated from the Russian of... by L. Bogdanov, in *BSOAS*, VI (1930-32).1: 151-77.

FOLK LITERATURE

1076. Monni ADAMS, "History in a Sumba Myth," in *AFS*, XXX (1971).2: 133-9.

1077. Anonymous, "The Well Diggers," in Garnett [item 3294], 175-7.

1078. Harley Harris BARTLETT, "A Batak and Malay Chant on Rice Cultivation, with Introductory Notes on Bilingualism and Acculturation in Indonesia," in *Proceedings of the American Philosophical Society*, 96 (1952).6: 629-52.

1079. *C. Tj. BERTLING, "Notes on Myth and Ritual in Southeast Asia," in *Bundel Prof. Dr F.D.K. Bosch*, published as *BTLV*, 114 (1958).1-2: 17-28.

1080. H.T. DAMSTÉ, "De legende van de Heilige Zeven Slapers in het Atjehsch," in *BTLVNI*, 98 (1939).4: 407-88.

1081. H.T. DAMSTÉ, "Hikajat Kisah OElat. Wormstekige stenen op Atjèh (en in Minangkabau?)," in *BTLV*, 104 (1948).4: 515-39.

1082. D.W.N. de BOER, "Het Toba-Bataksche verhaal van Si Tadjom Bolak en Si Radja Mebangebang (Met één facsimilé)," in *BTLV*, 104 (1948). 1: 45-88.

1083. Adèle de LEEUW, *Indonesian Legends and Folk Tales*, Told by... Illustrated by Ronni Solbert (New York: Thomas Nelson & Sons, 1964).

1084. Adèle Louise de LEEUW, *Indonesian Fairy Tales*, Told by... Illustrated by Harry Toothill (London: Muller, 1966).

1085. Walter DREESEN, *Märchen aus Bali / Balinese Fairy Tales*. With brush drawings by Walter Dreesen. English version revised by Freddy Beermann (Hamburg: Karl F. Wede, 1947).

1086. Usman EFFENDI, *Si Penidur und der Riese: Legenden und Volksmärchen aus Indonesien*, frei nacherzählt von... (Berlin: Alfred Holz, [c 1967]).

1087. James J. FOX, "Semantic Parallelism in Rotinese Ritual Language," in *BTLV*, 127 (1971).2: 215-55.

1088. *Peter R. GOETHALS, *The Seven Nymphs*. Collected, translated from the Sumbawan, and edited by... Scholarly translation of a Sumbawan version of the Swan Maiden tale, of special interest because of its faithfulness to the original. Typescript.

1089. *Peter R. GOETHALS, *Lakasiasi*. Collected, translated from the Sumbawan, and edited by... Scholarly translation of a Sumbawan version of the Cupid and Psyche tale. Typescript.

1090. *Peter R. GOETHALS, *Ahmad and Muhamad*. Collected, translated from the Sumbawan, and edited by... The quest for Princess Rembajang Bulan and her rescue, illustrating the loose structure of the longer oral tale and containing numerous familiar motifs. Typescript.

1091. J. GONDA, "Some Notes on the Relation between Syntactic and Metrical Units in a Javanese Kidung," in *Bundel Prof. Dr F.D.K. Bosch* [item 1079], 98-116.

1092. *Dr Jacoba HOOYKAAS, "A Journey into the Realm of Death. Balinese Folktales with Translations," in *BTLV*, 111 (1955).3: 236-73. Texts with translation.

1093. *Dr Jacoba HOOYKAAS - van LEEUWEN BOOMKAMP, *Sprookjes en Verhalen van Bali*, met 33 illustraties van Balische kunstenaars ('S-Gravenhage / Bandung: W. van Hoeve, 1956). See item 1098.

1094. Jacoba HOOYKAAS, "A Yantra of Speech Magic in Balinese Folklore and Religion," in *BTLV*, 115 (1959).2: 176-91.

1095. *Jacoba HOOYKAAS, "The Changeling in Balinese Folklore and Religion," in *BTLV*, 116 (1960).4: 424-36.

1096. *Jacoba HOOYKAAS, "The Myth of the Young Cowherd and the Little Girl," in *BTLV*, 117 (1961).2: 267-78.

1097. *Dr* Jacoba HOOYKAAS, "A Balinese Folktale on the Origin of Mice," in *BTLV*, 117 (1961).2: 279-81.

1098. *Jacoba HOOYKAAS - van LEEUWEN BOOMKAMP, *Märchen aus Bali*, mit 33 Illustrationen balinesischer Maler (Zürich: Die Waage, [c 1963]). Translation of item 1093.

1099. Ismail HUSSEIN, "A Batak Folk Tale," translated by..., in *Tenggara*, II (1968).1: 59-62.

2000. *J.C.J.G. JONKER, "Soembawareesche Teksten met Vertaling," in *BTLVNI*, 92 (1934).2: 211-334. Seven folktales from Sumbawan, edited by P. Voorhoeve.

2001. *J.C.J.G. JONKER and P. VOORHOEVE, *Seven Sumbawan Folktales*. Translated [from item 2000] by Peter R. Goethals. Delightful tales,

containing numerous familiar motifs and affording insights into
Sumbawan attitudes. Typescript.

2002. R.A. KERN, "Het Soendasche pantoen-verhaal Loetoengkasaroeng," in
       BTLVNI, 99 (1940).3: 467-500.

2003. R.A. KERN, "Zang en tegenzang," in *BTLV*, 104 (1948).1: 119-36.

2004. R.A. KERN, "Een episode uit het La Galigo epos," in *BTLV*, 117
       (1961).3: 363-83.

2005. H. LAGEMANN, "Das niassische Mädchen," in *Tijdschrift voor Indi-
       sche Taal-, Land- en Volkenkunde*, 36 (1893): 296-324.

2006. H. LAGEMANN, "Ein Heldensang der Niasser," in *Tijdschrift voor In-
       dische Taal-, Land- en Volkenkunde*, 48 (1906): 341-407.

2007. *Philip Frick McKEAN, "The Mouse-deer (*Kantjil*) in Malayo-Indone-
       sian Folklore: Alternative Analyses and the Significance of a
       Trickster Figure in South-East Asia," in *AFS*, XXX (1971).1: 71-84.

2008. *P. MIDDELKOOP, "Four Tales with Mythical Features Characteristic
       of the Timorese People," in *BTLV*, 114 (1958).4: 384-405.

2009. *P. MIDDELKOOP, "A Timorese Myth and Three Fables," in *BTLV*, 115
       (1959).2: 157-75.

2010. *Rodney NEEDHAM, "Jātaka, Pañcatantra, and Kodi Fables," in *BTLV*,
       116 (1960).2: 232-62.

2011. James L. PEACOCK, "Comedy and Centralization in Java: The *Ludruk*
       Plays," in *JAF*, 80.318 (October-December 1967): 345-56.

2012. C.H. SCHAAP, *Indonesische volksverhalen*, in het Nederlands bewerkt
       door... Kramers Pocket kpF 11 ('S-Gravenshage: W. van Hoeve, n.d.).

2013. *Hans SCHÄRER, *Der Totenkult der Ngadju Dajak in Süd-Borneo* [item
       1058]. Ngadju texts with translation.

2014. *Dra Mrs* THIO, *Indonesian Folk Tales*, selected and translated by
       ... Illustrated by Oey Liep Sioe (Tunas, 1962).

2015. G.C. van der HORST - van DOORN, *Indische sprookjes: Legenden en
       Fabeln*, verzameld door... geïllustreerd door Suzon Beijnon (Den
       Haag: Van Goor, n.d.).

2016. *Justus M. van der KROEF, "Rice Legends of Indonesia," in *JAF*, 65.
       255 (January-March 1952): 49-55.

2017. *Justus M. van der KROEF, "Folklore and Tradition in Javanese Soci-
       ety," in *JAF*, 68.267 (January-March 1955): 25-33.

2018. Petrus VOORHOEVE, *Overzicht van de volksverhalen der Bataks...*
       Doctoral dissertation, 1927.

2019. *R.O. WINSTEDT, "A Pandji Tale from Kelantan," in *JMBRAS*, XII.1
       (March 1949): 53-60.

2020. *Dr C.W. WORMSER, Het hooge heiligdom: Legenden, tempelruïnes en
       heilige graven van Java's bergen* (Deventer / Bandung: W. van Hoe-
       ve, 1942).

2021. *F.A.E. van WOUDEN, "Myths and Social Structure in the Timorese Ar-
       chipelago," in his *Types of Social Structure in Eastern Indonesia*.
       Translated by Rodney Needham. Preface by G.W. Locher. Koninklijk
       Instituut voor Taal-, Land- en Volkenkunde, Translation Series 11
       (The Hague: M. Nijhoff, 1968).

HINDU LITERATURE

2022. C. BULCKE, "An Indonesian Birth-story of Hanuman," in *JOIUB*, III
       (1953).2: 147-51.

2023. Lokesh CHANDRA, "A New Indonesian Episode of the *Mahabharata* Cyc-
       lus," in *ArOr*, 4 (1959): 565-71.

2024. *Prof Juan R. FRANCISCO, "The Ráma Story in the Post-Muslim Malay
       Literature of South-east Asia," in *SMJ*, New Series, X (1962).19-20:
       468-85.

2025. T. GOUDRIAAN, "The Balinese *Indrastava*," in *ALB* (Dr V. Raghavan
       Felicitation Volume), 31-32 (1967-68): 158-70.

2026. C. HOOYKAAS, "Sanskrit Kavya and Old-Javanese Kakawin (New Light
       from the *Ramayana*)," in *JOIUB*, IV (December 1954 / March 1955):
       143-8.

2027. C. HOOYKAAS, "Bharata's Departure: a Passage on Arthasastra in the
       Old-Javanese *Ramayana* Kakawin," in *JOIUB*, V (December 1955): 187-
       92.

2028. C. HOOYKAAS, *The Old-Javanese* Rāmāyaṇa: *an exemplary kakawin as to
       form and content* (Amsterdam: Hollandsch Uitgevers Maatschaapij,
       1958).

2029. C. HOOYKAAS, "An Exorcist Litany from Bali," in *BTLV*, 125 (1969).
       2: 356-70. Bilingual texts.

2030. *J. KATS, "The *Rāmāyaṇa* in Indonesia," in *BSOAS*, IV (1926-28).3:
       579-85.

2031. R.N. POERBATJARAKA, *Ardjuna Wiwaha* (The Hague: Martinus Nijhoff, 1926).

2032. *Dr* POERBATJARAKA, "Onbegrepen ontkenning in het Oudjavaanse Râmâyaṇa," in *BTLV*, 106 (1950).1: 79-90.

2033. Mysu SEDAH and Mysu PANULUH, *"Bharata-yuddha,"* translated by R.N. Poerbatjaraka and C. Hooykaas, in *Djawa*, XIV (1934): 1-88.

2034. SOEWITO-SANTOSO, *Boddhakawya-Sutasoma: A Study in Javanese Wajrayana. Text, Translation, Commentary.* Doctoral dissertation, The Australian National University, 1968.

2035. W.F. STUTTERHEIM, *Rama-Legenden und Rama-Reliefs in Indonesien* [in two volumes] (Münich: Georg Müller, 1925).

INSCRIPTIONS

2036. *J.G. de CASPARIS, *Inscripties uit de Çailendra-tijd* (Bandung: Nix, 1950).

2037. *J.G. de CASPARIS, *Selected Inscriptions from the 7th to the 9th century A.D.* Prasasti Indonesia, 2 (Bandung: Masa Baru, 1956).

2038. B.R. CHATTERJEE, *History of Indonesia, Early and Medieval.* 3d edition (Meerut: Meenakshi Prakashan, 1967), 107-98.

2039. Himansu Bhusan SARKAR, "South-India in Old-Javanese and Sanskrit Inscriptions," in *BTLV*, 125 (1969).2: 193-205.

2040. M.M. SUKARTO K. ATMODJO, "Preliminary Report on the Copper-plate Inscription of Asahduren," in *BTLV*, 126 (1970).2: 215-27.

CHRONICLES

2041. Anthony H. JOHNS, "The Role of Structural Organisation and Myth in Javanese Historiography," in *JAS*, XXIV (1964).1: 91-9.

2042. *Theodoor PIGEAUD, *Java in the 14th Century: The* Nāgara Kertā gama *by Rakawi Prapañca of Majapahit, 1365 A.D.* [in five volumes]. Third edition, revised and enlarged by some contemporaneous texts, with notes, translations, commentaries and a glossary (The Hague: M. Nijhoff, 1960-1963).

2043. J.E. van LOHUIZEN - de LEEUW, "The beginnings of Old-Javanese historical literature," in *BTLV*, 112 (1956).4: 383-94.

PRE-MODERN PROSE AND POETRY

2044. G.W.J. DREWES, "Javanese Poems dealing with or attributed to the
       Saint of Bonań," in *BTLV*, 124 (1968).2: 209-40.

2045. *C. HOOYKAAS, *The Lay of Jaya Prana, the Balinese Uriah*. Introduc-
       tion, Text, Translation and Notes by... (London: Luzac, 1958).
       Outstanding work of scholarship providing numerous insights into
       literary esthetics and many familiar motifs.

2046. C. HOOYKAAS, "Korte mededelingen: Interpolated or guine? Khili
       Suchi, the Royal Nun," in *BTLV*, 116 (1960).2: 278-9.

2047. *C. HOOYKAAS, *Bagus Umbara, Prince of Koripan: The Story of a Prince
       of Bali and a Princess of Java*. Illustrated on palm leaves by a
       Balinese artist, with Balinese text and English translation, by...
       (London: The Trustees of the British Museum, 1968). Based on a
       modern manuscript representing one episode from the epic (see item
       2049], of unusual interest by reason of the juxtaposition of il-
       lustrations and text.

2048. SOEBARDI, *The Book of Cabolek: A Critical Edition with Introduc-
       tion, Translation, and Notes. A Contribution to the Study of the
       Javanese Mystical Tradition*. Doctoral dissertation, The Australian
       National University, 1967.

2049. *R. van ECK, "Bagoes Hoembårå of Mantri Koripan, Balineesch Ge-
       dicht. Tekst en Nederlandsche Vertaling met Aanteekeningen bewerkt
       door...," in *BTLVNI*, III (1876).11: 1-137, 177-368. Only available
       translation of full epic.

2050. P. VOORHOEVE, "Three Old Achehnese Manuscripts," in *BSOAS*, XIV
       (1952).2: 335-45.

MODERN PROSE

2051. *Soetan* Takdir ALISJAHBANA, "With Sails Unfurled," excerpt trans-
       lated by Patricia Marks, in Echols [item 1033], 23-30.

2052. Chairil ANWAR, "Excerpts from Letters to H.B. Jassin," in Burton
       Raffel, *The Complete Poetry and Prose of Chairil Anwar*. Edited
       and Translated by... (Albany: State University of New York Press,
       1970), 185.

2053. Chairil ANWAR, "Four Aphorisms," in Raffel [item 2052], 184.

2054. Chairil ANWAR, "Hoppla! (*Hoppla!*)," in Raffel [item 2052], 174-6.

2055. Chairil ANWAR, "Looking It In the Eye (*Berhadapan mata*)," in Raffel [item 2052], 170-4.

2056. Chairil ANWAR, "Radio Talk, 1946," in Raffel [item 2052], 178-81.

2057. Chairil ANWAR, "Three Against Fate (*Tiga menguak takdir*)," in Raffel [item 2052], 163.

2058. Chairil ANWAR, "Three Approaches, One Idea," in Raffel [item 2052], 181-4.

2059. Chairil ANWAR, "An Untitled Speech: 1943," in Raffel [item 2052], 163-70.

2060. Chairil ANWAR, "Writing Poems, Looking at Pictures (*Membuat sadjak, melihat lukisan*)," in Raffel [item 2052], 176-8.

2061. Rosihan ANWAR, "The Voice of the People," translated by Karl Strange, in Echols [item 1033], 68-85.

2062. Harry G. AVELING, "*Sitti Nurbaja*: Some Reconsiderations," and comments by Taufik Abdullah, in *BTLV*, 126 (1970).2: 228-45.

2063. M. BALFAS, "The Knock on the Door," translated by Adrienne Balfas, in *Tenggara*, II (1968).2: 68-79. Bilingual text.

2064. *Suwarsih DJOJOPUSPITO, "The Tale of the Flamboyant Tree," translated by Muriel B. Lechter, in Echols [item 1033], 57-61.

2065. *Suwarsih DJOJOPUSPITO, "The Story of Sibuntjit (*Tjerita Sibuntjit*)," translated from her *Tudjuh tjeritera pendek* (1950) by Marian De Walt Morgan. Typescript.

2066. HAMKA [= *Hadji* Abdul Malik Karim Amrullah], "Under the Protection of the Ka'bah," a chapter, translated by Patricia Marks, in Echols [item 1033], 34-7.

2067. HAMKA, "My Father," selections, translated by Harry J. Benda, in Echols [item 1033], 38-51.

2068. *HAMKA, "A Deserted Child (*Anak tinggal*)," in Hendon [item 2070], 1-18.

2069. Amal HAMZAH, "Spy-glass," translated by Malcolm Willison, in Echols [item 1033], 87-9.

2070. *Rufus S. HENDON, *Six Indonesian Short Stories*. Yale University

Southeast Asia Studies. Translation Series No. 7 (New Haven: Yale University Southeast Asia Studies, [c 1968]).

2071. IDRUS, "Aki's Song," translated by John M. Echols, in Echols [item 1033], 91-117.

2072. *Raden Adjeng KARTINI, Letters of a Javanese Princess. Translated from the Dutch by Agnes Louise Symmers. Edited and with an introduction by Hildred Geertz. Preface by Eleanor Roosevelt. The Norton Library, N207. UNESCO Collection of Representative Works, Indonesian Series (New York: W.W. Norton, 1964).

2073. *Denys LOMBARD, Histoires courtes d'Indonésie: soixante-huit "tjerpén" (1933-1965), Traduits et présentés par... avec la collaboration de Winarsih Arifin et Minnie Wibisono. Publications de l'Ecole Française d'Extrême-Orient, Volume LXIX (Paris: Ecole Française d'Extrême-Orient, 1968). Excellent anthology.

2074. Mochtar LUBIS, "Djamal, City Guerrilla," translated by Judith Rosenberg, in Echols [item 1033], 119-23.

2075. Mochtar LUBIS, "Djamal Infiltrating," translated by Dean J. Almy, Jr., in Echols [item 1033], 124-7.

2076. *Mochtar LUBIS, "The Lotteries of Haji Zakaria," translated by Robert MacQuaid, in Perspective of Indonesia [item 1050], 142-4.

2077. *Mochtar LUBIS, "The Lotteries of Haji Zakaria," translated by Robert MacQuaid, in Wigmore [item 3300], 51-6.

2078. *Mochtar LUBIS, "The Lotteries of Haji Zakaria," translated by Robert MacQuaid, in Hanrahan [item 3295], 361-7.

2079. Mochtar LUBIS, A Road With No End. Translated from the Indonesian and edited by Anthony H. Johns (London: Hutchinson, [c 1968]).

2080. *Mochtar LUBIS, "A House of Teak (Rumah djati)," translated by Alberta J. Freidus. Typescript.

2081. *Achdiat K. MIHARDJA, "Hamid," translated by Robert J. MacQuaid, in Echols [item 1033], 129-41.

2082. *Achdiat K. MIHARDJA, "Hamid," translated by Robert MacQuaid, in Perspective of Indonesia [item 1050], 159-63.

2083. *Achdiat K. MIHARDJA, "Hamid," translated by Robert MacQuaid, in Wigmore [item 3300], 236-46.

2084. *Achdiat K. MIHARDJA, "Hamid," translated by Robert MacQuaid, in Hanrahan [item 3295], 352-61.

2085. Achdiat K. MIHARDJA, "Sensation at the Top of a Coconut Tree,"
       translated by Benedict Anderson, in Milton [item 3298], 143-56.

2086. *Achdiat K. MIHARDJA, "Van Buren and the Village Girl," in José
       [item 3297], 173-8.

2087. *Achdiat K. MIHARDJA, "Van Buren and the Village Girl," in *Of Love
       and Hope* [item 3291], 141-7.

2088. Abdul MUIS, "Meant For Each Other," Chapter I, translated by An-
       drea Wilcox, in Echols [item 1033], 11-22.

2089. MULTATULI [= Eduard Douwes Dekker], *Max Havelaar: or, The Coffee
       Auctions of the Netherlands Trading Company*. Translated from the
       Dutch by W. Siebenhaar, with an Introduction by D.H. Lawrence (New
       York & London: A.A. Knopf, 1927).

2090. MULTATULI, *Max Havelaar: or, The Coffee Auctions of the Dutch
       Trading Company*. With an Introduction by D.H. Lawrence. [Transla-
       ted,] edited and introduced by Roy Edwards (Leyden: Sijthoff /
       New York: London House & Maxwell, 1967).

2091. Armijn PANÉ, "Imperialists Fenced In," translated by Dean J. Almy,
       Jr., in Echols [item 1033], 53-5.

2092. *Armijn PANÉ, "The Chicken Coop," translated by A. Brotherton, in
       Perspective of Indonesia [item 1050], 122-3.

2093. *Armijn PANÉ, "Toothache *(Sakit Gigi)*," in Hendon [item 2070], 60-
       96.

2094. M.A.M. RENES-BOLDINGH, *Batakoche Sagen en Legenden* (Nijkerk: G.F.
       Callenbach, n.d.).

2095. *Asrul SANI, "Three Village Sketches from Sumatra," translated by
       Boyd Compton, in *Perspective of Indonesia* [item 1050], 150-4.

2096. *Bakri SIREGAR, "Behind the Hills *(Dibalik Bukit)*," in Hendon [item
       2070], 97-123.

2097. *Barus SIREGAR, "The Lute Player *(Pemain Gambus)*," in Hendon [item
       2070], 19-29.

2098. Ras SIREGAR, "He Came By Night *(Ia datang malam hari)*," translated
       by Alberta J. Freidus. Typescript.

2099. *Sitor SITUMORANG, "Mother's Pilgrimage to Paradise," translated
       by Oentoeng Soebroto, in Wigmore [item 3300], 156-63.

2100. *Sitor SITUMORANG, "The Djinn," translated by John M. Echols, in
       Echols [item 1033], 173-7.

2101. *Sitor SITUMORANG, "Snow in Paris (*Saldju di Paris*)," Translated from the Indonesian by Rufus S. Hendon, in *Ventures: Magazine of the Yale Graduate School*, IX (1969).1: 48-54.

2102. Oentoeng SOEBROTO, "The Wish," in Wigmore [item 3300], 332-6.

2103. *Rusman SUTIASUMARGA, "On the Outskirts of the City (*Meminggir Kota*)," in Hendon [item 2070], 30-40.

2104. Pramoedya Ananta TOER, "Happy Associations," from *They Who Are Paralyzed* (1951), translated by Robert C. Bishton, in Echols [item 1033], 143-52.

2105. Pramoedya Ananta TOER, "Vanished Childhood," from *Stories of Blora* (1952), translated by Harry J. Benda, in Echols [item 1033], 153-71.

2106. *Pramoedya Ananta TOER, "Born Before the Dawn," translated by A. Brotherton, in *Perspective of Indonesia* [item 1050], 114-6.

2107. *Pramoedya Ananta TOER, "Born Before the Dawn," translated by A. Brotherton, in Wigmore [item 3300], 118-24.

2108. Pramoedya Ananta TOER, "Inem (*Inem*)," in Hendon [item 2070], 41-59.

MODERN POETRY

2109. *Soetan* Takdir ALISJAHBANA, "Oh Most Beautiful," translated by Burton Raffel and Nurdin Salam, in Echols [item 1033], 31.

2110. *Soetan* Takdir ALISJAHBANA, "Meeting," translated by Burton Raffel and Nurdin Salam, in Echols [item 1033], 31.

2111. *S. Takdir ALISJAHBANA, "Meeting," translated by Burton Raffel and Nurdin Salam, in *Perspective of Indonesia* [item 1050], 121.

2112. *S. Takdir ALISJAHBANA, "Meeting (*Bertemu*)," translated by Burton Raffel and Nurdin Salam, in Burton Raffel, *Anthology of Modern Indonesian Poetry*. Edited by... (Berkeley & Los Angeles: University of California Press, 1964), 36.

2113. *S. Takdir ALISJAHBANA, "Meeting (*Bertemu*)," translated by Burton Raffel and Nurdin Salam, in José [item 3297], 159.

2114. Chairil ANWAR, "Affandi's Slut / *"Betina"-nja Affandi*," in Raffel [item 2052], 108-9. Bilingual text.

2115.   Chairil ANWAR, "Agreement with Friend Soekarno / *Persetudjuan dengan bung Karno*," in Raffel [item 2052], 130-1. Bilingual text.

2116.   Chairil ANWAR, "Alone / *Sendiri*," in Raffel [item 2052], 14-5. Bilingual text.

2117.   Chairil ANWAR, "At the Mosque," translated by Burton Raffel and Nurdin Salam, in Shimer [item 3299], 67.

2118.   Chairil ANWAR, "At the Mosque / *Dimesdjid*," in Raffel [item 2052], 50-1. Bilingual text.

2119.   Chairil ANWAR, *The Complete Poetry and Prose of Chairil Anwar*, in Raffel [item 2052].

2120.   Chairil ANWAR, "D.S.: For Her Album / *Buat Album D.S.*," in Raffel [item 2052], 94-5. Bilingual text.

2121.   Chairil ANWAR, "Dipo Negoro," in Raffel [item 2052], 6-7. Bilingual text.

2122.   Chairil ANWAR, "Dusk in the Harbour," in Wigmore [item 3300], 165.

2123.   Chairil ANWAR, "Dusk in a Little Harbor," in José [item 3297], 241.

2124.   Chairil ANWAR, "Empty / *Hampa*," in Raffel [item 2052], 40-1. Bilingual text.

2125.   Chairil ANWAR, "Evening / *Malam*," in Raffel [item 2052], 84-5. Bilingual text.

2126.   Chairil ANWAR, "Evening in the Mountains / *Malam di pegunungan*," in Raffel [item 2052], 122-3. Bilingual text.

2127.   Chairil ANWAR, "Fir Trees in Rows / *Derai-derai tjemara*," in Raffel [item 2052], 152-3. Bilingual text.

2128.   Chairil ANWAR, "For Mrs. N. / *Buat njonja N.*," in Raffel [item 2052], 146-7. Bilingual text.

2129.   Chairil ANWAR, "For Miss Gadis Rasid / *Buat Gadis Rasid*," in Raffel [item 2052], 140-1. Bilingual text.

2130.   Chairil ANWAR, "For the Poet Bohang / *Kepada penjair Bohang*," in Raffel [item 2052], 80-1. Bilingual text.

2131.   Chairil ANWAR, "Forward / *Madju*,"[1] in Raffel [item 2052], 6-7. Bilingual text.

2132.   Chairil ANWAR, "Forward / *Madju*,"[2] in Raffel [item 2052], 8-9. Bilingual text.

2133. Chairil ANWAR, "Free / *Merdeka*," in Raffel [item 2052], 60-1. Bilingual text.

2134. Chairil ANWAR, "From Her / *Dari dia*," in Raffel [item 2052], 112-3. Bilingual text.

2135. Chairil ANWAR, "A Fugitive / *Pelarian*," in Raffel [item 2052], 16-7. Bilingual text.

2136. Chairil ANWAR, "Goodbye / *Selamat tinggal*," in Raffel [item 2052], 54-5. Bilingual text.

2137. Chairil ANWAR, "Gravestone / *Nisan*," in Raffel [item 2052], 2-3. Bilingual text.

2138. Chairil ANWAR, "Heaven (*Sorga*)," translated by Burton Raffel and Nurdin Salam, in Raffel [item 2112], 68.

2139. Chairil ANWAR, "Heaven / *Sorga*," in Raffel [item 2052], 120-1. Bilingual text.

2140. Chairil ANWAR, "I Run Around With Them / *Aku bersikar antara mereka*," in Raffel [item 2052], 144-5. Bilingual text.

2141. Chairil ANWAR, "I'm Back Again (title supplied)," in Raffel [item 2052], 156-7. Bilingual text.

2142. Chairil ANWAR, "In the Train / *Dalam kereta*," in Raffel [item 2052], 74-5. Bilingual text.

2143. Chairil ANWAR, "In Vain," translated by Burton Raffel and Nurdin Salam, in Echols [item 1033], 66.

2144. Chairil ANWAR, "In Vain / *Sia-sia*," in Raffel [item 2052], 10-1. Bilingual text.

2145. Chairil ANWAR, "Ina Mia / *Ina Mia*," in Raffel [item 2052], 134-5. Bilingual text.

2146. Chairil ANWAR, "Invitation / *Adjakan*," in Raffel [item 2052], 12-3. Bilingual text.

2147. Chairil ANWAR, "Jesus Christ / *Isa*," in Raffel [item 2052], 68-9. Bilingual text.

2148. Chairil ANWAR, "Krawang-Bekasi / *Krawang-Bekasi*," in Raffel [item 2052], 126-9. Bilingual text.

2149. Chairil ANWAR, "The Law / *Hukum*," in Raffel [item 2052], 22-3. Bilingual text.

2150.   Chairil ANWAR, "Let's Leave Here (title supplied)," in Raffel [item 2052], 158-9. Bilingual text.

2151.   Chairil ANWAR, "Let This Evening Go By (title supplied)," in Raffel [item 2052], 154-5. Bilingual text.

2152.   Chairil ANWAR, "Life / *Penghidupan*," in Raffel [item 2052], 4-5. Bilingual text.

2153.   Chairil ANWAR, "Like This (title supplied)," in Raffel [item 2052], 132-3. Bilingual text.

2154.   Chairil ANWAR, "Me," translated by Burton Raffel and Nurdin Salam, in Echols [item 1033], 66.

2155.   Chairil ANWAR, "Me / *Aku*,"[1] in Raffel [item 2052], 20-1. Bilingual text.

2156.   Chairil ANWAR, "Me / *Aku*,"[2] in Raffel [item 2052], 46-7. Bilingual text.

2157.   Chairil ANWAR, "Memories / *Kenangan*," in Raffel [item 2052], 36-7. Bilingual text.

2158.   Chairil ANWAR, "Mirat's Young, Chairil's Young / *Mirat muda, Chairil muda*," in Raffel [item 2052], 148-9. Bilingual text.

2159.   Chairil ANWAR, "My Friend and I / *Kawanku dan aku*," in Raffel [item 2052], 42-3. Bilingual text.

2160.   Chairil ANWAR, "My House / *Rumahku*," in Raffel [item 2052], 38-9. Bilingual text.

2161.   Chairil ANWAR, "My Love's On a Far-away Island," translated by Burton Raffel and Nurdin Salam, in *Chapbook of Contemporary Asian Poetry* [item 3289], 21-2.

2162.   Chairil ANWAR, "My Love's On a Faraway Island," translated by Burton Raffel and Nurdin Salam, in Shimer [item 3299], 68.

2163.   Chairil ANWAR, "My Love Far in the Islands," translated by Derwent May, in Shimer [item 3299], 68-9.

2164.   Chairil ANWAR, "My Love's on a Faraway Island / *Tjintaku djauh dipulau*," in Raffel [item 2052], 106-7. Bilingual text.

2165.   Chairil ANWAR, "News from the Sea / *Kabar dari laut*," in Raffel [item 2052], 102-3. Bilingual text.

2166.   Chairil ANWAR, "1943 / *1943*," in Raffel [item 2052], 66-7. Bilingual text.

2167.   Chairil ANWAR, "Nocturno (fragment)," translated by Burton Raffel
        and Nurdin Salam, in Echols [item 1033], 65.

2168.   Chairil ANWAR, "Nocturno: a Fragment / *Nocturno (Fragment),*" in
        Raffel [item 2052], 96-7. Bilingual text.

2169.   Chairil ANWAR, "Notes for 1946," translated by Burton Raffel and
        Nurdin Salam, in Echols [item 1033], 63-4.

2170.   Chairil ANWAR, "Notes for 1946 / *Tjatetan th. 1946,*" in Raffel
        [item 2052], 92-3. Bilingual text.

2171.   Chairil ANWAR, "On Top of the Mountain / *Puntjak,*" in Raffel [item
        2052], 138-9. Bilingual text.

2172.   Chairil ANWAR, "An Ordinary Song / *Lagu biasa,*" in Raffel [item
        2052], 26-7. Bilingual text.

2173.   Chairil ANWAR, "Our Garden / *Taman,*" in Raffel [item 2052], 24-5.
        Bilingual text.

2174.   Chairil ANWAR, "Paradise," translated by Ahmed Ali and Idham, in
        Perspective of Indonesia [item 1050], 123.

2175.   Chairil ANWAR, "Parting / *Bertjerai,*" in Raffel [item 2052], 44-5.
        Bilingual text.

2176.   Chairil ANWAR, "Patience / *Kesabaran,*" in Raffel [item 2052], 32-
        3. Bilingual text.

2177.   Chairil ANWAR, "Poem for Basuki Resobowo / *Sadjak buat Basuki Re-
        sobowo,*" in Raffel [item 2052], 118-9. Bilingual text.

2178.   Chairil ANWAR, "Prayer / *Doa,*" in Raffel [item 2052], 70-1. Bilin-
        gual text.

2179.   Chairil ANWAR, "A Proclamation / *Pemberian tahu,*" in Raffel [item
        2052], 116-7. Bilingual text.

2180.   Chairil ANWAR, "A Pure Rhyme / *Sadjak putih,*" in Raffel [item
        2052], 72-3. Bilingual text.

2181.   Chairil ANWAR, "A Reckoning-Up / *Perhitungan,*" in Raffel [item
        2052], 34-5. Bilingual text.

2182.   Chairil ANWAR, "Revenge / *Dendam,*" in Raffel [item 2052], 58-9.
        Bilingual text.

2183.   Chairil ANWAR, "A Room," translated by Burton Raffel and Nurdin
        Salam, in *Chapbook of Contemporary Asian Poetry* [item 3289], 22-3.

2184.   Chairil ANWAR, "A Room / *Sebuah kamar*," in Raffel [item 2052], 88-
        9. Bilingual text.

2185.   Chairil ANWAR, *Selected Poems*. Translated by Burton Raffel and
        Nurdin Salam. With an Introduction by James S. Holmes. The World
        Poets Series [No. 4] (New York: New Directions, n.d. [*ca* 1962]).

2186.   Chairil ANWAR, "A Sentry at Night / *Perdjurit djaga malam*," in
        Raffel [item 2052], 136-7. Bilingual text.

2187.   Chairil ANWAR, "Situation / *Situasi*," in Raffel [item 2052], 110-
        1. Bilingual text.

2188.   Chairil ANWAR, "Some Are Plundered, Some Escape / *Jang terampas
        dan jang luput*," in Raffel [item 2052], 150-1. Bilingual text.

2189.   Chairil ANWAR, "A Story / *Tjerita*," in Raffel [item 2052], 48-9.
        Bilingual text.

2190.   Chairil ANWAR, "Story for a Girl, Dien Tamaela," translated by
        Ahmed Ali and Idham, in *Perspective of Indonesia* [item 1050], 113.

2191.   Chairil ANWAR, "Story for a Girl, Dien Tamaela," in Wigmore [item
        3300], 338-9.

2192.   Chairil ANWAR, "A Tale for Dien Tamaela," translated by Burton
        Raffel and Nurdin Salam, in José [item 3297], 158.

2193.   Chairil ANWAR, "A Tale for Dien Tamaela," translated by Burton
        Raffel and Nurdin Salam, in Raffel [item 2112], 69-70.

2194.   Chairil ANWAR, "A Tale for Dien Tamaela / *Tjerita buat Dien Tama-
        ela*," in Raffel [item 2052], 98-101. Bilingual text.

2195.   Chairil ANWAR, "To a Beggar / *Kepada peminta-minta*," in Raffel
        [item 2052], 52-3. Bilingual text.

2196.   Chairil ANWAR, "To a Friend," translated by Burton Raffel and Nur-
        din Salam, in Echols [item 1033], 65.

2197.   Chairil ANWAR, "To a Friend," translated by Burton Raffel and Nur-
        din Salam, in José [item 3297], 162.

2198.   Chairil ANWAR, "To a Friend / *Kepada kawan*," in Raffel [item
        2052], 114-5. Bilingual text.

2199.   Chairil ANWAR, "To Gadis," in Wigmore [item 3300], 246.

2200.   Chairil ANWAR, "To the Painter Affandi / *Kepada pelukis Affandi*,"
        in Raffel [item 2052], 90-1. Bilingual text.

2201. Chairil ANWAR, "Together / *Orang berdua*," in Raffel [item 2052],
       86-7. Bilingual text.

2202. Chairil ANWAR, "Tuti's Ice Cream," translated by Burton Raffel
       and Nurdin Salam, in Echols [item 1033], 64.

2203. Chairil ANWAR, "Tuti's Ice Cream / *Tuti artic*," in Raffel [item
       2052], 124-5. Bilingual text.

2204. Chairil ANWAR, "Twilight at a Little Harbor / *Sendja di pelabuhan
       ketjil*," in Raffel [item 2052], 104-5. Bilingual text.

2205. Chairil ANWAR, "The Voice of the Night / *Suara malam*," in Raffel
       [item 2052], 18-9. Bilingual text.

2206. Chairil ANWAR, "We Wobble Along (title supplied)," in Raffel [item
       2052], 62-3. Bilingual text.

2207. Chairil ANWAR, "We're Ready / *Siap-sedia*," in Raffel [item 2052],
       76-9. Bilingual text.

2208. Chairil ANWAR, "While the Moon Gleams (title supplied)," in Raffel
       [item 2052], 142-3. Bilingual text.

2209. Chairil ANWAR, "Whistling Song / *Lagu siul*," in Raffel [item
       2052], 82-3. Bilingual text.

2210. Chairil ANWAR, "A Whore and My Wife / *Kupu malam dan biniku*," in
       Raffel [item 2052], 28-9. Bilingual text.

2211. Chairil ANWAR, "Willingness," translated by Burton Raffel and Nur-
       din Salam, in Echols [item 1033], 64.

2212. Chairil ANWAR, "Willingness / *Penerimaan*," in Raffel [item 2052],
       30-1. Bilingual text.

2213. Chairil ANWAR, "Your Mouth (title supplied)," in Raffel [item
       2052], 56-7. Bilingual text.

2214. Chairil ANWAR, "?," in Raffel [item 2052], 64-5. Bilingual text.

2215. Rivai APIN, "Elegy," translated by Burton Raffel and Nurdin Salam,
       in Echols [item 1033], 63.

2216. *Rivai APIN, "Between Two Worlds," translated by Ahmed Ali and
       Idham, in·*Perspective of Indonesia* [item 1050], 163.

2217. *Rivai APIN, "Between Two Unfinished Worlds," translated by Jean
       Kennedy and Burton Raffel, in Raffel [item 2112], 72-3.

2218. Rivai APIN, "The Wanderer," in Wigmore [item 3300], 125.

2219. Harry AVELING, "Contemporary Indonesian Poetry," in *Twentieth Century*, December 1970: 101-9.

2220. Toto Sudarto BACHTIAR, "Djakarta in the Evening," translated by Derwent May, in Shimer [item 3299], 71.

2221. *Louis-Charles DAMAIS, *Cent deux poèmes indonésiens (1925-1950)*, mis en français par... Préface du Prof. Dr R. Prijono. Illustrations de M. Salim (Paris: Adrien-Maisonneuve, 1965). Excellent selection from the work of the early poets.

2222. Donna M. DICKINSON, *Sharp Gravel: Indonesian Poems by Chairil Anwar*. Translated by... (Berkeley: Center for Southeast Asia Studies, [c 1960]). Bilingual text, mimeographed.

2223. *[Amir HAMZAH], "Because of You," in Wigmore [item 3300], 337.

2224. *Amir HAMZAH, "Because of You," translated by S.T. Alisjahbana, Sabina Thornton, and Burton Raffel, in Shimer [item 3299], 66-7.

2225. *Amir HAMZAH, "In Praise of You (*Memudji dikau*)," translated by Burton Raffel and Nurdin Salam, in Raffel [item 2112], 23.

2226. *Amir HAMZAH, "In Praise of You (*Memudji dikau*)," translated by Burton Raffel and Nurdin Salam, in José [item 3297], 164.

2227. *Amir HAMZAH, "Prayer," translated by Burton Raffel and Nurdin Salam, in Echols [item 1033], 32.

2228. *Amir HAMZAH, "Prayer," translated by Burton Raffel and Nurdin Salam, in *Perspective of Indonesia* [item 1050], 158.

2229. *Amir HAMZAH, "Prayer," translated by Burton Raffel and Nurdin Salam, in Raffel [item 2112], 30.

2230. Taufiq ISMAIL, "*Sajak2 dari Indonesia* / Poems from Indonesia," translated by Adrienne Balfas, in *Tenggara*, I (1967): 104-11.

2231. A.H. JOHNS, "Chairil Anwar: An interpretation," in *BTLV*, 120 (1964).4: 393-408.

2232. Joke MOELJONO, "In Alien Land," translated by James S. Holmes, in *Perspective of Indonesia* [item 1050], 105.

2233. J. MOELJONO, "*Pemuda*," in Wigmore [item 3300], 164-5.

2234. M. NURDIN ABD, "The False," translated by Oentoeng Soebroto and Robert Chapman, in Wigmore [item 3300], 57-8.

2235. *Burton RAFFEL, *Anthology of Modern Indonesian Poetry* [item 2112].

2236. *Burton RAFFEL, *The Development of Modern Indonesian Poetry* (Albany: State University of New York Press, [c 1967]).

2237. *Burton RAFFEL, *The Complete Poetry and Prose of Chairil Anwar* [item 2052].

2238. W.S. RENDRA, "Ballad of the Men of Limestone Soil," translated by Derwent May, in *Chapbook of Contemporary Asian Poetry* [item 3289], 19-20.

2239. W.S. RENDRA, "Ballad of the Men of the Limestone Stoil," translated by Derwent May, in Raffel [item 2112], 144-5.

2240. W.S. RENDRA, "Ballad of the Men of the Limestone Soil," translated by Derwent May, in José [item 3297], 165-6.

2241. W.S. RENDRA, "Little Sister Narti," translated by Burton Raffel, in Shimer [item 3299], 72.

2242. W.S. RENDRA, "A Pickpocket's Advice to His Mistress," translated by H.G. Aveling, in *Tenggara*, II (1968).2: 26-31.

2243. W.S. RENDRA, "Prostitutes of Jakarta, Unite!," translated by H.G. Aveling, in *Tenggara*, II (1968).2: 20-5.

2244. W.S. RENDRA, "Swan Song," translated by H.G. Aveling, in *Tenggara*, II (1968).2: 4-21.

2245. Asrul SANI, "Remember Father, Remember Father," translated by Jean Kennedy, in Shimer [item 3299], 69-70.

2246. *Sitor SITUMORANG, "Chartres Cathedral," in Wigmore [item 3300], 247-8.

2247. *Sitor SITUMORANG, "Cathédrale de Chartres (Chartres Cathedral)," translated by S. Thornton, in José [item 3297], 160-1.

2248. Sitor SITUMORANG, "Swimming Pool: For Rulan," translated by Jean Kennedy and Burton Raffel, in Shimer [item 3299], 69.

2249. Sitor SITUMORANG, "Waking," translated by Jean Kennedy and Burton Raffel, in *Chapbook of Contemporary Asian Poetry* [item 3289], 21.

2250. R.B. SLAMETMULJANA, *Poëzie in Indonesia: Een literaire en taalkundige studie*, door... (Leuven: Instituut voor Oriëntalisme, Universiteit te Leuven, 1954).

2251. [Mme] Hurustati SUBANDRIO, "Indonesian," in Hatto [item 3296], 196-8. Statement on the traditional *alba*, somewhat anachronistic in view of the recency of the language.

2252.   E. TATENGKENG, "Traveler First Class (*Penumpang Kelas I*)," trans-
        lated by James S. Holmes, in Raffel [item 2112], 48.

2253.   E. TATENGKENG, "Traveler First Class (*Penumpang Kelas I*)," trans-
        lated by James S. Holmes, in José [item 3297], 163.

2254.   J.E. TATENGKENG, "Traveler First Class," translated by James S.
        Holmes, in *Chapbook of Contemporary Asian Poetry* [item 3289], 23.

2255.   J.E. TATENGKENG, "Traveler First Class," translated by James S.
        Holmes, in Shimer [item 3299], 65-6.

2256.   J.E. TATENGKENG, "On the Shore: Twilight," translated by Burton
        Raffel and Nurdin Salam, in Shimer [item 3299], 66.

2257.   A. TEEUW, review of *Sharp Gravel* [item 2222], in *BTLV*, 117 (1961).
        3: 396-8.

2258.   A. TEEUW, review of *Chairil Anwar. Pelopor Angkatan 45* by H.B.
        Jassin, in *BTLV*, 117 (1961).3: 398-9.

2259.   *Louise WALUJATI SUPANGAT, "Parting," translated by Burton Raffel
        and Nurdin Salam, in Echols [item 1033], 66.

2260.   *WALUJATI, "Parting," translated by Burton Raffel and Nurdin Salam,
        in *Perspective of Indonesia* [item 1050], 144.

2261.   *Louise WALUJATI HATMOHARSOIO, "Parting (*Berpisah*)," translated by
        Burton Raffel and Nurdin Salam, in Raffel [item 2112], 96.

                                    DRAMA

2262.   Harry G. AVELING, "An Analysis of Utuy Tatang Sontani's 'Suling',"
        in *BTLV*, 125 (1969).2: 328-43.

2263.   Hubert S. BANNER, "Java's Shadow Shows and the Kawi Epics," in
        London Mercury, XVI (August 1928): 389-99.

2264.   S. BLOCK and A.K. COOMARASWAMY, "Javanese Theatre," in *Asia* (July
        1929): 536-9.

2265.   *James R. BRANDON, *On Thrones of Gold: Three Javanese Shadow Plays*.
        Edited with an introduction by... (Cambridge: Harvard University
        Press, 1970).

2266.   *James R. BRANDON, "The Reincarnation of Rama (*Wahju Purba Sedja-
        ti*)," translated by Pandam Guritno Siswoharsojo and Stephen R.
        Alkire. English version by..., in Brandon [item 2265], 81-170.

2267. *James R. BRANDON, "Irawan's Wedding (*Irawan Rabi*)," translated by Stephen R. Alkire and Pandam Guritno Siswoharsojo. English version by..., in Brandon [item 2265], 171-267.

2268. *James R. BRANDON, "The Death of Karna (*Karna Tanding*)," Javanese version and English translation by Pandam Guritno Siswoharsojo. English version by James R. Brandon and Stephen R. Alkire, in Brandon [item 2265], 269-359.

2269. Miguel COVARRUBIAS, *The Island of Bali* (New York: Alfred A. Knopf, 1942), 205-55.

2270. Tyra de KLEEN, *Wayang (Javanese Theatre)*. Second Edition. The Ethnographical Museum of Sweden, Stockholm (Statens Etnografiska Museum), New Series, Publication No. 4 (Stockholm: Gothia, 1947).

2271. *Tyra de KLEEN, "The Story of Arayana," in her *Wayang* [item 2270], 23-30.

2272. Beryl de ZOETE and Walter SPIES, *Dance and Drama in Bali* (New York and London: Harper, 1939).

2273. Gerd HÖPFNER, *Südostasiatische Schattenspiele: Masken und Figuren aus Java und Thailand im Museum für Völkerkunde, Berlin*. Katalog von... (Berlin: Museum von Völkerkunde, Staatliche Museen, Stiftung Preussischer Kulturbesitz, Abteilung Südasien, 1967).

2274. MANGKUNAGARA VII *of Surakarta, On the Wayang Kulit (Purwa) and Its Symbolic and Mystical Elements*. Translated from the Dutch by Claire Holt. Data Paper No. 27 (Ithaca, N.Y.: Southeast Asia Program, Cornell University, 1957).

2275. H. MEINHARD, "The Javanese Wajang and Its Indian Prototype," in *Man*, 39 (1939): 109-11.

2276. James L. PEACOCK, *Rites of Modernization: Symbolic and Social Aspects of Indonesian Proletarian Drama* (Chicago: University of Chicago Press, 1968).

2277. J. RADHAKRISHNAN, "The Development of Drama and Stage in Indonesia," in *Indonesian Spectator*, XI (1 November 1958): 15-6.

2278. T. ROORDA, *Pandji-Verhalen*. Twee *wajang gedog* verhalen in 1869 in het Javaansch uitgegeven door... Op nieuw uitgegeven (met aanvulling der aanteekeningen en voorzien vaan een alfabetische lijst van eigennamen) door J.G.H. Gunning (Leiden: E.J. Brill, 1896).

2279. G.D. van WENGAN, review of *Wajang purwa (Le jeu d'ombres d'Indonésie)* by Moebirman, in *BTLV*, 118 (1962).3: 394-6.

V. LAOS

GENERAL

2280. Hubert DESCHAMPS and anonymous, "Laos: History," in *EB (1962)*, 13: 712ab.

2281. *Henri DEYDIER, *Introduction à la connaissance du Laos* (Saigon: Imprimerie Française d'Outre-Mer, 1952). Useful survey of Lao culture by an outstanding fieldworker.

2282. *Louis FINOT, "Recherches sur la littérature laotienne," in *BEFEO*, XVII (1917).5: 84-113. Classic description of main genres with tally of known works; not yet superseded.

2283. *Thao* KÉNE, *Bibliographie du Laos*. Comité Littéraire Lao, Ministère de l'Education Nationale (Vientiane: Editions du Comité Littéraire, 1958).

2284. Pierre-Bernard LAFONT, "Les écritures 'tay du Laos," in *BEFEO*, L (1962).2: 367-93.

2285. Pierre-Bernard LAFONT, "Les écritures pāli du Laos," in *BEFEO*, L (1962).2: 395-405.

2286. *Pierre-Bernard LAFONT, *Bibliographie du Laos*. Publications de l'Ecole Française d'Extrême-Orient, Volume L (Paris: Ecole Française d'Extrême-Orient, 1964). Best work of its kind available, with literature in translation listed on 119-23.

2287. *Pierre-Bernard LAFONT, "Inventaire des manuscrits des Pagodes du Laos," in *BEFEO*, LII (1965).2: 429-545. Valuable as providing an exact statement of monastic library holdings.

2288. Frank M. LeBAR and Adrienne SUDDARD (ed.), *Laos: Its People, Its Society, Its Culture*, by the Staff and Associates of the Human Relations Area Files. Survey of World Cultures, [No. 8] (New Haven: HRAF Press, [c 1960]), 91-3.

2289. François MARTINI, "La langue," in *Présence du Royaume Lao* [item 2295], 999-1005.

2290. Georges MASPERO, "Littérature laotienne," in *Un empire colonial français: l'Indochine*. Ouvrage publié sous la direction de M. Georges Maspero (Paris et Bruxelles: G. Van OEst, 1929), I: 305-7.

2291.   John McKINSTRY, *Bibliography of Laos and Ethnically Related Areas*.
        Laos Project Paper No. 22 (Los Angeles: Department of Anthropolo-
        gy, University of California, n.d. [1961]).

2292.   Ronald PERRY, "Translations from the Lao," in *The Hudson Review*,
        XIII (1960).1: 74-86.

2293.   Phouvong PHIMMASONE, "La littérature," in *Présence du Royaume Lao*
        [item 2295], 1006-13.

2294.   *Thao PHOUVONG, *Initiation à la littérature laotienne*. Cours et
        Conférences de l'Ecole Française d'Extrême-Orient, 1948-1949 (Ha-
        noi: Imprimerie Minsang, n.d. [*ca* 1950]). Best available overview
        of literature.

2295.   *Présence du Royaume Lao, pays du Million d'Eléphants et du Parasol
        blanc*. Numéro spécial de *FA*, XII.118-119-120 (1956).

2296.   *Rains in the Jungle (Lao Short Stories)* (Hanoi: Neo Lao Haksat
        Publications, 1967).

2297.   *The Wood Grouse*. Cover and illustration by Kham Deng (Hanoi: Neo
        Lao Haksat Publications, 1968). More short stories by Pathet Lao
        writers.

                            FOLK LITERATURE

2298.   *Thao* Nhouy ABHAY, "Quelques contes," in his *Aspects du pays lao*.
        Préface de Charles Rochet (Vientiane: Editions Comité Littéraire
        Lao / Saigon: Imprimerie d'Extrême-Orient, 1956), 107-19.

2299.   *Thao* Nhouy ABHAY, "Les verrats et le tigre (conte lao)," in *FA*,
        XIII.128 (1957): 526-30.

2300.   *Thao* Nhouy ABHAY, "Quatre légendes lao," in *FA*, XIV.138-139 (1957):
        390-4.

2301.   Anonymous, "Une légende de la tentation du Bouddha," in *FA*, III.
        27 (1948): 746-8.

2302.   Anonymous, "Dinner for the Monk," in Courlander, *The Tiger's Whis-
        ker* [item 3293], 111-4.

2303.   Anonymous, "Dinner for the Monk," in Garnett [item 3294], 155-7.

2304.   *Charles ARCHAIMBAULT, "Le cycle de *Nang* Oua - *Nang* Malong et son
        substrat sociologique," in *FA/A*, Nouvelle Série, XVII.170 (1961):
        2581-604.

2305. Pierre BITARD, "Boua-Rah, légende Tay-lu," in *BSEI*, Nouvelle Sé-
       rie, XXXIII (1958).4: 451-70.

2306. *D^r* Jean BRENGUES, *Contes et légendes du pays laotien* (Saigon:
       Coudurier et Montégout, 1906). Remarkably full and valuable an-
       thology.

2307. *D^r* Jean BRENGUES, "Contes et fables populaires," in his *Contes et
       légendes* [item 2306], 5-63. Comprises "Les grenouilles" (5); "Com-
       ment la petite grenouille *khiet* tua le lion" (5-6); "Le chat et
       la chèvre" (6); "Comment la grenouille tue [*sic*] un éléphant"
       (7); "Le tigre et le coq sauvage" (7-8); "La grenouille *ũng*" (8);
       "Les deux loutres" (9); "La petite barque et l'homme" (9-10);
       "Les petits oiseaux" (10-1); "Pourquoi les lièvres n'aiment que
       l'eau de la rosée" (11-2); "Le tigre vieux" (12); "Le canard et
       la poule sultane" (13); "Le cheval qui aime son maître" (13-4);
       "Le lièvre qui tombe dans un puits" (14-5); "Histoire d'un trou-
       peau de rats" (15-6); "L'éléphant sauvage" (16-7); "Pourquoi les
       bœufs ne poursuivent pas les chasseurs" (17); "Pourquoi les cor-
       beaux sont noirs et les paons de couleur bigarrée" (17-8); "Pour-
       quoi les crocodiles n'aiment pas les chiens" (18-9); "Le crocodile
       et le singe" (19-20); "Le tigre, le singe et le lièvre" (20-2);
       "Le *Nok seng*" (22-4); "Comment les marabouts sont devenus chauves"
       (24-5); "Conte du corbeau qui veut manger le ver" (25-6); "His-
       toire du Souei qui tue son fils" (27-8); "Les deux camarades" (28-
       9); "Le bœuf Phijisan" (30-1); "Histoire d'hommes chauves" (31-3);
       "Légende de l'oiseau *Hatsadiling*" (34-7); "Un petit bœuf" (37-41);
       "Le paon d'or" (41-3); "Histoire du bonze au jacquier et du bonze
       aux bambous" (43-6); "Histoire des deux *Chao-hua-pho*, dont l'un
       avait un jardin d'aubergines et l'autre une bambouseraie" (46-7);
       "Histoire du bonze au buffle" (47-8); "Histoire du vieux bonze à
       qui l'on fit manger de la crotte de chien" (49-50); "Fable du
       bonze avare" (50); "Histoire du bonze qu'on réveille de bonne
       heure" (51-2); "Histoire du bonze *saramok*" (52-3); "Histoire du
       bonze au crabe" (53-4); "Histoire du bonze au cou coupé" (55);
       "Le bonze mystifié" (55-7); "Le vieux bonze badigeonné de piment"
       (57-9); "Le bonze avare tombé du palmier" (59-61); "Le vieux bonze
       au *mak mi*" (61-3).

2308. *D^r* Jean BRENGUES, "Contes judiciaires," in his *Contes et légendes*
       [item 2306], 63-8. Comprises "Quand une bille de bois entraîne une
       barque" (64); "Sur l'assassinat du fils du *phaya*" (65); "Découverte
       d'un trésor en fendant du bois" (65-6); "Le paon du *phaya*" (66-7);
       "Etre dévoré par un génie malfaisant est un grand malheur" (67);
       "Histoire de deux femmes allant au bain" (68).

2309. *D^r* Jean BRENGUES, "Un récit de *Molam*: *Thao*-Singsai," in his *Contes
       et légendes* [item 2306], 68-88. A fine oral version of the *Sang
       Thong* tale.

2309. *D^r* Jean BRENGUES, "*Thao* Sinsay." Translated [by PNJ from item

2308, 72-88]. Typescript.

2310. *Dr Jean BRENGUES, "*Nang* Munlatantai," in his *Contes et légendes* [item 2306], 88-155. Collection of tales bound together by the Sheherazad motif, translated from an incomplete manuscript. Comprises "Fable du bœuf Utsupharat" (91-3); "Fable du puceron et de la punaise" (93); "Conte du *Nok jang*" (93-5); "Fable du puceron et de la punaise (suite)" (95-6); "Fable de la Tortue et des deux Cygnes" (96-7); "Fable du bœuf Utsupharat (suite)" (97); "Fable du lion et de l'éléphant" (97-8); "Fable du *Nok têt té*" (98-9); "Fable du chasseur et du singe" (99); "Fable du tigre, du singe, du serpent et de l'homme tombés dans un puits" (99-101); "Fable du chasseur et du singe (suite)" (101); "Fable du tigre et de l'ermite" (101-2); "Fable du renard et du tigre" (102); "Fable du tisserin, de la mouche luisante et du singe" (102-3); "Fable du chasseur et du singe" (103); "Fable du singe qui a appris à porter une épée" (103-4); "Fable du chasseur et du singe (suite)" (104); "Fable du *Nok têt té*" (104-5); "Fable du bœuf Utsupharat (suite)" (105-6); "Fable des deux *Nok sai*" (106); "Fable du *phaya* Corbeau" (106-7); "Fable des deux *Nok sai* (suite)" (107); "Fable du *phaya Khut* et de la tortue" (108); "Fable du tigre *khong* et des deux *Nok sai kon*" (109); "Fable du *Nok sai* (suite)" (109-10); "Fable du brigand Baphuttaka" (110-2); "Fable des trois poissons" (112); "Fable du bœuf Utsupharat (suite)" (112-3); "Fable du *phaya* Kéjaraxa" (113-6); "Fable du bœuf Utsupharat (suite)" (116-8); "Fable des grenouilles et du serpent" (119-20); "Fable du singe Buthala" (120-4); "Fable du mari Vithayakham" (124-5); "Fable du serpent d'eau et des grenouilles (suite)" (125); "Fable du charmeur de serpents" (125-7); "Fable du chasseur, de l'éléphant, de la vipère et du renard" (127-8); "Fable de Phana et Vapha" (128-30); "Fable de Mullakari" (131-4); "Fable de Phana et Vapha (suite)" (134-6); "Fable du serpent et des grenouilles (suite)" (136); "Fable du charpentier et du singe" (136-7); "Visaovasurat. -Fable des deux *phayas*" (137-40); "Fable du *phaya* Thatsaratharaxa" (140-3); "Fable du chasseur et du génie de la forêt" (143-4); "Fable du *phaya* Tulaxathana" (144); "Fable du serpent et des grenouilles (suite)" (145); "Fable des deux boucs, du renard, du chat, du *Nok jang*, d'un brahme voyageur et de trois femmes" (145-52); "Fable du serpent et des grenouilles (suite)" (152-4).

2311. *Mme* M. GERNY-MARCHAL, "Contes cambodgiens et laotiens," in *Revue indochinoise*, Nouvelle Série, XXXII (1919).7-8: 71-7. Contains "La reconnaissance d'un roi: Conte laotien" (72-7).

2312. Andrée-Yvette GOUINEAU, "Les élèves du Lycée Pavie de Vientiane vous racontent quelques fables et légendes de leur pays, telles que la tradition orale les leur a transmises," textes recueillis par..., in *Présence du Royaume Lao* [item 2295], 1087-1103.

2313. *Pierre-Bernard LAFONT, "Contes p'u tai," in *BSEI*, Nouvelle Série, XLVI (1971).1: 21-48. Translation, with analytical commentary, of five P'u-tai tales from northeastern Laos collected in 1925.

2314. Banyen LÉVY, "La Phi-Kong-Koy," légende recueillie par..., in *Présence du Royaume Lao* [item 2295], 1083-4.

2315. Banyen LÉVY, "La tortue d'or," légende recueillie par..., in *Présence du Royaume Lao* [item 2295], 1084-6.

2316. Paul LÉVY et Pierre NGINN, "Proverbes," in *Présence du Royaume Lao* [item 2295], 1079-82.

2317. Ronald PERRY, "The Animals' Children," in his "Translations from the Lao" [item 2292], 82-5.

2318. Ronald PERRY, "The Origin of Monkeys," in his "Translations from the Lao" [item 2292], 80-2.

2319. Ronald PERRY, "The Two Sparrows," in his "Translations from the Lao" [item 2292], 85-6.

HINDU-BUDDHIST LITERATURE

2320. *Dr J. BRENGUES, "Une version laotienne du *Pañcatantra*," in *JA*, XI (1908): 357-434.

2321. Henri DEYDIER, "Les origines et la naissance de Rāvaṇa dans le *Rāmāyaṇa* laotien," in *Mélanges publiés en l'honneur du Cinquantenaire de l'Ecole Française d'Extrême-Orient*, published as *BEFEO*, XLIV (1951): 141-6 + plates.

2322. Henri DEYDIER, "Le Râmâyana au Laos," in *FA*, 78 (Novembre 1952): 871-3.

2323. *Prince* DHANI, "The Rama Jataka (a Lao version of the story of Rama)," in *JSS*, XXXVI (1946).1: 1-22.

2324. *Louis FINOT, "Le *Pañcatantra* laotien," in his "Recherches sur la littérature laotienne" [item 2282], 84-113.

2325. G. TERRAL-MARTINI, "*Velāmajātaka*," in *BEFEO*, XLIX (1959).2: 609-16 + plate.

INSCRIPTIONS

2326. Auguste PAVIE, *Recherches sur l'histoire du Cambodge, du Laos et du Siam*. Mission Pavie Indo-Chine, 1879-1895. Etudes diverses, II (Paris: Ernest Leroux, 1898), 169-488.

CHRONICLES

2327. *Charles ARCHAIMBAULT, "Les Annales de l'ancien Royaume de S'ieng Khwang," in *BEFEO*, LIII (1967).2: 557-673 + plates.

2328. *G. COEDÈS, *Documents sur l'histoire politique et religieuse du Laos occidental.* Extrait du *BEFEO*, XXV (1925).1-2 (Hanoi: Imprimerie d'Extrême-Orient, 1925). Primarily on Northeast Thailand but including valuable material on Laos.

2329. Louis FINOT, "Origines légendaires," traduction [des *Annales du Lan Xang*] de..., in *Présence du Royaume Lao* [item 2295], 1047-9.

2330. Louis FINOT, "Fondation du Royaume de Lan Xang Hom Khao," traduction [des *Annales du Lan Xang*] de..., in *Présence du Royaume Lao* [item 2295], 1057-60.

2331. Louis FINOT, "Etablissement du Bouddhisme," traduction [des *Annales du Lan Xang*] de..., in *Présence du Royaume Lao* [item 2295], 1073-6.

2332. M.L. MANICH, *History of Laos, including the History of Lannathai, Chiengmai* (Bangkok: Nai Vitaya Rajiravanichathep, 1967).

2333. Auguste PAVIE, *Recherches sur l'histoire du Cambodge, du Laos et du Siam.* Mission Pavie Indo-Chine, 1879-1895. Etudes diverses, II (Paris: Ernest Laroux, 1898), 1-144.

2334. Auguste PAVIE, "Le testament du Khun Borom," traduction [des *Annales du Lan Xang*] de..., in *Présence du Royaume Lao* [item 2295], 1051-5.

2335. Auguste PAVIE, "Le sacre de Fa Ngoum," traduction [des *Annales du Lan Xang*] de..., in *Présence du Royaume Lao* [item 2295], 1061-5.

2336. Auguste PAVIE, "Naissance du Pra Bang," traduction [des *Annales du Lan Xang*] de..., in *Présence du Royaume Lao* [item 2295], 1067-71.

2337. *Maha Sila* VIRAVONG, *History of Laos.* Translated from the Laotian by the U.S. Joint Publications Research Service (New York: Paragon Book Reprint Corp., 1964).

PRE-MODERN PROSE AND POETRY

2338. *Thao* Nhouy ABHAY, "Folklore laotien: Xine Xay," in *BSEI*, Nouvelle Série, IX (1934).4: 75-91. Literary version of the *Sang Thong* tale.

2339. *Thao* Nhouy ABHAY, "The Court of Love and Poetry in Laos," in *A/AQCS*, II (1952).6: 219-22.

2340. *Thao* Nhouy ABHAY, "Cour d'amour et poésie," in his *Aspects du pays lao*. Préface de Charles Rochet (Vientiane: Editions Comité Littéraire Lao / Saigon: Imprimerie d'Extrême-Orient, 1956), 39-42.

2341. *Thao* Nhouy ABHAY, "La versification," in *Présence du Royaume Lao* [item 2295], 1014-27.

2342. *Thao* Nhouy ABHAY, "Sin Xay," in his *Aspects du pays lao* [item 2340], 91-105.

2343. *Thao* Nhouy ABHAY, "Sin Xay," traduction de..., in *Présence du Royaume Lao* [item 2295], 1028-42.

2344. *Pierre BITARD, "Un manuscrit laotien illustré: La légende de Nang Têng On," in *BSEI*, Nouvelle Série, XXXI (1956).2: 113-33 + plates. Of special interest by reason of the juxtaposition of illustrations and text.

2345. *PANGKHAM, *Sinsay (Chef d'œuvre de la littérature lao)*, par... Traductions de *Thao* Nhouy Abhay et P.S. Nginn. Illustrations de Thit Phou (Bangkok: Tiew-chuy Sae Tiew, 1965). A literary version of the *Sang Thong* tale.

2346 *PANGKHAM, *The Sinsay of Pangkham*. Translated [by PNJ from item 2345]. Typescript. See item 2349.

2347. Auguste PAVIE, "Les douze jeunes filles," in his *Recherches sur la littérature du Cambodge, du Laos et du Siam*. Mission Pavie Indo-Chine, 1879-1895. Etudes diverses, I (Paris: Ernest Leroux, 1898), French translation (27-52) with Lao text (343-9).

2348. Auguste PAVIE, "*Néang* Kakey," in his *Recherches sur la littérature du Cambodge, du Laos et du Siam*. Mission Pavie Indo-Chine, 1879-1895. Etudes diverses, I (Paris: Ernest Leroux, 1898), French translation (155-68) with Lao text (365-7).

2349. Ronald PERRY, "The Sin Xai, after the Lao of Pang Kham," in *The Hudson Review*, XX (1967).1: 11-48.

2350. Ronald PERRY, "Invocation: Namathu," in his "Translations from the Lao" [item 2292], 75-6.

2351. Ronald PERRY, "Song of Mahaxay," in his "Translations from the Lao" [item 2292], 79-80.

2352. Ronald PERRY, "The Song of Sétaphon," in his "Translations from the Lao" [item 2292], 78.

2353. Ronald PERRY, "Two Invocations," in his "Translations from the
       Lao" [item 2292], 79.

                          MODERN PROSE AND POETRY

2354. BOUN X.K., "Ballot No 15," in *Rains in the Jungle* [item 2296], 41-
       61.

2355. BOUN X.K., "One Hundred Silver Piastres," in *Rains in the Jungle*
       [item 2296], 62-77.

2356. Phay BUN, "Return," in *The Wood Grouse* [item 2297], 32-47.

2357. *Thao* Boun LIN, "The Exploit of Old Xieng May and His Daughter,"
       in *Rains in the Jungle* [item 2296], 33-40.

2358. *Thao* Boun LIN, "Kham Fong and His Village," in *The Wood Grouse*
       [item 2297], 23-31.

2359. *Thao* Boun LIN, "Rains in the Jungle," in *Rains in the Jungle*
       [item 2296], 11-22.

2360. *Thao* Bun [*sic*] LIN, "A Lao Youngster," in *The Wood Grouse* [item
       2297], 91-102.

2361. *Thao* Bun LIN, "The Teacher with a Rifle," in *The Wood Grouse*
       [item 2297], 48-56.

2362. *Thao* Bun LIN, "The Wood Grouse," in *The Wood Grouse* [item 2297],
       65-74.

2363. Kham MAN, "An Iron Fighter," in *The Wood Grouse* [item 2297], 57-
       64.

2364. Kham MAN, "A Nam Bac Guerilla," in *The Wood Grouse* [item 2297],
       103-12.

2365. Xieng MOUAN, "Joining the Guerillas," in *The Wood Grouse* [item
       2297], 75-90.

2366. Xieng MOUAN, "Revenge," in *The Wood Grouse* [item 2297], 9-22.

2367. *Katay D. SASORITH, *Souvenirs d'un ancien écolier de Paksé* (Sai-
       gon: Editions Lao Sédone / Imprimerie Nationale d'Extrême-Orient,
       1958). Deft autobiographical sketches of the boyhood of the well-
       known political leader, written originally in French.

2368. THAMNARET, "Nightsong," in Perry, "Translations from the Lao"
       [item 2292], 76-7. Modern verse.

2369. Thoong Van VICHIT, "A laissez-passer," in *Rains in the Jungle*
       [item 2296], 23-32.

                                DRAMA

2370. Henri DEYDIER, *Introduction à la connaissance du Laos* [item
       2281], 88.

GENERAL

2371. Asmah binti *Haji* OMAR, "Towards the Unification of *Bahasa Melayu* and *Bahasa Indonesia*" [item 1027].

2372. *L.F. BRAKEL, "Persian Influence on Malay Literature," in *Abr-Nahrain*, IX (1969-1970).

2373. John F. CADY, *Southeast Asia* [item 1028].

2374. G.W.J. DREWES, review of *Malay Sufism...* by A.H. Johns [item 2387], in *BTLV*, 115 (1959).3: 280-304.

2375. Ivor H.N. EVANS, *Papers on the Ethnology & Archaeology of the Malay Peninsula* (Cambridge: at the University Press, 1927).

2376. Ivor H.N. EVANS, *The Negritoes of Malaya* (Cambridge: at the University Press, 1937).

2377. Ivor H.N. EVANS, *The Religion of the Tempasuk Dusuns of North Borneo* (Cambridge: at the University Press, 1953).

2378. Lloyd FERNANDO, "Picture of the Artist as a Eurasian," review of *A Mortal Flower* by Han Suyin, in *Tenggara*, II (1968).1: 92-5.

2379. *Sir* Hamilton A.R. GIBB, *Mohammedanism* [items 1036 and 1037].

2380. Alfred GUILLAUME, *Islam* [item 1038].

2381. D.G.E. HALL, *A History of South-East Asia* [item 1039].

2382. *T. HARRISSON, *Borneo Writing and Related Matters*, edited by... Published as Special Monograph No.1, *Sarawak Museum Bulletin* (Kuching: Sarawak Museum, 1966).

2383. C. HOOYKAAS, *Over maleische literatuur* (Leiden: E.J. Brill, 1937).

2384. *Ismail HUSSEIN, "A Selected Bibliography of Traditional Malay Literature," in *Tenggara*, 4 (1969): 94-115.

2385. *Yahya ISMAIL, "Malay Literary Guide for 1965," in *Tenggara*, I (1967): 127-31.

2386. *Yahya ISMAIL, "Malay Literary Guide for 1966 and 1967," in *Tenggara*, II (1968).2: 90-7.

2387. A.H. JOHNS, "Malay Sufism as illustrated in an anonymous collection of 17th century tracts," in *JMBRAS*, XXX (1957).2: 1-111. See item 2374.

2388. Armand KAHN, *La littérature arabe* [item 1048].

2389. R.S. KARNI, review of *Malaya, a Background Bibliography* by Beda Lim [item 2391], in *BTLV*, 120 (1964).4: 479-81.

2390. *J. KATS, "The *Rāmāyaṇa* in Indonesia" [item 2030].

2391. Beda LIM, "Malaya, a Background Bibliography," in *JMBRAS*, XXXV (1962).2-3: v + 199.

2392. Mohammad Taib OSMAN, *Modern Malay Literature* (Kuala Lumpur: Dewan Bahasa dan Pustaka / Ministry of Education, 1964).

2393. Mohd. Taib OSMAN, "Mythic Elements in Malay Historiography," in *Tenggara*, II (1968).2: 80-9.

2394. Cyril Northcote PARKINSON and anonymous, "Malaya: History," in *EB* *(1962)*, 14: 711a-2b.

2395. Hans SCHÄRER, *Ngadju Religion* [items 1056 and 1057].

2396. Hans SCHÄRER, *Der Totenkult der Ngadju Dajak* [item 1058].

2397. Idris SHAH, *The Sufis* [item 1059].

2398. Idries SHAH, *Tales of the Dervishes* [item 1060].

2399. *Walter William SKEAT, *Malay Magic, being an introduction to the folklore and popular religion of the Malay Peninsula*. With a preface by Charles Otto Blagden (London: Macmillan 1900).

2400. *Walter William SKEAT, *Malay Magic, being an introduction to the folklore and popular religion of the Malay Peninsula*. With a preface by Charles Otto Blagden (New York: Dover, 1967).

2401. Wilfred Cantwell SMITH, *Islam in Modern History* [item 1061].

2402. John A. SUBHAN, *Sufism* [item 1063].

2403. A. TEEUW, "The History of the Malay Language," in *BTLV*, 115 (1959). 2: 138-56.

2404. Xavier S. THANI NAYAGAM, *A Reference Guide to Tamil Studies: Books* (Kuala Lumpur: University of Malaysia Press, 1966). Lists 1,322 publications, the first section covering translations and summaries of Tamil literature.

2405. P. VOORHOEVE, "The Origin of the Malay Sja'ir," in *BTLV*, 124 (1968).2: 277-8.

2406. C.W. WATSON, "Some Preliminary Remarks on the Antecedents of Modern Indonesian Literature" [item 1071].

2407. John Alden WILLIAMS, *Islam* [item 1072].

2408. *R.O. WINSTEDT, "A History of Malay Literature," in *JMBRAS*, XVII. (1939).1: 1-243.

2409. R.O. WINSTEDT, "Sanskrit in Malay Literature," in *BSOAS*, XX (1957): 599-600.

2410. Robert YOUNG, "Land Dayaks at Sunset," in *SMJ*, New Series, VIII (1958).11: 429-31. Commentary on Geddes, *Nine Dayak Nights* [item 2443].

2411. *V.A. ZHUKOVSKY, "Persian Ṣūfiism" [item 1074].

2412. *V. ZHUKOVSKY, "The Idea of Man and Knowledge in the Conception of Persian Mystics" [item 1075].

FOLK LITERATURE

2413. Anonymous, *Choo and His Melons*. Illustrated by Hussaini Sulaiman (Kuching: Borneo Literature Bureau, [c 1968]).

2414. Anonymous, *Clever Mouse-deer*. Illustrated by Mohammed Sahari (Kuching: Borneo Literature Bureau, [c 1964]). Dayak versions of a selection of *Pelandok* tales.

2415. Anonymous, *Dayang Isah Tandang Sari: A Tale of Sarawak* (Kuching: Borneo Literature Bureau, [c 1962]).

2416. Anonymous, *Ebin*. Illustrated by Hussaini Sulaiman (Kuching: Borneo Literature Bureau, [c 1968]).

2417. Anonymous, *Foolish Saloi*. Illustrated by Aini Abdul Rahman (Kuching: Borneo Literature Bureau, [c 1964]).

2418. *Anonymous, *Tales by Lamplight*. Illustrated by Daud bin Napis (Kuching: Borneo Literature Bureau, [c 1964]).

2419. *Anonymous, *Sarawak Stories*. Illustrated by Mohammed Sahari (Kuching: Borneo Literature Bureau, [c 1965]).

2420. Anonymous, "The War of the Plants," a Malay tale, in Courlander,

The Tiger's Whisker [item 3293], 127-31.

2421. Gallih BALANG, "The Origin of Poison inside Borneo," in *SMJ*, New
       Series, XII (1965).25-26: 235.

2422. BIGAR anak Deboi, "Rang Dungo: A Murut Story of Creation," in *SMJ*,
       New Series, VII (1956).7: 205-7.

2423. BIRAI anak Dap, "Two Dayak Chants," in *SMJ*, New Series, V (1949).
       1: 73-6.

2424. *A. BOLANG and Tom HARRISSON, "The Javanese Dog and related stories
       from Emperoh Gerong," in *SMJ*, New Series, V (1951).3: 417-41. Land
       Dayak legends and tales.

2425. Alexander BOLANG and Tom HARRISSON, "Nakoda Ragam: from Sambas to
       Brunei," in *SMJ*, New Series, VI (1954).4: 57-60. Version of a
       legend of Bulkiah, fifth Sultan of Brunei, collected in southwest-
       ern Borneo in August 1951.

2426. Joan CRAEN, "Tales by Lamplight," in *Tales by Lamplight* [item
       2418].

2427. M.G. DICKSON, "Four Saribas Dayak Songs," with notes by A.J.N.
       Richards, in *SMJ*, New Series, V (1951).3: 457-61.

2428. P Donatus DUNSELMAN, "Kana Sera of Zang der Zwangerschap: Een
       sacrale hymne der Mualang-Dajaks," in *BTLV*, 110 (1954).1: 52-63.

2429. Laing Jau ENG, *Mount Murud: a Kayan Legend*. Illustrated by Husai-
       ni [*sic*] bin Sulaiman (Kuching: Borneo Literature Bureau,
       [c 1962]).

2430. Pabit ENJOK, "Leppo Tau Punishment Stories," in *SMJ*, New Series,
       XII (1965).25-26: 176-8.

2431. I.H.N. EVANS, "Fifty Dusun Riddles," in *SMJ*, New Series, V (1951).
       3: 553-61.

2432. *Ivor H.N. EVANS, "Some Dusun Proverbs and Proverbial Sayings," in
       SMJ, New Series, VI (1952).5: 233-44.

2433. *Ivor H.N. EVANS, "Some Dusun Fables," in *SMJ*, New Series, VI
       (1952).5: 245-7.

2434. *Ivor H.N. EVANS, "Stories from North Borneo," in *SMJ*, New Series,
       VI (1952).5: 250-3.

2435. Ivor H.N. EVANS, "More Dusun Riddles," in *SMJ*, New Series, VI
       (1954).4: 20-35.

2436. *Prof Juan R. FRANCISCO, "Some Philippine Tales Compared with Parallels in North Borneo," in SMJ, New Series, X (1962).19-20: 511-23.

2437. William Henry FURNESS, Folk-lore in Borneo: A Sketch. [Privately printed.] (Wallingford, Pa., 1899).

2438. Very Rev. A.D. GALVIN, "Mamat Chants and Ceremonies, Long Moh (Upper Baram)," in SMJ, New Series, V (1951).3: 235-48.

2439. Bishop [Very Rev. A.D.] GALVIN, "Bilian Limanjong (A Morik Song)," in SMJ, New Series, XII (1965).25-26: 163-5. Text, translation, commentary.

2440. Bishop GALVIN, "The Child of Padau Sigau (A Sebob Saga)," in SMJ, New Series, XII (1965).25-26: 166-70. Translation, commentary, Sebob text.

2441. Bishop GALVIN, "Some Baram Kenyah Songs," in SMJ, New Series, XIV (1966).28-29: 6-14.

2442. Bishop GALVIN and Rev. T. BAARTMANS, "Dressing Up for a Dance (Baram Kenyah)," in SMJ, New Series, XII (1965).25-26: 171-2. Song of self-exhortation to the dance.

2443. W.R. GEDDES, Nine Dayak Nights. Oxford Paperbacks, No 36 (London / Melbourne / New York: Oxford University Press, 1961). Includes epic "The Story of Kichapi" (77-142). See items 2410 and 2459.

2444. Edward GEORGIE, "A Dayak (Love) Song," in SMJ, New Series, IX (1959).13-14: 21-4. Translation, notes, Iban text.

2445. A.W. HAMILTON, Malay Proverbs / Bidal melayu. Malayan Heritage Series, No. 6 (Singapore: D. Moore for Eastern Universities Press, 1955).

2446. A.W. HAMILTON, Malay Pantuns / Pantun melayu. Fourth Edition. Malayan Heritage Series, No. 8 (Singapore: D. Moore, [c 1956]).

2447. Lim Beng HAP, "Poonek," in Tales by Lamplight [item 2418], 36-46.

2448. Lim Beng HAP, "Tricked Again," in Tales by Lamplight [item 2418], 47-59.

2449. A.C. HADDON, "The Tortoise and the Mouse Deer (Kenyah)," in SMJ, New Series, X (1962).19-20: 535-6.

2450. Tom HARRISSON, Borneo Writing [item 2382].

2451. Tom HARRISSON, "The Gibbon in West Borneo folklore and augury," in

SMJ, New Series, XIV (1966).28-29: 132-45.

2452. Tom HARRISSON and Pulu RIBU, "Two Underground Tales from Indonesian Central Borneo," in *SMJ*, New Series, VI (1952).5: 275-83.

2453. A.T. HATTO, "Dayak," in his *Eos* [item 3296], 202. On the *alba* or dawn song.

2454. S. HOLLY, "The Origin of the Idahan People," in *SMJ*, New Series, VI (1952).5: 257-62.

2455. Ismail HUSSEIN, "A Malay Folk-story / *Sebuah Cherita Rakyat Melayu*," edited and introduced by..., in *Tenggara*, I (1967): 60-75. Bilingual text.

2456. George JAMUH, "Three Strange Events," in *SMJ*, New Series, VII (1956).7: 182-5. Dayak yarns.

2457. George JAMUH, "*Penghulu* Lasong Piri Speaks from Kalimantan," in *SMJ*, New Series, X (1962).19-20: 554-8. Traditions collected from a Murut informant.

2458. *George JAMUH, Tom HARRISSON and Benedict SANDIN, "'Pelandok', the Villain-Hero---in Sarawak and Interior Kalimantan," in *SMJ*, New Series, X (1962).19-20: 524-34. Borneo versions of the mouse-deer cycle.

2459. Russel A. JUDKINS, "Silanting Kuning's Transformation: Liminality in a Land Dayak Myth. An Analysis of *Nine Dayak Nights*," in *SMJ*, New Series, XVII (1969).34-35: 123-38. See item 2443.

2460. Philip Frick McKEAN, "The Mouse-deer (*Kantjil*) in Malayo-Indonesian Folklore" [item 2007].

2461. Malan NOHJ [*sic*], "Sabah Queen," in *Tales by Lamplight* [item 2418], 60-91.

2462. R. NYANDOH, "Two Tapuh Stories," in *SMJ*, New Series, V (1951).3: 414-6. Collected in 1951 in Serian District.

2463. R. NYANDOH, "How Bear and Deer bear Human Babies," in *SMJ*, New Series, V (1951).3: 590-9. Tapuh Land Dayak tale.

2464. R. NYANDOH, "Two Land Dayak Fish Stories," in *SMJ*, New Series, VI (1954).4: 39-41.

2465. R. NYANDOH, "The Story of Kumang Ruwai," in *SMJ*, New Series, VII (1956).7: 208-20. Translation with Land Dayak text in alternating lines.

2466. R. NYANDOH, "Head-Hunting Revenge (Land Dayak)," in *SMJ*, New
       Series, VIII (1958).12: 732-5. Tale collected in Serian District
       in October 1958.

2467. R. NYANDOH, "Lingagat and the Magical Faeces (a Land Dayak Bird
       Story)," in *SMJ*, New Series, IX (1959).13-14: 49-52. Translation
       and text in alternating paragraphs.

2468. *R. NYANDOH, "Seven Land Dayak Stories," in *SMJ*, New Series, XI
       (1963).21-22: 114-31.

2469. *R. NYANDOH, "Man weds Sow: three versions," in *SMJ*, New Series,
       XIV (1966).28-29: 124-31. Tales (translation only) on the same
       theme collected from a Niah Melanau informant, a Land Dayak, and
       an Iban.

2470. NYELONG, "Baya China Batangan (A Murut Tale)," translated by R.A.
       Bewsher, in *SMJ*, New Series, VI (1952).5: 263-74.

2471. Ann PARKINSON, *Malayan Fables*. Book I. Illustrated by S.L. Goh
       (Singapore: Donald Moore, 1956).

2472. Lu'un RIBU, "The Perfect Fool," in *SMJ*, New Series, VII (1956).7:
       186-9. Kelabit Murut story edited by Tom Harrisson.

2473. Lu'un RIBU and Tom HARRISSON, "Agan Plandok, the Noble Mouse-Deer,"
       in *SMJ*, New Series, V (1951).3: 573-9. Kelabit versions of the
       pelandok cycle.

2474. Lu'un RIBU and Pulu RIBU, "The Dead Monkey That Spoke," in *SMJ*,
       New Series, VII (1956).7: 190-7. Kelabit-Murut story edited by Tom
       Harrisson.

2475. Pulu RIBU, "The Man-Eating Elephant," in *SMJ*, New Series, VII
       (1956).7: 198-204. Kelabit-Murut story edited by Tom Harrisson.

2476. A.J.N. RICHARDS, "The Migrations of the Ibans and their Poetry,"
       in *SMJ*, New Series, V (1949).1: 77-87.

2477. Anthony RICHARDS and T.K. JARO, "Pasai Siong," in *SMJ*, New Series,
       VI (1954).4: 36-8. Kanowit tale.

2478. Owen RUTTER, *The Dragon of Kinabalu*. With Eight Illustrations in
       Colour by Mary Penrose-Thackwell (London: Clement Ingleby, n.d.
       [*ca* 1923]). Fourteen tales from North Borneo adapted for general
       readership.

2479. Che'gu Abang bin SAID, "How the old men of Bintulu put the pirates
       to flight," in *SMJ*, New Series, V (1951).3: 462. Malay yarn.

2480. *Benedict SANDIN, "Some Niah Folklore and Origins," in *SMJ*, New Series, VIII -(1958).12: 646-62.

2481. *Benedict SANDIN, "Tragi-Comic Tales of Apai Salui (Iban)," in *SMJ*, New Series, IX (1960).15-16: 638-47. Five Iban tales.

2482. *Benedict SANDIN, "The Owl Marries the Moon (a Saribas Story)," in *SMJ*, New Series, XI (1964).23-24: 534-6. Followed by Tom Harrisson, "The Sea-going Cuckoo and other themes significant in the Saribas Story" (537-40), commenting on the Sandin translation, and by Iban text (541-3).

2483. Benedict SANDIN, "A Saribas Iban Death Dirge (*sabak*)," in *SMJ*, New Series, XIV (1966).28-29: 15-80. Introduction, texts, translation, Notes.

2484. *Benedict SANDIN, "Apai Salui Sleeps with a Corpse (an Iban folk story)," in *SMJ*, New Series, XV (1967).30-31: 223-7. Translation, with no commentary, followed by Iban text.

2485. *Benedict SANDIN, "Simpulang or Pulang Gana: the Founder of Dayak Agriculture," in *SMJ*, New Series, XV (1967).30-31: 245-406. Detailed study of Dayak beliefs and practices associated with agri-culture, with numerous texts and translations. *Cf.* Maurice et Proux, "L'âme du riz" [item 3091].

2486. *Benedict SANDIN, "Five Mythological Stories of the Ibans," in *SMJ*, New Series, XVII (1969).34-35: 99-112.

2487. Clifford SATHER, "Bajau Riddles," in *SMJ*, New Series, XII (1965). 25-26: 162.

2488. Mubin SHEPPARD, *The Magic Kite, and Other Ma'yong Stories* (Singa-pore: Federal Publications, [c 1960]).

2489. Walter SKEAT, *Fables and Folk-Tales from an Eastern Forest*. Illus-trated by F.H. Townsend (Cambridge: at the University Press, 1901). Twenty-six tales from the Malay Peninsula.

2490. W. SKEAT, *Fables and Folk Tales from an Eastern Forest,* Collected and Translated by... Illustrated by F.H. Townsend (Singapore: Donald Moore, 1955).

2491. SUNGA, "Kumang Kidundung," in *SMJ*, New Series, V (1951).3: 580-5. Land Dayak tale transcribed and translated by R. Nyandoh and T. Harrisson.

2492. Stephen Wan ULOK and *Rev* A.D. GALVIN, "A Kenyah Song," in *SMJ*, New Series, VI (1952).5: 287-9. Illustrating modern influences in Baram river region.

2493. Walter UNJAH, "The Stone of Demong," in *SMJ*, New Series, VI
       (1954).4: 61-4. Iban origin myth.

2494. *R.J. WILKINSON and R.O. WINSTEDT, *Pantun Melayu*. Malay Literature
       Series, No. 12 (Singapore: Donald Moore, 1961).

2495. Thomas Rhys WILLIAMS, "A Tambunan Dusun Origin Myth," in *JAF*, 74.
       291 (January-March 1961): 68-73.

2496. Thomas Rhys WILLIAMS, "The Form and Function of Tambunan Dusun
       Riddles," in *JAF*, 76.300 (April-June 1963): 95-110.

2497. R.O. WINSTEDT, "Malay," in Hatto [item 3296], 199-201. On the *al-
       ba* or dawn song.

2498. R.O. WINSTEDT, "A Pandji Tale from Kelantan," in *JMBRAS*, XXII.1
       (March 1949): 53-60.

INDIAN LITERATURE

2499. *Prof* Juan R. FRANCISCO, "The Ráma Story in the Post-Muslim Malay
       Literature of South-east Asia" [item 2024].

2500. *S.M. PONNIAH, *Sri Paduka: the Exile of the Prince of Ayodhya*,
       translated by....Papers in International Studies, Southeast Asia
       Series No. 7 (Athens, Ohio: Center for International Studies,
       Southeast Asia Program, Ohio University, 1969). Dramatic render-
       ing of the second canto (*Ayodhya Kandam*) of Kamban's Tamil *Rāmā-
       yaṇa*.

2501. Rama SUBBIAH, "Selections from *Kuruntokai*: love poems from classi-
       cal Tamil literature," translated and introduced by..., in *Tengga-
       ra*, I (1967): 52-9.

2502. Rama SUBBIAH, "Further Selections from *Kuruntokai*[:] love poems
       from classical Tamil literature," translated by..., in *Tenggara*,
       4 (1969): 60-6.

2503. Alexander ZIESENISS, *The Rama Saga in Malaysia*. Translated by P.
       W. Burch (Singapore: Malaysian Sociological Research Institute,
       1963).

CHRONICLES

2504. Zainal Abidin bin ABDUL WAHID, "*Sejarah Melayu*," in *AS*, IV (1966).

3: 445-51.

2505. C.C. BROWN, "A Malay Herodotus," in *BSOAS*, XII (1948).3-4: 730-6.

2506. T. ISKANDAR, "Three Malay Historical Writings in the First Half of the 17th Century," in *JMBRAS*, 40 (1967).2: 38-53.

2507. J. RAS, *Hikajat Bandjar: A Study in Malay Historiography* (The Hague: Martinus Nijhoff, 1968).

2508. P.L. Amin SWEENEY, "The Connection between the *Hikayat Raja2 Pasai* and the *Sejarah Melayu*," in *JMBRAS*, 40 (1967).2: 94-105.

2509. David K. WYATT, "A Thai Version of Newbold's *Hikayat Patani*," translated and introduced by..., in *JMBRAS*, 40 (1967).2: 16-37.

PRE-MODERN PROSE AND POETRY

2510. Anonymous, "The Epic of Bidasari: Song IV," in Garnett [item 3294], 178-89.

2511. Kassim bin AHMAD, *Characterisation in* Hikayat Hang Tuah; *A General Survey of Methods of Character-Portrayal and Analysis and Interpretation of the Characters of Hang Tuah and Hang Jebat* (Kuala Lumpur: Dewan Bahasa dan Pustaka, 1966).

2512. *BOKHARI, "The Sultan of Kembajat," modern adaptation by Gene Z. Hanrahan, in Hanrahan [item 3295], 382-8.

2513. *G.W.J. DREWES, "Hikajat Muhammad Mukabil (The Story of the Kadi and the Learned Brigand)," in *BTLV*, 126 (1970).3: 309-31.

2514. *Hans OVERBECK, "Hikayat Maharaja Ravana," in *JMBRAS*, XI.2 (December 1933): 111-32. *Cf*. Francisco, *Maharadia Lawana* [item 2722].

MODERN PROSE

2515. Cynthia ANTHONY, "Nannan," in *Tenggara*, II (1968).1: 50-4.

2516. Cynthia ANTHONY, "A Certain Cry," in *Tenggara*, 4 (1969): 67-9.

2517. Tom HARRISSON, *Borneo Writing* [item 2382].

2518. Pretam KAUR, "Through the Wall," in *Tenggara*, II (1968).1: 70-2.

2519. Siew Yue KILLINGLEY, "Everything's Arranged," in *Tenggara*, I
       (1967): 38-51.

2520. Ssu LANG, *Nostalgia for Jesselton*. Translated by Tak-Wa Kwok from
       a series entitled *"Huai Nien Ya Pi"* in *The Borneo Times*, summer
       1958 (Honolulu: Research Translations, Institute for Advanced Pro-
       jects, East-West Center, 1965).

2521. Gabriel LEE, "The Madman of Mempawah," in *Tumasek*, III (September
       1964): 12-7.

2522. Lee Kok LIANG, "It's All In a Dream," in *Tumasek*, II (April 1964):
       6-17.

2523. Lee Kok LIANG, "When the Saints Go Marching," in *Tumasek*, III
       (September 1964): 34-50.

2524. *Lee Kok LIANG, "Ibrahim Something," in *Tenggara*, I (1967): 16-24.

2525. Shirley LIM, "The Touring Company," in *Tenggara*, II (1968).2: 58-
       62.

2526. Shirley LIM, "On Christmas Day in the Morning," in *Tenggara*, 4
       (1969): 52-7.

2527. Chua Cheng LOCK, "Down by the Sea," in *Tumasek*, I (January 1964):
       14-8.

2528. Keris MAS, *"Menjelang Merdeka* / The Approach of Independence," di-
       petek dari majailah *Dewan Bahasa*, Oktober 1957, Malay text with
       English translation by Fadzilah Amin, in *Tenggara*, I (1967): 4-15.

2529. Keris MAS, "Runtuh," in *Tenggara*, II (1968).1: 18-33. Bilingual
       text.

2530. *Keris MAS, *"Mereka Tidak Mengerti* / They Do Not Understand,"
       translated by Adibah Amin, in *Tenggara*, 4 (1969): 4-25.

2531. Patrick Ng Kah ONN, "The Interview," in Wigmore [item 3300], 217-
       26.

2532. *S. RAJARATNAM, "The Tiger," in Wigmore [item 3300], 44-50.

2533. *S. RAJARATNAM, "The Tiger," in Hanrahan [item 3295], 368-74.

2534. Goh Poh SENG, "If We Dream Too Long," extract from a novel, in
       Tumasek, I (January 1964): 27-34.

2535. Goh Poh SENG, "The Temple Bells," in *Tumasek*, II (April 1964): 39-
       43.

2536. Maria STRANSKA, "A Journey," in *Tumasek,* II (April 1964): 20-6.

2537. Lam Chih SUNG, "The Crutch on the Wall," in *Tumasek,* III (September 1964): 7-9.

2538. Han SUYIN, "Big Dog Tsou," in Wigmore [item 3300], 95-105.

2539. Han SUYIN, "Big Dog Tsou," in Hanrahan [item 3295], 388-98.

2540. Pun Tzoh WAH, "No Place for the Esoteric," review article on *Malaysian Chinese Short Stories,* Selected and Translated by Ly Singko, in *Tenggara,* 4 (1969): 89-91.

MODERN POETRY

2541. A.S. AMIN, "The Child in the Red Shirt," in José [item 3297], 340.

2542. Usman AWANG, "Gift (for my child's birthday)," in José [item 3297], 343.

2543. Usman AWANG, *"Chahaya: Tablo untuk Jymy Asmara* / Light," translated by Adibah Amin, in *Tenggara,* I (1967): 30-7. Bilingual text.

2544. *Usman AWANG, *"Suara dari Pusara* / Voice from the Grave," translated by Adibah Amin, in *Tenggara,* 4 (1969): 48-51. Bilingual text.

2545. Sean BRESLIN, "Poem," in *Tumasek,* I (January 1964): 46.

2546. Yeo Bock CHENG, "Malacca Mosaic," in *Tenggara,* II (1968).2: 50.

2547. Yeo Bock CHENG, "Of Dragons and Lions," in *Tenggara,* II (1968).2: 51.

2548. R. Yeo Cheng CHUAN, "Blood-debt Rally," in *Tumasek,* I (January 1964): 12.

2549. R. Yeo Cheng CHUAN, "Annexation," in *Tumasek,* I (January 1964): 13.

2550. R. Yeo Cheng CHUAN, "Sympathy," in *Tumasek,* II (April 1964): 27.

2551. Ee Tiang HONG, "The Loan," in *Tumasek,* III (September 1964): 27.

2552. Ee Tiang HONG, "New Poems," in *Tenggara,* I (1967): 83-4.

2553. Ee Tiang HONG, "Cycle," in *Tenggara,* II (1968).1: 63.

2554. Ee Tiang HONG, "Mood," in *Tenggara,* II (1968).1: 64.

2555. Ee Tiang HONG, "Heeren Street, Malacca," in *Tenggara*, II (1968). 1: 65.

2556. Ee Tiang HONG, "To a Shrub," in *Tenggara*, II (1968).1: 66.

2557. Ee Tiang HONG, "Likes and Dislikes," in *Tenggara*, II (1968).1: 66.

2558. Ee Tiang HONG, "Pengkalan Chepa, Kelantan," in *Tenggara*, 4 (1969): 70-1.

2559. Ee Tiang HONG, "Telephone and Sticker," in *Tenggara*, 4 (1969): 72.

2560. Pretam KAUR, "Gone With the Peacocks," in *Tenggara*, II (1968).1: 16.

2561. Chiew Seen KONG, "Lawyers," in *Tumasek*, III (September 1964): 28.

2562. Lee Geok LAN, "Twenty-one...," in *Tumasek*, I (January 1964): 47.

2563. Lee Geok LAN, "Two Poems," in *Tenggara*, I (1967): 101-2.

2564. Abdul LATIFF, "Poems and Sketches from His Notebooks," translated by Adibah Amin, in *Tenggara*, II (1968).1: 40-5. Bilingual text.

2565. Gabriel LEE, "In Time of Riot: 9 a.m.," in *Tumasek*, III (September 1964): 26.

2566. Margaret LEONG, "Japanese Cemetery - Singapore," in Wigmore [item 3300], 50.

2567. Chua Cheng LOCK, "Lines for a Postcard from a Beach," in *Tumasek*, I (January 1964): 19.

2568. *MASURI S.N. [*sic*], "I Do Not Care," translated by Abdullah Majid and Oliver Rice, in *Chapbook of Contemporary Asian Poetry* [item 3289], 36.

2569. *MASURI S.N., "My Lion City," in José [item 3297], 341-2.

2570. Chandran NAIR, "Hindu Cremation," in *Tenggara*, II (1968).2: 49.

2571. Wong Phui NAM, "Prospect of Spring," after Tu Fu, in *Tumasek*, I (January 1964): 6.

2572. Wong Phui NAM, "Candles for a Local Osiris," in *Tumasek*, I (January 1964): 35-41.

2573. *Wong Phui NAM, "Poems," in *Tenggara*, I (1967): 85-7.

2574. Wong Phui NAM, *Now the Hills Are Distant*. Supplement to *Tenggara*,

I (1967) (Kuala Lumpur: Tenggara, [c 1968]).

2575. Wong Phui NAM, "My Uncle, Dying," in *Tenggara*, II (1968).1: 55.

2576. Wong Phui NAM, "Remembering Grandma," in *Tenggara*, II (1968).1: 56-8.

2577. Wong Phui NAM, "What Larkins," review of *A Private Landscape* ["A collection of verse very representative of the Malaysian-Singapore literary landscape"], edited by David Ormerod, in *Tenggara*, II (1968).1: 90-1.

2578. Wong Phui NAM, "A Death in Ward 13," in *Tenggara*, 4 (1969): 26-7.

2579. Omar Mohd. NOR, "An Advertisement," in *Tenggara*, II (1968).1: 73.

2580. Omar Mohd. NOR, "Three Layers," in *Tenggara*, II (1968).1: 74.

2581. Omar Mohd. NOR, "The Mosque," in *Tenggara*, II (1968).1: 74.

2582. Omar Mohd. NOR, "e.e. cummings talked to me from his grave," in *Tenggara*, II (1968).1: 75-8.

2583. Omar Mohd. NOR, "Malaysian Sun Misbehaves," in *Tenggara*, II (1968).1: 78.

2584. Hew Chee PENG, "To a Friend," in *Tumasek*, II (April 1964): 29.

2585. Lee Tzu PHENG, "Still-life," in *Tenggara*, II (1968).2: 47.

2586. Lee Tzu PHENG, "Orphans," in *Tenggara*, II (1968).2: 48.

2587. *Oliver RICE and Abdullah MAJID, *Sajak2 Melayu Baru / Modern Malay Verse, 1946-61*. Selected by....Translated by Abdullah Majid, Asraf and Oliver Rice with the assistance of James Kirkup and the poets. Introduction by James Kirkup. Seri Sastera Timur dan Barat (Kuala Lumpur: Oxford University Press, 1963). Best anthology available.

2588. *Samad SAID, "Embers," translated by Abdullah Majid and Oliver Rice, in *Chapbook of Contemporary Asian Poetry* [item 3289], 35-6.

2589. *A. Samad SAID, "Direction," in José [item 3297], 344.

2590. Mohamad *Hj*. SALLEH, "The Ice-cream Boys," in *Tenggara*, II (1968). 2: 44.

2591. Mohamad *Hj*. SALLEH, "Breaking," in *Tenggara*, II (1968).2: 45.

2592. Mohamad *Hj*. SALLEH, "The City Is My Home," in *Tenggara*, II (1968).2: 46.

2593.   Goh Poh SENG, "On Looking At the Moon and Thinking," in *Tumasek*, I (January 1964): 26.

2594.   Goh Poh SENG, "The History of War," in *Tumasek*, II (April 1964): 18.

2595.   Goh Poh SENG, "As a Wind," in *Tumasek*, II (April 1964): 19.

2596.   Goh Poh SENG, "Spring at Wu Ling," after Li Ch'ing Chao, in *Tumasek*, III (September 1964): 29.

2597.   Pabitra SEYNE, "It ain't gonna rain no more," in *Tumasek*, III (September 1964): 11.

2598.   Lam Chih SUNG, "Rain," in *Tumasek*, III (September 1964): 10.

2599.   Edwin THUMBOO, "Philosophy," in *Tumasek*, I (January 1964): 45.

2600.   Edwin THUMBOO, "Deepavali," in *Tumasek*, II (April 1964): 38.

2601.   Edwin THUMBOO, "Cremation," in *Tumasek*, III (September 1964): 32.

2602.   *Edwin THUMBOO, "Seven Poems," in *Tenggara*, I (1967): 25-9.

2603.   Edwin THUMBOO, "In Africa," in *Tenggara*, II (1968).1: 67.

2604.   Edwin THUMBOO, "Proposals," in *Tenggara*, II (1968).1: 68-9.

2605.   I. ULAGANATHAN, "The Rubbish Bin," translated from the Tamil by Rama Subbiah, in *Tenggara*, II (1968).1: 34-5.

2606.   *I. ULAGANATHAN, "Request and Reply," translated from the Tamil by Rama Subbiah, in *Tenggara*, II (1968).1: 36-7.

2607.   Chong Yoon WAH, "Leaves of Acacia," in *Tumasek*, III (September 1964): 31.

DRAMA

2608.   Usman AWANG, "Visitors at Kenny Hill (*Tamu di-Bukit Kenny*)," translated by Adibah Amin, in *Three South East Asian Plays*. Supplement to *Tenggara*, 4 (1969): 25-48.

2609.   Jeanne CUISINIER, *Le théâtre d'ombres à Kelantan*. Préface de Jean Filliozat. 6e édition (Paris: Gallimard, [c 1957]).

2610.   Lee Joo FOR, "Son of Zen," in *Three South East Asian Plays* [item

2608], 59-113. Written originally in English.

2611. Lim Chor PEE, "Is Drama Non-existent in Singapore?," in *Tumasek*, I (January 1964): 42-4.

2612. Lim Chor PEE, "Drama and the University," in *Tumasek*, II (April 1964): 49-51.

2613. Goh Poh SENG, "The Moon Is Less Bright," from a new play, in *Tumasek*, III (September 1964): 60-71.

VII. PHILIPPINES

GENERAL

2614. *Domingo ABELLA, "Some Notes on the Historical Background of Philippine Literature," in Manuud [item 2634], 34-48.

2615. Estanislao ALINEA, "Philippine Literature in Spanish from the Literature of Protest to Efflorescence," in Manuud [item 2634], 508-17.

2616. Anonymous, *Literature at the Crossroads:* 3 Symposia on the Filipino Novel, Filipino Poetry, the Filipino Theater. Sponsored by the Congress for Cultural Freedom (Manila: Alberto S. Florentino, 1965).

2617. Miguel A. BERNAD, *S.J.*, "The Church and Philippine Literature in the Spanish Era," in Manuud [item 2634], 518-26.

2618. *Leonard CASPER, *The Wounded Diamond:* Studies in Modern Philippine Literature (Manila: Bookmark, 1964).

2619. Teófilo del CASTILLO y TUAZON [and] Buenaventura S. MEDINA, *Jr.*, *Philippine Literature from ancient times to the present* (Quezon City: Teófilo del Castillo, [c 1966]).

2620. *Clodualdo del MUNDO, "Spanish and American Colonial Literature in Tagalog," in Manuud [item 2634], 361-84.

2621. Clodualdo del MUNDO, "Literary Criticism in Tagalog," in Manuud [item 2634], 436-56.

2622. *Francisco R. DEMETRIO, *Dictionary of Philippine Folk Beliefs and Customs* [in four volumes]. Foreword by Wayland D. Hand. A Museum and Archives Publication, No. 2 (Cagayan de Oro City: Xavier University, 1970). Valuable tool for elucidation of motifs, tale types, and subliterary features.

2623. *Juan R. FRANCISCO, *Indian Influences in the Philippines, with Special Reference to Language and Literature.* Published as *Philippine Social Sciences and Humanities Review,* XXVIII.1-3 (January-September 1963), Chapters IV and V, "Indian Literature in the Philippines," 131-252.

2624. N.V.M. GONZALEZ, "In a Borrowed Tongue," in *BA,* 29 (1955).1: 26-30.

2625. *Lucila V. HOSILLOS, "The Emergence of Filipino Literature Toward National Identity," in *AS*, IV (1966).3: 430-44.

2626. *Lucila V. HOSILLOS, *Philippine-American Literary Relations, 1898-1941* (Quezon City: University of the Philippines Press, 1969).

2627. *F. Landa JOCANO, "Some Aspects of Filipino Vernacular Literature," in Manuud [item 2634], 287-307.

2628. Felix M. KEESING, "Cultural Trends in the Philippines," in *FEQ*, IV (1945).2: 102-8.

2629. Amparo S. LARDIZABAL and Felicitas TENSUAN-LEOGARDO, *Readings on Philippine Culture and Social Life* (Manila: Rex Book Shop, [c 1970]).

2630. *Bienvenido LUMBERA, "Philippine Literature and the Filipino Personality," in Manuud [item 2634], 1-15.

2631. *Bienvenido LUMBERA, "The Literary Relations of Tagalog Literature," in Manuud [item 2634], 308-30.

2632. Bienvenido LUMBERA, "Alliance and Revolution: Tagalog Writing During the War Years," in Manuud [item 2634], 385-402.

2633. Bienvenido LUMBERA, "Rehabilitation and New Beginnings: Tagalog Literature Since the Second World War," in Manuud [item 2634], 403-35.

2634. *Antonio G. MANUUD, *Brown Heritage: Essays on Philippine Cultural Tradition and Literature* (Quezon City: Ateneo de Manila University Press, 1967). Massive collection of critical and historical essays by writers of proven competence.

2635. José Villa PANGANIBAN and Consuelo Torres PANGANIBAN, *A Survey of the Literature of the Filipinos*. Based on the Findings and Readings of... Fifth mimeoscription (San Juan, Rizal: Limbagang Pilipino, 1963).

2636. *Máximo RAMOS, *Philippine Harvest: An Anthology of Filipino Writing in English*. Edited by... and Florentino B. Valeros. Revised Edition (Quezon City: Phoenix Publishing House, 1964).

2637. *Miss* Ramona RIVERA, *Philippine Literature:* Excerpts Read from the Works of... Oscar de Zuniga, Manuel Arguillo, and Dr José Rizal. Magnetic tape recording (27 minutes) by... Asia Society Presents series.

2638. E. SAN JUAN, *Jr.*, "*Panikitan*: A Critical Introduction to Tagalog Literature," in *AS*, IV (1966).3: 412-29.

2639. *Bienvenido SANTOS, "The Filipino Novel in English," in Manuud [item 2634], 634-47.

2640. *Herbert SCHNEIDER, *S.J.*, "The Period of Emergence of Philippine Letters (1930-1944)," in Manuud [item 2634], 575-88.

2641. *Herbert SCHNEIDER, *S.J.*, "The Literature of the Period of Emergence," in Manuud [item 2634], 589-602.

2642. John N. SCHUMACHER, *S.J.*, "The Literature of Protest: Pelaez to the Propagandists," in Manuud [item 2634], 483-507.

2643. *Mrs* Leticia Ramos SHAHANI, *Origins of Philippine Culture*. Magnetic tape recording (27 minutes) by... Asia Society Presents series.

2644. Francisco G. TONOGBANUA, *A Survey of Filipino Literature* (Manila: privately issued, 1959). Mimeographed.

FOLK LITERATURE

2645. Anonymous, "The Turtle and the Monkey Share a Tree," in Courlander, *Ride with the Sun* [item 3292], 25-7.

2646. Manuel and Lyd ARGUILLA, *Philippine Tales and Fables* (Manila: Capitol Publishing House, 1957).

2647. *Roy Franklin BARTON, *The Mythology of the Ifugaos*. Published as *Memoirs of the American Folklore Society*, 46 (1956).

2648. *R.F. BARTON, "Myths and Their Magic Use in Ifugao," in *AFS*, XVII (1958): 209-12.

2649. *Laura Watson BENEDICT, "Bagobo Myths," in *JAF*, XXVI (1913): 13-63.

2650. *Francisco BILLIET and Francis LAMBRECHT, *Studies on Kalinga Ullálim and Ifugaw Orthography*. Publications of The Catholic School Press (Baguio City: The Catholic School Press, 1970). Transcription and translation of four *ullálim* or 'eulogies of gravery', with detailed analysis of their cultural significance.

2651. Juan T. BURGOS, *A Guide to the Ilocano Metrical Romance*. Thesis for the M.A. in English. Manila, 1924.

2652. Cecile CARIÑO, "The Golden Tree of the Ibalois. A Folktale," in *AFS*, XVII (1958): 201-3.

2653. Eric CASIÑO, "*Lunsay*: Song-Dance of the Jama Mapun of Sulu," in
       AS, IV (1966).2: 316-23.

2654. Fay-Cooper COLE, *The Wild Tribes of Davao District, Mindanao*.
       The R.F. Cummings Philippine Expedition. Published as Field Muse-
       um of Natural History Publication 170. Anthropological Series,
       Vol. XII, No. 2 (Chicago: Field Museum of Natural History, 1913),
       125-8 (Bagobo mythology), 172-5 (Mandaya mythology and religion).

2655. Maria Della CORONEL, *Stories and Legends from Filipino Folklore*.
       Illustrated by Cenon M. Rivera (Manila: University of Santo Tomás
       Press, 1967).

2656. Toribio de CASTRO, "The Weird Tale of the Twelve Hunchbacks. A
       Tagalog Folktale," in *AFS*, XVII (1958): 199-201.

2657. Leopoldo A. DELACRUZ, *Sr.*, *Fables in Aklani* (San Juan, Rizal: Ka-
       lantiao Press, [c 1958]). Twenty-two tales in Aklani (1-30) with
       English translation (31-59).

2658. Eugenio EALDAMA, "Two Folktales of the Monteses of Panay," in *AFS*,
       XVII (1958): 226-8.

2659. Fred EGGAN, "Ritual Myths Among the Tinguian," in *JAF*, 69.274
       (October-December 1956): 331-9.

2660. *Dean S. FANSLER, *Filipino Popular Tales*. Memoirs of The American
       Folk-lore Society, Volume XII (Lancaster, Pa., and New York: The
       American Folk-lore Society, 1921).

2661. *Dean S. FANSLER, *Filipino Popular Tales*. Collected and edited,
       with comparative notes, by... (Hatboro, Pa.: Folklore Associates,
       1965).

2662. *Prof Juan R. FRANCISCO, "Some Philippine Tales Compared with
       Parallels in North Borneo" [item 2436].

2663. *Juan R. FRANCISCO, "Foreign Elements in Philippine Folk Litera-
       ture," in *ALB* (Dr V. Raghavan Felicitation Volume), 31-32 (1967-
       68): 450-71.

2664. Maria Colina GUTTIEREZ, "The Cebuano *Balitao* and How It Mirrors
       Visayan Culture and Folklife," in *AFS*, XX (1961): 15-135.

2665. Donn V. HART, *Riddles in Filipino Folklore: An Anthropological
       Analysis* (Syracuse: Syracuse University Press, 1964).

2666. Donn V. HART and Harriet C. HART, "'Maka-andog': A Reconstructed
       Myth from Eastern Samar, Philippines," in *JAF*, 79.311 (January-
       March 1966): 84-108.

2667. *Donn V. HART and Harriet C. HART, "Cinderella in the Eastern Bisayas: With a Summary of the Philippine Folktale," in *JAF*, 79. 312 (April–June 1966): 307–37.

2668. F. Landa JOCANO, "Twenty-three Place-name Legends from Antigue Province, Philippines," in *AS*, III (1965).1: 16–40.

2669. *F. Landa JOCANO, *The Epic of Labaw Donggon* (Quezon City: University of the Philippines, 1965. Kiniray epic with English translation.

2670. F. Landa JOCANO, *Outline of Philippine Mythology* (Manila: Centro Escolar / University Research and Development Center, 1969). For secondary school use.

2671. Bacil F. KIRTLEY, "A Bohol Version of the Earth-Diver Myth," in *JAF*, 70.278 (October–December 1957): 362–3.

2672. *Francis LAMBRECHT, "The Ifugaw Sagas or *Hudhud*," in *Little Apostle of The Mountain Province* (Baguio), 7.7 (December 1930), 8. 11 (April 1932).

2673. *Francis LAMBRECHT, "The Saga of Aginaya," in *Little Apostle of The Mountain Province* (Baguio), 1932–34.

2674. *Francis LAMBRECHT, "The Saga of Guminingin and Bugan," in *Little Apostle of The Mountain Province* (Baguio), 1934.

2675. *Francis LAMBRECHT, "Ifugao Tales," in *AFS*, XIV (1955): 149–96.

2676. *Francis LAMBRECHT, "Ifugao Tales, Banawe and Mayawyaw," in *AFS*, XVI (1957): 107–84.

2677. *Francis LAMBRECHT, "Ifugao Epic Story: *Hudhud* of Aliguyun at Hananga," in *JEAS*, 6 (1957).3–4: 1–203.

2678. *Francis LAMBRECHT, "Ifugao Ballads," in *JEAS*, 7 (1958).2: 169–207.

2679. *Francis LAMBRECHT, "Ifugaw *Hu'dhud*," in *AFS*, XIX (1960): 1–174; XX (1961): 136–273.

2680. *Francis LAMBRECHT, "Ifugaw *Hudhud* Literature," in *Saint Louis Quarterly*, 3 (1965).2: 191–214.

2681. *Francis LAMBRECHT, "Ifugaw *Hudhud* Literature," in Manuud [item 2634], 816–37. Reprinted from item 2680.

2682. *Francis LAMBRECHT, "The *Hudhud* of Dinulawan and Bugan at Gonhadan," in *Saint Louis Quarterly*, V (1967).3–4: iii–vi + 267–713.

2683. *Francis LAMBRECHT, *The* Hudhúd *of Dinulawan and Bugan at Gonhadan*
      (Baguio: St. Louis University, 1967). Reprinted from item 2682.

2684. *Frank C. LAUBACH, "The *Darangan*: I. How Bantugan Died Below the
      Mountain by the Sea. II. How Bantugan Came Back from Heaven," in
      JH, X.3 (September 1962): 330–58. Reprinted from *Philippine Pub-
      lic Schools: A Monthly Magazine for Teachers*, 3.8 (November 1930):
      359–73. Portions of a Maranao epic.

2685. *Frank C. LAUBACH, "The *Darangan*: I. How Bantugan Died Below the
      Mountain by the Sea. II. How Bantugan Came Back from Heaven,"
      typescript by W.C. Mijares, University Research Center, Mindanao
      State University, from *JH*, X.3: 330–58 [item 2684].

2686. Leon LINDEMANS, "A Kalinga Story," in *AFS*, XIV (1955): 197–201.

2687. José L. LLANES, "An Annotated Dictionary of Philippine Mythology,"
      in *JEAS*, V (1956).2: 14–35 and 3: 35–85. Incomplete.

2688. Bienvenido LUMBERA, "The Folk Tradition in Tagalog Poetry," in
      Manuud [item 2634], 331–60.

2689. I.V. MALLARI, *Tales from The Mountain Province*, from materials
      gathered by Laurence L. Wilson (Manila: Philippine Education Com-
      pany, [c 1958]).

2690. *E. Arsenio MANUEL, "Notes on Philippine Folk Literature," in *JEAS*,
      IV (1955).2: 137–55.

2691. *E. Arsenio MANUEL, "The Maiden of the Buhong Sky," in *Philippine
      Social Sciences and Humanities Review*, XXII (1957).4: 435–97. Bi-
      lingual text. See item 2692.

2692. *E. Arsenio MANUEL, *The Maiden of the Buhong Sky: A Fragment of
      the Bagobo Tuwaang Epic Cycle*, Recorded and translated, with the
      assistance of Saddani Pagayaw, by... (Quezon City: University of
      the Philippines, 1958).

2693. E. Arsenio MANUEL, "Bagobo Riddles," in *AFS*, XXI (1962): 123–85.

2694. *E. Arsenio MANUEL, *Upland Bagobo Narratives*, recorded with the
      help of Bagobo friends and translated with the assistance of Sad-
      dani Pagayaw (Quezon City: University of the Philippines, 1962).

2695. *E. Arsenio MANUEL, "A Survey of Philippine Folk Epics," in *AFS*,
      XXII (1963): 1–76.

2696. E. Arsenio MANUEL, *Philippine Folklore Bibliography: A Prelimina-
      ry Survey*. Philippine Folklore Society, Paper number 1 (Quezon·
      City: Philippine Folklore Society, 1965).

2697. *E. Arsenio MANUEL, "On the Study of Philippine Folklore," in Ma-
      nuud [item 2634], 253-86.

2698. *Melchizadeck MAQUISO, "*Ulahingan* - Part I: An English Edition of
      the Manobo Epic," Appendix to William R. Pfeiffer, *Manobo Music
      Traditions and Some Other Ethnic Music Traditions of Mindanao: A
      Preliminary Report of Field Research, February to July 1969.* Uni-
      versity of Hawaii Music Department.

2699. *H. Arlo NIMMO, "Songs of the Sulu Sea," in *Etc: A Review of Gene-
      ral Semantics,* XXV (1968).4: 489-94. Nineteen Bajau *kalangan baliu*
      or 'wind songs' from the Tawi-Tawi and Sibutu islands, with help-
      ful introductory comment.

2700. *H. Arlo NIMMO, "Posong, Trickster of Sulu," in *Western Folklore,*
      XXIX (1970).3: 185-91.

2701. *William R. PFEIFFER, "Seven Manobo Songs with modern texts,"
      translated by... with the assistance of Miss Lolita Bidangan, in
      his *Manobo Music Traditions* [item 2698].

2702. Antonio POSTMA, "The *Ambahan*: a Mangyan-Hanúnoo Poetic Form," in
      AS, III (1965).1: 71-85.

2703. Pieter Jan RAATS, *A Structural Study of Bagobo Myths and Rites*
      (Cebu City: University of San Carlos, 1969).

2704. Rudolf RAHMANN, "Quarrels and Enmity Between the Sun and the Moon.
      A Contribution to the Mythologies of the Philippines, India, and
      the Malay Peninsula," in *AFS,* XIV (1955): 202-14.

2705. Máximo RAMOS, *The Creatures of Midnight: Faded Deities of Luzon,
      the Visayas and Mindanao.* Decorations by Monina Parina (Quezon
      City: Island Publishers, [c 1967]).

2706. Lucetta K. RATCLIFF, "Filipino Folklore," Collected by..., in *JAF,*
      62.245 (July-September 1949): 259-89.

2707. Dr James A. ROBERTSON, *The Robertson Translations of the Pavon
      Manuscripts of 1838-1839. A - Stories of the Indios of This Island
      (Negros).* Transcript No. 5-A (Chicago: Philippine Studies Program,
      Department of Anthropology, University of Chicago, n.d. [*ca* 1957]).
      Stories and legends collected on Negros by Padre José María Pavón
      y Araguro, translated by Dr James A. Robertson.

2708. *Mamitua SABER, "*Darangen*: the Epic of the Maranao," in *JH,* X.3
      (September 1962): 322-9.

2709. *Mamitua SABER, "*Darangen*: the Epic of the Maranao," typescript by
      W.C. Mijares, University Research Center, Mindanao State Universi-
      ty, from *JH,* X.3: 322-9 [item 2708].

2710. William Henry SCOTT, "The Legend of Biag, An Igorot Culture Hero," in *AFS*, XXIII (1964).1: 93-110.

2711. Elizabeth Hough SECHRIST, *Once in the First Times: Folk Tales from the Philippines*. Illustrated by John Sheppard (Philadelphia: Macrae Smith, [c 1969]).

2712. Morice VANOVERBERGH, "Isneg Riddles," in *AFS*, XII (1953): 1-95.

2713. *Morice VANOVERBERGH, "Isneg Tales," in *AFS*, XIV (1955): 1-148.

2714. *Leopoldo Y. YABES, *The Ilocano Epic; A Critical Study of the 'Life of Lam-ang,' Ancient Ilocano Popular Poem*, with a Translation of the Poem into English Prose (Manila, 1935). See item 2715.

2715. *Leopoldo Y. YABES, "The Ilocano Epic: A Critical Study of 'The Life of Lam-ang'," in *Philippine Social Sciences and Humanities Review*, XXIII (1958).2-4: 283-337. Secondary (literary) epic or metrical romance attributed to Pedro Bukaneg, comprising about 1,290 lines and based upon an Ilokano legend dating from the early days of the Spanish occupation.

2716. Leopoldo Y. YABES, "The Adam and Eve of the Ilocanos," in *AFS*, XVII (1958): 220-5.

2717. Gregorio F. ZAIDE, *"Darangan*: The Epic of Mindanao," in *Far Eastern University Journal*, 1952: 34-7. Convenient synopsis of the Maranao epic.

CHRONICLES

2718. R.A. BEWSHER, "Bisayan Accounts of Early Settlements in the Philippines Recorded by Father Santaren," in *SMJ*, New Series, VII (1956).7: 48-53.

2719. *Dr Manuel L. CARREÓN, *"Maragtas*: the Datus from Borneo (The Earliest Known Visayan Text)," in *SMJ*, New Series, VIII (1957).10: 51-99. Translation of quasi-historical Hiligaynon traditions describing settlement of Panay from North Borneo.

2720. *Father [Tomás] SANTAREN, "Bisayan Accounts of early Bornean Settlements in the Philippines," translated by Enriqueta Fox, in *SMJ*, New Series, VII (1956).7: 22-42.

PRE-MODERN METRICAL WORKS

2721. Francisco BALTAZAR [= "Balagtás"], *Florante at Laura*. Translated by Tarrosa Subido and Arranged in Modern Tagalog by J.C. Balmaseda (Manila: J. Martinez, 1950). Most celebrated Tagalog *awit* or dodecasyllabic metrical romance, composed in 1837 and comprising 1,708 lines.

2722. *Juan R. FRANCISCO, *Maharadia Lawana*. Text Edited and Translated with the Collaboration of Nagasura T. Madale. Philippine Folklore Society Reprint Issue No. 1 (Quezon City: Philippine Folklore Society, 1969). Reprinted from *AS*, VII (1969).2. Maranao prose adaptation of part of the *Rāmāyaṇa*, edited from a romanized transcription of a Maranao manuscript; bilingual text.

2723. E. Arsenio MANUEL, "Tayabas Tagalog *Awit* Fragments from Quezon Province," in *AFS*, XVII (1958): 54–98.

2724. *Leopoldo Y. YABES, "A Critical Study of 'The Life of Lam-ang'" [items 2714 and 2715].

MODERN SHORT STORIES

2725. Estrella ALFÓN, "English," in Arcellana, *PEN Short Stories* [item 2728], 1–5.

2726. César R. AQUINO, "In the Smithy of My Soul," in Arcellana, *PEN Short Stories* [item 2728], 10–6.

2727. *Francisco ARCELLANA, "Flowers of May," in Polotan, *Prize Stories* [item 2780], 16–26.

2728. *Francisco ARCELLANA, *PEN Short Stories*. Edited, with an introduction, by... (Manila: Philippine Chapter, International PEN, 1962).

2729. *Francisco ARCELLANA, "Period of Emergence: The Short Story," in Manuud [item 2634], 603–17.

2730. Manuel E. ARGUILLA, "The Socialists," in Casper, *New Writing* [item 2736], 205–16.

2731. Manuel ARGUILLA, "The Long Vacation," in Arcellana, *PEN Short Stories* [item 2728], 6–9.

2732. Gregorio C. BRILLANTES, "A Wind Over the Earth," in Casper, *New Writing* [item 2736], 226–35.

2733. Gregorio C. BRILLANTES, "Journey to the Edge of the Sea," in Ar-
       cellana, *PEN Short Stories* [item 2728], 17-41.

2734. Leopoldo N. CACNIO, "To Her Alone," in Arcellana, *PEN Short
       Stories* [item 2728], 42-50.

2735. *Leonard CASPER, *Modern Philippines Short Stories* [*sic*] (Albuquer-
       que, 1962).

2736. *Leonard CASPER, *New Writing from the Philippines: A Critique and
       Anthology* (Syracuse: Syracuse University Press, 1966).

2737. Erwin E. CASTILLO, "Tomorrow Is a Downhill Place," in Arcellana,
       PEN Short Stories [item 2728], 51-60.

2738. Gilda CORDERO-FERNANDO, "The Morning Before Us," in Polotan,
       Prize Stories [item 2780], 208-19.

2739. Gilda CORDERO-FERNANDO, "People in the War," in Arcellana, *PEN
       Short Stories* [item 2728], 80-91.

2740. Andrés Cristóbal CRUZ, "The Quarrel," in Polotan, *Prize Stories*
       [item 2780], 85-100.

2741. Andrés Cristóbal CRUZ, "So," in Casper, *New Writing* [item 2736],
       178-85.

2742. *Amador DAGUIO, "Wedding Dance," in Shimer [item 3299], 358-65.

2743. Amador T. DAGUIO, "The Woman Who Looked Out of the Window," in
       Arcellana, *PEN Short Stories* [item 2728], 61-4.

2744. Morli DHARAM, "Dada," in Arcellana, *PEN Short Stories* [item 2728],
       65-79.

2745. Rony V. DIAZ, "The Centipede," in Polotan, *Prize Stories* [item
       2780], 152-60.

2746. *Rony V. DIAZ, "Death in a Sawmill," in Polotan, *Prize Stories*
       [item 2780], 161-74.

2747. S.V. EPISTOLA, "The Beads," in Polotan, *Prize Stories* [item 2780],
       175-207.

2748. Federico Licsi ESPINO, *Jr., The Country of Sleep: Five Stories*
       (Quezon City: Bustamente Press, [c 1969]).

2749. Ligaya Victorio FRUTO, *Yesterday and Other Stories* (Quezon City:
       Vibal Printing Co., [c 1969]).

2750. *Juan T. GATBONTON, "Clay," in Polotan, *Prize Stories* [item 2780],
       1-15.

2751. *N.V.M. GONZALEZ, "Children of the Ash-Covered Loam," in Polotan, *Prize Stories* [item 2780], 49-69.

2752. *N.V.M. GONZALEZ, "Lupo and the River," in Polotan, *Prize Stories* [item 2780], 101-51.

2753. *N.V.M. GONZALEZ, "The Bread of Salt," in José [item 3297], 108-15.

2754. *N.V.M. GONZALEZ, "The Bread of Salt," in *Of Love and Hope* [item 3291], 84-93.

2755. *N.V.M. GONZALEZ, "A Warm Hand," in Shimer [item 3299], 365-74.

2756. *N.V.M. GONZALEZ, *Selected Stories*. Introduction by Leonard Casper (Denver: Alan Swallow, [c 1964]).

2757. *N.V.M. GONZALEZ, "The Sea Beyond," in Casper, *New Writing* [item 2736], 217-25.

2758. *N.V.M. GONZALEZ, "The Calendar Christ," in Arcellana, *PEN Short Stories* [item 2728], 92-6.

2759. *Sinai C. HAMADA, "Tanabata's Wife," in Arcellana, *PEN Short Stories* [item 2728], 97-104.

2760. Nick JOAQUIN, *Prose and Poems*. With an Introduction by Teodoro M. Locsin (Manila: Graphic House, [c 1952]).

2761. Nick JOAQUIN, *Nick Joaquin's Selected Stories* (Manila: Alberto S. Florentino, 1962).

2762. Nick JOAQUIN, *La naval de Manila and other essays* (Manila: Alberto S. Florentino, 1964).

2763. Nick JOAQUIN, "Difficulties of a Diplomat," in Arcellana, *PEN Short Stories* [item 2728], 105-18.

2764. Nick JOAQUIN, "Difficulties of a Diplomat," in his *Selected Stories* [item 2761], 53-70.

2765. Nick JOAQUIN, "Guardia de Honor," in Hanrahan [item 3295], 408-25.

2766. Nick JOAQUIN, "May Day Eve," in Wigmore [item 3300], 266-76.

2767. Nick JOAQUIN, "May Day Eve," in Milton and Clifford [item 3298], 156-65.

2768. Nick JOAQUIN, "May Day Eve," in his *Selected Stories* [item 2761], 24-36.

2769. Nick JOAQUIN, "May Day Eve," in José [item 3297], 68-76.

2770. Nick JOAQUIN, "Summer Solstice," in his *Selected Stories* [item 2761], 37-52.

2771. Nick JOAQUIN, "Three Generations," in his *Selected Stories* [item 2761], 5-23.

2772. F. Sionil JOSÉ, "The Ancestor," in Wigmore [item 3300], 295-308.

2773. F. Sionil JOSÉ, "The Refugee," in Arcellana, *PEN Short Stories* [item 2728], 119-38.

2774. F. Sionil JOSÉ, "The Heirs," in *Tenggara*, I (1967): 88-100.

2775. Francisco Sionil JOSÉ, *The God Stealer, and Other Stories* (Quezon City: R.P. Garcia, 1968).

2776. Anthony MORLI, "Dada," in Casper, *New Writing* [item 2736], 236-54.

2777. Wilfrido D. NOLLEDO, "Rice Wine," in Arcellana, *PEN Short Stories* [item 2728], 139-54.

2778. Wilfrido D. NOLLEDO, "Rice Wine," in Casper, *New Writing* [item 2736], 186-204.

2779. Laura S. OLOROSO, "Nick Joaquin and His Brightly Burning Prose Works," in Manuud [item 2634], 765-92.

2780. *Kerima POLOTAN, *The Carlos Palanca Memorial Awards for Literature: Prize Stories, 1950-1955*. Edited by... (Manila: La Tondeña, [c 1957]).

2781. *Kerima POLOTAN, *Stories* (Manila: Bookmark, 1968).

2782. *Kerima POLOTAN-TUVERA, "The Sounds of Sunday," in Arcellana, *PEN Short Stories* [item 2728], 241-54.

2783. *Kerima POLOTAN-TUVERA, "The Sounds of Sunday," in José [item 3297], 1-14. *Asia Magazine* award story.

2784. José A. QUIRINO, *Three Faces of the Hero, and Other Stories* (Manila: Benipayo Press, 1969).

2785. Aida L. RIVERA, *Now and At the Hour, and other short stories* (Manila: Benipayo Press, 1957).

2786. Aida L. RIVERA, "Love in the Cornhusks," in her *Now and At the Hour* [item 2785], 3-10.

2787. *Aida L. RIVERA, "The Madonna Face," in her *Now and At the Hour* [item 2785], 11-20.

2788. Aida L. RIVERA, "Young Liberator," in her *Now and At the Hour* [item 2785], 21-34.

2789. *Aida L. RIVERA, "The Chieftest Mourner," in her *Now and At the Hour* [item 2785], 35-45.

2790. *Aida L. RIVERA, "Now and At the Hour," in her *Now and At the Hour* [item 2785], 46-65.

2791. Vicente RIVERA, *Jr.*, "The Open Door," in Arcellana, *PEN Short Stories* [item 2728], 155-64.

2792. *Alejandro R. ROCES, "Of Cocks and Kings," in Wigmore [item 3300], 29-36.

2793. *Alejandro R. ROCES, "Portrait of a Cocker, Poet - and Lover," in Arcellana, *PEN Short Stories* [item 2728], 165-77.

2794. Arturo B. ROTOR, "Zita," in Casper, *New Writing* [item 2736], 165-77.

2795. V.R. SAMONTE, "The Other Woman," in Polotan, *Prize Stories* [item 2780], 254-66.

2796. Wilfredo Pascua SANCHEZ, "Moon Under My Feet," in Arcellana, *PEN Short Stories* [item 2728], 178-84.

2797. *Bienvenido N. SANTOS, "Even Purple Hearts," in Polotan, *Prize Stories* [item 2780], 70-84.

2798. *Bienvenido N. SANTOS, "The Day the Dancers Came," in Arcellana, *PEN Short Stories* [item 2728], 185-99.

2799. *Bienvenido N. SANTOS, "The Day the Dancers Came," in Casper, *New Writing* [item 2736], 255-72.

2800. *Bienvenido N. SANTOS, "The Enchanted Plant," in José [item 3297], 134-43.

2801. *Bienvenido N. SANTOS, *You Lovely People* (Manila: Benipayo Press, 1966). Prose sketches.

2802. Edilberto K. TIEMPO, "To Be Free," in Arcellana, *PEN Short Stories* [item 2728], 200-9.

2803. *Edith L. TIEMPO, "The Black Monkey," in Polotan, *Prize Stories* [item 2780], 27-37.

2804. *Edith L. TIEMPO, "The Dam," in Polotan, *Prize Stories* [item 2780], 234-53.

2805. *Edith L. TIEMPO, "The Dimensions of Fear," in Arcellana, *PEN Short Stories* [item 2728], 210-20.

2806. Patricia S. TORRES, "The Virgin," in Polotan, *Prize Stories* [item 2780], 38-48.

2807. *J.C. TUVERA, "Ceremony," in Polotan, *Prize Stories* [item 2780], 220-33.

2808. *J.C. TUVERA, "Ceremony," in Hanrahan [item 3295], 399-407.

2809. *Juan C. TUVERA, "High Into Morning," in Arcellana, *PEN Short Stories* [item 2728], 221-40.

THE NOVEL

2810. Magdalena B. BAUTISTA, *Diwata: A Novel* (Manila, 1958).

2811. Maguel A. BERNAD, *S.J.*, "Some Aspects of Rizal's Novels," in Manuud [item 2634], 527-38.

2812. Leonard CASPER, *New Writing from the Philippines* [item 2736].

2813. Ricaredo DEMETILLO, *Barter in Panay* (Quezon City: University of the Philippines, 1961). An historical novel about Sumakwel, first *datu* and lawgiver of Panay.

2814. *Nick JOAQUIN, *The Woman Who Had Two Navels*. Stonehill Award Novel (Manila: Regal Publishing Co., 1961).

2815. Elena Prado POLO, *Themes and Meanings in the American and Filipino Novels of the Second World War in the Pacific*. Doctoral dissertation, Michigan State University, 1970.

2816. José RIZAL, selections from his *Noli me tangere*, translated by León Ma. Guerrero, in Shimer [item 3299], 251-74.

MODERN POETRY

2817. Carlos A. ANGELES, "Dusk," in José [item 3297], 238.

2818. Carlos A. ANGELES, four poems, in Casper, *New Writing* [item 2736],

"Ferns" (276), "Landscape II" (276-7), "Asylum Piece" (277-8), "The Eye" (278).

2819. Cirilo F. BAUTISTA, *The Cave, and Other Poems* (Baguio City: Ato Bookshop, 1968).

2820. Tomás P. BOQUIREN, *The Unvanquished and Others (Philosophical Poems)*. Introduction by Federico Licsi Espino (Manila: Liwayway Publishing Co., [c 1969]).

2821. Rafael Zulueta da COSTA, "Like the Molave," in Shimer [item 3299], 77-9.

2822. Amador T. DAGUIO, "Off the Aleutian Islands," in Casper, *New Writing* [item 2736], 286.

2823. *Ricaredo DEMETILLO, "The Ambitious Failure," in Wigmore [item 3300], 276-7.

2824. *Ricaredo DEMETILLO, *The Authentic Voice of Poetry* (Quezon City: University of the Philippines Press, 1962).

2825. *Ricaredo DEMETILLO, *Masks and Signatures* (Quezon City: University of the Philippines Press, n.d.)

2826. *Ricaredo DEMETILLO, from "Barter in Panay," in Casper, *New Writing* [item 2736], 305-10.

2827. Federico Licsi ESPINO, Jr., *Burnt Alphabets: Poems in English, Tagalog and Spanish* (Manila: Pioneer Printing Press, [c 1969]).

2828. Federico Licsi ESPINO, Jr., *Counterclockwise: Poems, 1965-1969*. Preface by Ricaredo Demetillo (Quezon City: Bustamente Press, [c 1969]).

2829. Federico Licsi ESPINO, Jr., *Dark Sutra*. Introduction by Francisco Arcellana (Quezon City: Pioneer Press, [c 1969]). In tandem with his *Tomo 2: Toreng Bato . . . bastilyong pawid*. See item 2836.

2830. Federico Licsi ESPINO, Jr., *Dawn and Downsitting: Poems* (Quezon City: Pioneer Press, [c 1969]).

2831. *N.V.M. GONZALEZ and Jean EDWARDSON, *Six Filipino Poets*. With an Introduction by Leonard Casper and Notes by... (Manila: Benipayo Press, 1954).

2832. Alejandrino G. HUFANA, three poems, in Casper, *New Writing* [item 2736], "Pygmy Reservation" (279), "Farmer in a Wrong Career" (280), "Keeper of the Lighthouse" (281-2).

2833. Nick JOAQUIN, *Prose and Poems* [item 2760].

2834. Nick JOAQUIN, "*Verde, yo te quiero, verde!*," in Wigmore [item 3300], 37-8.

2835. Nick JOAQUIN, "Six P.M.," in Shimer [item 3299], 81.

2836. Edgar C. KNOWLTON, *Jr.*, review of *Toreng bato . . . kastilyong pawid* by Federico Licsi Espino [item 2829], in *BA*, 42.1 (Winter 1968): 171.

2837. Pablo LASLO y Raúl GUERRERO MONTEMAYOR, *Breve antología de la poesía filipina; poetas de habla española.* Selección y notas por ... Estudio preliminar del ingeniero Luis G. Miranda (México: B. Costa-Amic, 1966).

2838. Antonio G. MANUUD, "Toward a Theory Concerning the Development of Filipino Poetry in Spanish," in Manuud [item 2634], 457-82.

2839. Antonio MOLINA, "Philippine Music and Poetry," in Manuud [item 2634], 195-206.

2840. Virginia MORENO, "Lament of a Cathay Handmaiden in Marco Polo's Tent Pavilion," in *Chapbook of Contemporary Asian Poetry* [item 3289], 56-7.

2841. *Virginia R. MORENO, six poems, in Casper, *New Writing* [item 2736], "Sun Series" (287), "Shadow and Light" (287), "Night and Day" (288), "Sunset, Sunrise: (288), "Order for Masks" (289-90), "Batik Maker" (291).

2842. Valdemar OLAGUER, "In Answer to Cimabue," in José [item 3297], 237.

2843. José RIZAL, "My Last Farewell," translated by Nick Joaquin, in Shimer [item 3299], 75-7.

2844. E. SAN JUAN, *Jr.*, "Social Consciousness and Revolt in Modern Philippines Poetry," in *BA*, 39 (1965).4: 394-9.

2845. Epifanio SAN JUAN, two poems, in Casper, *New Writing* [item 2736], "Voyages" (298), "A Fable for Innocents" (299-304).

2846. Bienvenido N. SANTOS, "Cautery," in Wigmore [item 3300], 277.

2847. Bienvenido N. SANTOS, "The March of Death," in Shimer [item 3299], 79-81.

2848. José Mo. SINGSON, *Under the Eastern Sky: Collected Poems* (Manila: College Professors Publications Corp., 1969).

2849. *Edith L. TIEMPO, "Rowana, Playing in the Sun," in Wigmore [item 3300], 309.

2850. *Edith L. TIEMPO, "Mid-morning for Sheba," in José [item 3297], 332.

2851. *Edith L. TIEMPO, two poems, in Casper, *New Writing* [item 2736], "Green Hearts" (295-6), "The Fisherman" (297).

2852. Rolando S. TINIO, "Period of Awareness: The Poets," in Manuud [item 2634], 618-33.

2853. Emmanuel TORRES, two poems, in Casper, *New Writing* [item 2736], "Sung" (292), "The Hazards of Hearing an Explosion in Broad Daylight" (293-4).

2854. José García VILLA, "The Anchored Angel," in José [item 3297], 239-40.

2855. José García VILLA, four untitled poems, in Casper, *New Writing* [item 2736], 273-5.

2856. *Manuel A. VIRAY, "The Blind Woman Next Door," in *Chapbook of Contemporary Asian Poetry* [item 3289], 54-6.

2857. *Manuel A. VIRAY, "Morning of Ang Shiu, Chinese Storekeeper," in Casper, *New Writing* [item 2736], 285.

2858. Oscar de ZUÑIGA, "The Dogs," in *Chapbook of Contemporary Asian Poetry* [item 3289], 57.

2859. Oscar de ZUÑIGA, two poems, in Casper, *New Writing* [item 2736], "Suns Have Gone" (283), "The Ants and the Chandlers" (284).

DRAMA

2860. Julián C. BALMASEDA, "Philippine Drama," translated from the Pilipino, in *JH*, X.3 (September 1962): 299-321.

2861. Daisy HONTIVEROS-AVELLANA, "Philippine Drama: A Social Protest," in Manuud [item 2634], 668-88.

2862. Alejandrino G. HUFANA, *Curtain-raisers* (Quezon City: University of the Philippines Press, 1964).

2863. Nick JOAQUIN, "A Portrait of the Artist as Filipino (An Elegy in Three Scenes)," in Casper, *New Writing* [item 2736], 311-82.

2864. Ma. Teresa MUÑOZ, "Notes on Theater: Pre-Hispanic Philippines," in Manuud [item 2634], 648-67.

2865. Rolando S. TINIO, "Retracing Old Grounds: The Paradox of Philip-
       pine Theater," in Manuud [item 2634], 689-701.

VIII. THAILAND

GENERAL

2866. Anonymous, "The Society of Literature of Thailand," in *JSS*, XXXIV (1943).2: 203-4.

2867. Anonymous, *Thai Personal Names* (Washington, D.C.: Central Intelligence Agency, 1964).

2868. *Ruth BENEDICT, *Thai Culture and Behavior*. An Unpublished Wartime Study Dated September, 1943. Data Paper Number 4. Third Printing (Ithaca, N.Y.: Southeast Asia Program, Department of Far Eastern Studies, Cornell University, 1963). Eminent anthropologist's classic digest of Thai cultural patterns, invaluable as background to traditional and modern literatures.

2869. Jane BUNNAG, review of *Loosely Structured Social Systems: Thailand in Comparative Perspective* edited by Hans-Dieter Evers, in *BTLV*, 126 (1970).3: 358-61. Of interest in connection with item 2874.

2870. Anthony Herbert CHRISTIE, "Indonesia: Cultures in Historic Times," in *EB (1962)*, 12: 274a-6a.

2871. G. COEDÈS, review of *Etude sur la littérature siamoise* by P. Schweisguth [item 2880], in *BEFEO*, XLVI (1954).2: 657-61.

2872. D.N., review of *The Story of Phra Abhai Mani*, translated by H.H. Prince Prem Purachatra [item 2935], in *JSS*, XL (1952).2: 188-94.

2873. D.N., review of *The Story of Khun Chan Khun Phan*, translated by H.H. Prince Prem Chaya [item 2941], in *JSS*, XLIV (1956).1: 50-1.

2874. *John F. EMBREE, "Thailand - A Loosely Structured Social System," in *AmAn*, 52 (1950).2: 181-93. Controversial paper advancing point of view with which few scholars or knowledgable Thai agree, nevertheless valuable in offering a fresh perspective of Thai society and focusing attention on some of its unique features. See item 2869.

2875. Lucien M. HANKS, Jane R. HANKS and Lauriston SHARP, *Ethnographic Notes on Northern Thailand*. Edited by... Data Paper No. 58 (Ithaca, N.Y.: Southeast Asia Program, Department of Asian Studies, Cornell University, 1965).

2876. Robert B. JONES, *Thai Titles and Ranks*, Including a translation of *Traditions of Royal Lineage in Siam* by King Chulalongkorn. Data Paper Number 81 (Ithaca, N.Y.: Southeast Asia Program, Department of Asian Studies, Cornell University, 1971).

2877. Edgar C. KNOWLTON, *Jr.*, "A Conversation with M.R. Kukrit Pramoj in Bangkok," in *BA*, Autumn 1964.

2878. *Phya* Anuman RAJADHON, *Thai Literature and Swasdi Raksa*. Thailand Culture Series, No. 3. Fourth Edition (Bangkok: The National Culture Institute, B.E. 2499 [= A.D. 1956]). Useful synopsis of main genres.

2879. *Phya* Anuman RAJADHON, *Thai Literature in Relation to the Diffusion of Her Cultures*. Thai Culture, New Series, No. 9 (Bangkok: The Fine Arts Department, B.E. 2504 [= A.D. 1961]).

2880. *P. SCHWEISGUTH, *Etude sur la littérature siamoise*. Ouvrage publié avec le concours du Centre National de la Recherche Scientifique (Paris: Imprimerie Nationale / Adrien Maisonneuve, 1951). History of literature in considerable detail; best such work in a Western language. See items 2871 and 2881.

2881. E. SEIDENFADEN, "On Siamese Literature," review of *Etude sur la littérature siamoise* by P. Schweisguth [item 2880], in *AO*, XXII (1955).1-2: 8-9.

2882. S. SINGARAVELU, "Some Aspects of South Indian Cultural Contacts with Thailand: Historical Background," in *Proceedings of the First International Conference Seminar of Tamil Studies*, Kuala Lumpur - Malaysia, April 1966. Volume One (Kuala Lumpur: International Association of Tamil Research, 1966), I: 21-38.

2883. A. Neville J. WHYMANT, "Siam: Literature," in *EB (1962)*, 20: 596b-7a.

2884. A. Neville WHYMANT, Virginia THOMPSON, and Arthur Shane Beart OLVER, "Siam: History," in *EB (1962)*, 20: 590b-3a.

FOLK LITERATURE

2885. Anonymous, "The Adventures of Kawes and Honwichai," in *MS 1 Reader No. 2*.

2886. Anonymous, "Two Thai Stories: The Golden Carp and Chalawan the Crocodile King," in *MS III Reader No. 2*.

2887. Anonymous, "Why the Parrot Repeats Man's Words," in Courlander, *Ride With the Sun* [item 3292], 34-7.

2888. *Charles ARCHAIMBAULT, "Le cycle de *Nang* Oua - *Nang* Malong et son substrat sociologique" [item 2304].

2889. Solange BERNARD-THIERRY, "Notes de littérature populaire comparée," in *BSEI*, Nouvelle Série, XXVIII (1953).1: 19-24. Contains "I. Jataka et conte siamois" (19-21) and "II. Conte siamois et conte cambodgien" (22-4).

2890. *H.H. Prince* BIDYALANKARANA, "The Pastime of Rhyme-Making and Singing in Rural Siam," in *JSS*, XX (1926).2: 101-27.

2891. Eleanor BROCKETT, *Burmese and Thai Fairy Tales*. Retold by... (London: Frederick Muller, 1965).

2892. CHALERMNIT, *Thai Folk Tales* (Bangkok: Chalermnit Press, 1963). Comprises "The Story of Pra Law, or The Love of Two Women" (1-12), "The Love Story of a Notorious Woman, *Nang* Kaki" (13-30), "*Nang* Nak, or Love Never Dies" (31-9), "The Story of a Rose" (40-51), "Kamanit" (52-70).

2893. *J. CROSBY, "A Translation of 'The Book of the Birds' (*Paksi Pakaranam*)," in *JSS*, VII (1911).2: 1-90.

2894. Alan S. FEINSTEIN, *Folk Tales from Siam*. Illustrated by Pat Pibulsonggram (South Brunswick, N.J.: A.S. Barnes, 1969).

2895. *Col G.E. GERINI, "On Siamese Proverbs and Idiomatic Expressions," in *JSS*, I (1904): 11-158.

2896. Mary R. HAAS, "Thai Word Games," in *JAF*, 70.276 (April-June 1957): 173-5.

2897. Kermit KRUEGER, *The Golden Swans*. A Picture Story from Thailand, retold by... with pictures by Ed Young (New York: World, [c 1969]).

2898. Kermit KRUEGER, *The Serpent Prince: Folk Tales from Northeastern Thailand*. Illustrated by Yoko Mitsuhashi (New York: World, [c 1969]).

2899. *R.S. LE MAY, "Legends and Folklore of Northern Siam," in *JSS*, XVIII (1924).1: 1-49.

2900. *Reginald LE MAY, *Siamese Tales Old and New: The Four Riddles, and Other Stories*, translated by... With some Reflections on the Tales (London: Arthur Probsthain, 1958).

2901. Thomas E. LUX, "From Dream to Folklore in Northeast Thailand," in *AFS*, XXX (1971).1: 85-96.

2902. *Mom* Dusdi PARIBATRA, *The Reluctant Princess: A Legend of Love in*

Siam, Retold by... Illustrated by Sukit Chutama (Rutland / Tokyo: Charles E. Tuttle, 1963).

2903. *Phya* Anuman RAJADHON, "A Study on [the] Thai Folk Tale," in *JSS*, LIII (1965).2: 133-7.

2904. *Phraya* Anuman RAJADHON, *Essays on Thai Folklore* (Bangkok: Social Science Association Press of Thailand, 1968).

2905. *E. SEIDENFADEN, "Fairy Tales of common origin," in *JSS*, XXXIII (1941).2: 143-5.

2906. *E. SEIDENFADEN, "Further Notes on Fairy Tales of common origin," in *JSS*, XXXIV (1943).1: 59-62.

2907. *J. Kasem SIBUNRUANG, *Siamese Folktales*. Narrated in English by... With illustrations by Saeng Aroon Rataksikorn. Volume I (Bangkok: M. Gomiero, [c 1954]). Excellent renderings of some well-known tales. See item 2911.

2908. J. Kasem SIBUNRUANG, "The Golden Goby," in Wigmore [item 3300], 227-35.

2909. J. Kasem SIBUNRUANG, "The Golden Goby," in Hanrahan [item 3295], 374-82.

2910. J. Kasem SIBUNRUANG, "At the Country of the Bird-Women," in Garnett [item 3294], 158-64.

2911. *J. Kasem SIBUNRUANG, *Contes et légendes de Thaïlande*. Avant-propos de Thanat Khoman. Préface de J.M. Soulier. Illustrations de Prawat Laucharoen (Bangkok: Vipart's, [c 1969]). Good selection of tales supplementing those in item 2907.

2912. Marian Davies TOTH, *Tales from Thailand* (Tokyo and Rutland: Tuttle, 1971).

2913. W.A.M. URQUHART, *Tales from Old Siam*. Selected and edited by... (Bangkok: Progress Publishing Company, n.d. [*ca* 1963]).

2914. Ramadi VASNAVONG, "The Birth of the Mekong," a Thai folk tale retold by..., in *Bangkok World: Standard Bangkok Magazine*, Saturday 22 March 1970.

2915. *Ramadi VASNAVONG, "Prince of the Golden Conch," a Thai folk tale retold by..., in *Bangkok World: Standard Bangkok Magazine*, Saturday 1 May 1971. Another version of the *Sang Thong* tale.

2916. *Christian VELDER, *Märchen aus Thailand*, Herausgegeben und übertragen von... (Düsseldorf: E. Diederichs, [c 1968]).

2917. Christian VELDER, "Mong Lai's Beautiful Daughter," a Thai folk tale retold by... Translated by Hans Engelmann, in *Bangkok World: Standard Bangkok Magazine*, Saturday 30 October 1971.

2918. Margaretta B. WELLS, *Thai Fairy Tales* (Bangkok: Church of Christ in Thailand, 1965).

2919. William Alfred Rae WOOD, *Tales from Thailand: Fact and Fancy*, by Lotus [pseudonym]. Illustrated by Ben Kloezeman (Singapore: M.P. H. Publications, 1968).

INSCRIPTIONS

2920. G. COEDÈS, "L'inscription de Nagara Jum," in *JSS*, XIII (1919).3: 1–43.

2921. G. COEDÈS, "Nouvelles notes critiques sur l'inscription de Rāma Khamheng," in *JSS*, XVII (1923).3: 113–20.

2922. *G. COEDÈS, "Documents sur l'histoire politique et religieuse du Laos occidental" [item 2328].

2923. *G. COEDÈS, *Recueil des inscriptions du Siam*. Deuxième partie: in-scriptions de Dvāravatī, de Çrīvijaya et de Lavo. Editées et tra-duites par... (Bangkok: Bangkok Times Press, B.E. 2472 [= A.D. 1929]). Microfilm.

2924. *Thomas W. GETHING, "The Rām Khamhaeng Inscription," translated by ..., in Harry J. Benda and John A. Larkin, *The World of Southeast Asia: Selected Historical Documents* (New York: Harper & Row, [c 1967]), 40–5.

2925. Henry D. GINSBURG, *Ram Khamhaeng's Inscription: an introduction and translation*. Department of Asian Studies, University of Hawaii, 10 December 1965. Typescript research paper.

2926. *R. HALLIDAY, "Les inscriptions môn du Siam, éditées et traduites par...," in *BEFEO*, XXX (1930).1–2: 81–105.

2927. Auguste PAVIE, *Recherches sur l'histoire du Cambodge, du Laos et du Siam* [item 949], 169–488.

CHRONICLES

2928. J. BURNAY, "A propos de l'auteur de la recension Bradley de la

Grande Chronique d'Ayuthia," in *BSOAS*, XI (1943).1: 144-7.

2929. *Camille NOTTON, *Annales du Siam* [in three volumes] (Paris, 1930-39).

2930. Auguste PAVIE, *Recherches sur l'histoire du Cambodge, du Laos et du Siam* [item 949], 145-68.

2931. Larry STERNSTEIN, review of *The Dynastic Chronicles, Bangkok Era, The Fourth Reign (B.E. 2394-2411; A.D. 1851-1868)*, translated by Chadin (Kanjanavanit) Flood, in *JSS*, LIV (1966).2: 231.

2932. *W.A.R. WOOD, "The 'Pongsawadan of Luang Prasöt'," in *JSS*, XIX (1925).3: 153-7.

2933. David K. WYATT, "A Thai Version of Newbold's *Hikayat Patani*" [item 2509].

PRE-MODERN METRICAL WORKS

2934. Sunthorn BHU, *Swasdi Raksa*, in *Phya* Anuman Rajadhon, *Thai Literature and Swasdi Raksa* [item 2878], 15-9. Free prose translation of a late code of conduct for princes of the blood. See item 2936.

2935. *Sunthorn BHU, *The Story of Phra Abhai Mani*, told in English by Prem Chaya, with illustrations by Hem Vejakorn. Second Edition (Bangkok: Chatra Books, 1959). Readable abridged translation of a celebrated romance. See item 2872.

2936. *Sunthorn BHU, *The Sawatdii Raksaa of Sunthorn Bhu*. Translated by Sharon Bannon with the assistance of Sumitra Alexander. Close translation, with notes, of the same code of conduct as item 2934.

2937. *Sunthorn BHU, *The Subhāṣita Sāna Satarī* /suphaasĭt sàŋ sàtrĭĭ/ *or Code of Conduct for Young Women*. Translated by Mrs Thavitiya Sudara and Miss Dusdeporn Chummirokasant and edited with notes by Philip N. Jenner. Typescript.

2938. *H.H. Prince* BIDYA, "Sebhā Recitation and The Story of Khun Chāng Khun Phan," in *JSS*, XXXIII (1941).1: 1-22.

2939. *J.M. CADET, *The Ramakien: The Thai Epic*. Illustrated with the bas-reliefs of Wat Phra Jetubon, Bangkok (Tokyo and Palo Alto: Kodansha International, 1971). Sumptuous edition of the Thai version of the *Rāmāyaṇa*.

2940. *Prem CHAYA [= H.H. Prince Prem Purachatra], *Magic Lotus: A Romantic Fantasy*. An adaptation for the English Stage of the Fifteenth-

Century Siamese Classic *Pra Law*. Third Edition (Bangkok: Chatra Books, 1949). See item 2944.

2941. *Prem CHAYA, *The Story of Khun Chang Khun Phan*, told in English by ..., with illustrations by Hem Vejakorn (Bangkok: Chatra Books, 1955), Book One and Book Two [complete]. See items 2873 and 2957.

2942. Eugène DENIS, "L'origine cingalaise du *P'raḥ Malay*," in *Felicitation Volumes of Southeast Asian Studies* presented to His Highness Prince Dhaninivat... on the occasion of his eightieth birthday (Bangkok: The Siam Society, 1965), II: 329-38.

2943. *Prince DHANI NIVAT, "Madanabādhā, or The Romance of the Rose (King Rama VI's last work)," in *JSS*, XXXIX (1952).2: 181-9.

2944. *Prince* DHANI NIVAT, "The Date and Authorship of the Romance of Phra Lô," in *JSS*, XLI (1954).2: 179-83. See item 2940.

2945. DHANINIVAT, "The *Ramakien*. A Siamese Version of the Story of Rama," in *Burma Research Society, Fiftieth Anniversary Publications No. 1*: Some of the Papers read at the Fiftieth Anniversary Conference (Rangoon: Burma Research Society, 1961), 33-45.

2946. *Jean DRANS, *Histoire de Nang Manora et Histoire de Sang Thong*. Deux récits du recueil des Cinquante Jataka, Traduits du siamois (Tokyo: Presses Salésiennes, 1947), subsequently adopted as a Publication de la Maison Franco-Japonaise, Tokyo. Outstanding translation, with notes, of two traditional tales of unusual importance.

2947. *Edouard LORGÉOU, *Les entretiens de Nang Tantrai*, traduits du siamois par... Bois dessinés et gravés par A.-F. Cosyns. Les Classiques de l'Orient: collection publiée sous le patronage de l'Association Française des Amis de l'Orient et la direction de Victor Goloubew. Volume IX (Paris: Bossard, 1924).

2948. Auguste PAVIE, "*Néang* Kakey" [item 966], 155-68 (French translation), 357-61 (Thai text).

2949. Auguste PAVIE, "Les douze jeunes filles" [item 965], 27-52 (French translation), 335-42 (Thai text).

2950. *M.R.* Seni PRAMOJ, "Poetic Translations from the Siamese: Selected Verses of Sri Praj and Sunthon Bhu," in *JSS*, XLVI (1958).2: 215-6.

2951. *M.R.* Seni PRAMOJ, "A Poetic Translation from the Siamese: a *Lokanīti* Verse," in *JSS*, XLVII (1959).2: 179.

2952. *M.R.* Seni PRAMOJ, *Interpretative Translations of Thai Poets* (Bangkok: Southeast Asia Treaty Organization, 1965).

2953. Anuman RAJADHON, "*Thet Mahachet*," in *Burma Research Society, Fif-*

tieth Anniversary Publications No. 1: Some of the Papers read at the Fiftieth Anniversary Conference (Rangoon: Burma Research Society, 1961), 1-8.

2954. RAMA I, *Ramayana: Masterpiece of Thai Literature*, retold from the original version written by King Rama I of Thailand (Bangkok: Chalermit, 1965).

2955. P. SCHWEISGUTH, "Les '*Nirat*' ou poèmes d'adieu dans la littérature siamoise," in *JSS*, XXXVIII (1950).1: 67-78.

2956. P. SCHWEISGUTH, "Les '*Nirat*' ou poèmes d'adieu dans la littérature siamoise," in *The Siam Society Fiftieth Anniversary Commemorative Publication*: Selected Articles from The Siam Society *Journal*. Volume II: 1929-1953 (Bangkok: The Siam Society, 1954), 185-96.

2957. *Mme J. Kasem SIBUNRUANG, *La femme, le héros et le vilain: "Khun Chang, Khun Phèn," Poème populaire thaï*. Traduit par... Annales du Musée Guimet. Bibliothèque d'Etudes, Tome LXVe. Collection UNESCO d'œuvres représentatives, série thaïlandaise (Paris: Presses Universitaires de France, 1960). See items 2941 and 2942.

2958. E.H.S. SIMMONDS, "Thai Narrative Poetry: Palace and Provincial Texts of an Episode from *Khun Chang Khun Phaen*," in *AMaj*, New Series, X (1963).2: 279-99.

2959. E.H.S. SIMMONDS, "Siamese (Thai)," in Hatto [item 3296], 186-95. On the *alba* or dawn song.

2960. E.H.S. SIMMONDS, "Mahōrasap II. The Thai National Library manuscript," in *BSOAS*, XXXIV (1971).1: 119-31.

2961. *S. SINGARAVELU, "A Comparative Study of the Sanskrit, Tamil, Thai and Malay Versions of the Story of Rāma with Special Reference to the Process of Acculturation in the Southeast Asian Versions," in *JSS*, LVI (1968).2: 137-85.

2962. *Dr* Suraphol SUDARA and *Mrs* Thavitiya SUDARA, *A Selection of Classical Thai Poetry: from 1238 to 1925*. Magnetic tape recording (26 minutes) in Thai, illustrating traditional mode of chanting.

2963. Udom WAROTAMASIKKHADIT, "A Note on Internal Rhyme in Thai Poetry," in *JSS*, LVI (1968).2: 269-72.

2964. Saksri YAMNADDA, *The Mangalatthadīpanī, Chapters I and II*. Doctoral dissertation, University of Pennsylvania, 1971. On a Pāli text composed in Thailand in 1524 A.D.

MODERN PROSE

2965. *Manas CHANYONG, "Shoot to Kill," translated by Prince Prem Purachatra, in Wigmore [item 3300], 317-27.

2966. *Riem ENG [= Malai Chupinij], "Rising Flood," in José [item 3297],
189-96.

2967. *Riem ENG, "Rising Flood," in Siwasariyanon [item 2977], 6-17.

2968. *Riem ENG, *Nang* Phanthurat's Gold Mine," in José [item 3297], 274-
83.

2969. *Riem ENG, *Nang* Phanthurat's Gold Mine," in Siwasariyanon [item
2977], 36-49.

2970. Ute GLOCKNER, *Literatursoziologische Untersuchung des Thailändischen Romans im XX. Jahrhundert.* Doctoral dissertation, University
of Freiburg i. B., 1967.

2971. *Theb [Dhep] MAHAPAORYA, "Champoon," in José [item 3297], 299-309.

2972. *Theb MAHAPAORYA, "Champoon," in *Of Love and Hope* [item 3291], 41-
54.

2973. *Dhep MAHAPAORYA, "Champoon," in Siwasariyanon [item 2977], 50-69.

2974. V. na PRAMUANMARG, *Prisna.* Translated by Tulachandra (Bangkok:
Chatra Books, 1961), Book One [all published]. Novel, of interest
mainly as illustrating certain pitfalls in development of modern
literature.

2975. *Archin PANJABAN, "Heat and Heart," in Siwasariyanon [item 2977],
70-5.

2976. *Kukrit PRAMOJ, *Red Bamboo* (Bangkok: Progress Bookstore, [c 1961]).
Well-written political allegory in novel form.

2977. *Witt SIWASARIYANON, *Thai Short Stories.* With an introduction by
... Second Edition (Bangkok: International P.E.N., Thailand Centre, 1971). Best collection available.

2978. Dok Mai SOD, "The Good Citizen," translated by Nai K. Kitiyakara,
in Wigmore [item 3300], 106-16.

2979. *K. SURANGKHANANG, "The Grandmother," in José [item 3297], 310-21.

2980. *K. SURANGKHANANG, "The Grandmother," in Siwasariyanong [item 2977],
18-35.

2981. *Pratoomratha ZENG, "My Thai Cat," in Shimer [item 3299], 352-6.

MODERN POETRY

2982. *Prem CHAYA [= Prince Prem Purachatra], "On My Short-Sightedness,"
in Wigmore [item 3300], 116-7.

2983. *Prem CHAYA, four poems, in José [item 3297], "The Tropic Night"
(336), "The Canal of a Hundred Thousand Sores" (336), "The Flute"
(337), "An Early Morning Thought" (337).

2984. Angkarn KALAYANAPONG, "Four Poems," translated from the original
Thai by Sulak Sivaraksa and H. Woodward, in *Tenggara*, 1 (1967):
76-8.

2985. James N. MOSEL, "A Poetic Translation from the Siamese: Prince
Damrong's Reply in Verse to Rama V," in *JSS*, XLVII (1959).1: 103-
11.

2986. *James N. MOSEL, *Trends and Structure in Contemporary Thai Poetry*.
With Translations and Bibliography. Data Paper No. 43 (Ithaca,
N.Y.: Southeast Asia Program, Department of Far Eastern Studies,
Cornell University, 1961).

2987. Khukrit PRAMOT [= Kukrit Pramoj], "The Cold Winds," translated by
James N. Mosel and Burton Raffel, in *Chapbook of Contemporary
Asian Poetry* [item 3289], 61.

2988. *Chayasi SUNTHONPHIPHIT, "Till Heart's End," translated by James
N. Mosel and Burton Raffel, in *Chapbook of Contemporary Asian
Poetry* [item 3289], 60.

2989. *Chayasi SUNTHONPHIPHIT, "Till Heart's End," translated by James
N. Mosel and Burton Raffel, in Shimer [item 3299], 61-2.

2990. *H.R.H. Prince* Phanuphan YUKHON, "The White Lotus," translated by
James N. Mosel and Burton Raffel, in *Chapbook of Contemporary
Asian Poetry* [item 3289], 61.

2991. *H.R.H. Prince* Phanuphan YUKHON, "The White Lotus," translated by
James N. Mosel and Burton Raffel, in Shimer [item 3299], 61.

DRAMA

2992. Wallace CHAPPELL, "Manohra," translated by..., in James R. Brandon, *Traditional Asian Plays*. Edited by... (New York: Hill and Wang, 1972).

2993. G. COEDÈS, "Origine et évolution des diverses formes du théâtre traditionnel en Thaïlande," in *BSEI*, Nouvelle Série, XXXVIII (1963).3-4: 489-506.

2994. D., "*Nang Talung*," in *JSS*, XLVII (1959).2: 181.

2995. *Prince* DHANI NIVAT, "The Shadow-Play as a Possible Origin of the Masked-Play," in *JSS*, XXXVII (1948).1: 26-32.

2996. *Prince* DHANI NIVAT, "Traditional Dress in the Classic Dance of Siam," in *JSS*, XL (1952).2: 133-45.

2997. *Prince* DHANI NIVAT, "The Shadow-Play as a Possible Origin of the Masked-Play," in *The Siam Society Fiftieth Anniversary Commemorative Publication*. Selected Articles from The Siam Society *Journal*. Volume II: 1929-1953 (Bangkok: The Siam Society, 1954), 176-84.

2998. *Prince* DHANI NIVAT, "The *Dalang*," in *JSS*, XLIII (1956).2: 113-35.

2999. *H.H. Prince* DHANINIVAT..., *The Nang*. Thailand Culture Series, No. 12 (Bangkok: The National Culture Institute, B.E. 2497 [= A.D. 1954]).

3000. *H.H. Prince* DHANINIVAT....and Dhanit YUPHO, *The Khon*. Thailand Culture Series, No. 11 (Bangkok: The National Culture Institute, B.E. 2497 [= A.D. 1954]).

3001. Gerd HÖPFNER, *Südostasiatische Schattenspiele: Masken und Figuren aus Java und Thailand* [item 2273].

3002. R. NICOLAS, "Le *Lakhon Nora* ou *Lakhon Chatri* et les origines du théâtre classique siamois," in *JSS*, XVIII (1924).2: 85-110.

3003. *Miss* Ubon RAKHAMRUNG, *Manohra: a Thai Dance-Drama in Five Acts*. Translated by... Script for a performance by a group of East-West Center students on 5 March 1965. Typescript.

3004. *RAMA VI, *Madanabādhā, or The Romance of a Rose: A Play in Five Acts*. Edited by Dhani Nivat (Bangkok: Aksaraniti, 1925).

3005. J. Kasem SIBUNRUANG, "Le Roi Rama VI et le théâtre français," in *Présence de la France en Asie*. Numéro spécial de *FA*, XIII (1956). 125-126-127: 384-9.

3006. E.H.S. SIMMONDS, "New Evidence on Thai Shadow-Play Invocations," in *BSOAS*, XXIV (1961).3: 542-59.

3007. E.H.S. SIMMONDS, "*Mahōrasop* in a Thai *Manōrā* Manuscript," in

BSOAS, XXX (1967).2: 391-403.

3008.   Dhanit YUPHO, *The Khōn and Lakon: Dance Dramas presented by the Department of Fine Arts.* Programmes of the *Khōn, Lakon Jātri, Lakon Nok, Lakon Nai, Lakon Dŭkdamban* and *Lakon Phanthāng* for the years 1945-62. Illustrated and fully annotated, with libretto, historical background and technical notes on the dance dramas (Bangkok: The Department of Fine Arts, 1963).

3009. B.D. AIMY, "La lune dans la littérature vietnamienne," in *FA*, III (1948).23: 292-7; 25: 508-17.

3010. B.D. AIMY, "The Moon in the Literature of Viet-Nam," in *A/AQCS*, I (1951).2: 263-9; 3: 394-402.

3011. Anonymous, "The different systems of writing in Viet-Nam," in *Vietnam Bulletin*, V.5 (1 February 1971): 2.

3012. *Jacques BARUCH, *Essai sur la littérature du Viêt-Nam*. Etudes Orientales, No. 1 (Casteau: Thanh-Long, 1963).

3013. *Jacques BARUCH, *Bibliographie des traductions françaises des littératures du Viêt-Nam et du Cambodge* [item 858].

3014. Léopold CADIÈRE, *Croyances et pratiques religieuses des Viêt-namiens*. Publications hors série de l'Ecole Française d'Extrême-Orient, Volume I. Deuxième Edition (Saigon: Imprimerie Nouvelle d'Extrême-Orient, 1958), Volume II (Saigon: Ecole Française d'Extrême-Orient, 1955), Volume III (Paris: Ecole Française d'Extrême-Orient, 1957).

3015. CHEON, "L'argot annamite," in *Revue Indochinoise*, 2e Sem., 1906: 1266-97. On secret speech forms of various "professional" groups.

3016. Louis CHOCHOD, "Le climat indochinois et son influence sur la littérature populaire des Annamites," in *Bulletin des Sociétés de Géographie de Lyon et de la Région Lyonnaise*, 1935: 35-44.

3017. *G. CORDIER, "Littérature annamite," in *Un empire colonial français: l'Indochine*. Ouvrage publié sous la direction de M. Georges Maspero (Paris et Bruxelles: G. Van OEst, 1929), I: 309-18.

3018. Georges COULET, *Cultes et religions de l'Indochine annamite* (Saigon: C. Ardin, n.d. [1937]).

3019. H.G. CREEL, *Chinese Thought from Confucius to Mao Tsê-tung*. A Mentor Book, MP498 (New York: The New American Library, 1964). Useful introduction to main currents of Chinese philosophy reflected in Vietnamese literature.

3020. Hubert DESCHAMPS and anonymous, "Vietnam: History," in *EB (1962)*, 23: 146a-7b.

3021. *Maurice-G. DUFRESNE, "Littérature annamite," in *Indochine*. Ouvrage publié sous la direction de M. Sylvain Lévi. Exposition Coloniale Internationale de Paris, Commissariat Général (Paris: Société d'Editions Géographiques, Maritimes et Coloniales, 1931), I: 157-79.

3022. Maurice DURAND, "Les transcriptions de la langue vietnamienne et l'œuvre des missionnaires européens," in *Symposium on Historical, Archaeological and Linguistic Studies on Southern China, South-East Asia and the Hong Kong Region*, edited by F.S. Drake (Hong Kong: Hong Kong University Press, 1967), 288-94.

3023. *Maurice M. DURAND et Nguyen Tran-HUAN, *Introduction à la littérature viêtnamienne*. Collection UNESCO "Introduction aux Littératures Orientales" (Paris: G.-P. Maisonneuve et Larose, [c. 1969]). Best and fullest work available.

3024. Murray B. EMENEAU, "Vietnamese Language," in *EB (1962)*, 23: 147b-8a.

3025. C.P. FITZGERALD, *China: A Short Cultural History*. Third Edition. Praeger University Series, U-578 (New York and Washington: Frederick A. Praeger, 1961), Part I: Feudal China (34-105).

3026. Phan GIANG, "Literature in Annam: How a Popular Literature Was Born of French Inspiration," in *Asiatic Review*, New Series, 42 (1946): 382-4.

3027. *Pierre HUARD et Maurice DURAND, "La littérature viêtnamienne," Chapitre XXI in their *Connaissance du Viêt-Nam* (Paris: Imprimerie Nationale / Hanoi: Ecole Française d'Extrême-Orient, 1954), 267-98. Excellent synopsis.

3028. E.R. HUGHES, *Chinese Philosophy in Classical Times*. Edited and translated by... Everyman's Library, No. 973 (London: J.M. Dent, 1944). Well-chosen readings in early Chinese thought directly relevant to Vietnamese literature.

3029. Le-Xuan-KHOA, "Philosophy of Life in Classical Vietnamese Literature," in *Asian Culture*, 3 (1961).1: 41-8.

3030. D.C. LAU, *Lao Tzu, Tao Te Ching*. Translated, with an introduction, by... Penguin Classics, L131 (Harmondsworth, Essex: Penguin Books, 1970).

3031. James LEGGE, *Confucius: Confucian Analects, The Great Learning, and The Doctrine of the Mean*. Translated, with Critical and Exegetical Notes, Prolegomena, Copious Indexes, and Dictionary of All Characters by... Dover Books (New York: Dover, 1971). Reprint of second revised edition of 1893, with Chinese text. Invaluable as background to Vietnamese thought and literature.

3032. Anh-LIEN, "Pessimism in Vietnamien Poetry," in *A/AQCS*, III (1953). 11: 397-400.

3033. Nguyen-Phan-LONG, "Deux héroïnes viêtnamiennes," in *FA*, III (1948).22: 175-82; 23: 284-91.

3034. François MARTINI, "Langue viêtnamiennes. Notices bibliographiques," in *BEFEO*, XLIX (1958): 337-48.

3035. *P. MIDAN, "L'humour dans la littérature Annamite," in *BSEI*, Nouvelle Série, VIII (1933).3: 67-83. Entertaining essay on badly neglected topic.

3036. Cung-Giu-NGUYEN, "La conscience malheureuse chez Nguyen-Du," in *FA*, IV (1949).40: 1244-54.

3037. Cung giu NGUYEN, "Contemporary Vietnamese Writing," in *BA*, 29 (1955).1: 19-25.

3038. *Stephen O'HARROW, *The Growth of Modern Vietnamese Prose Fiction*, with special reference to the role of Nhât Linh in the *Tự Lực Van Đoàn* and some comparisons to parallel developments in modern Chinese literary history. Thesis presented . . . for the Degree [of] Master of Arts. School of Oriental and African Studies, University of London, 1965.

3039. Stephen O'HARROW, "Some Background Notes on Nhat Linh (Nguyên Tuong Tam, 1906-1963)," in *FA*, XXII (1968).2: 205-20.

3040. *Stephen O'HARROW, *L'histoire socio-littéraire de la langue vietnamienne (jusqu'au XXème siècle) et le rôle de Phạm Quỳnh (de 1917 à 1932)*. Thèse de doctorat, Université de la Sorbonne Nouvelle, Institut National des Langues et Civilisations Orientales, 1972.

3041. P.B., "Pour mieux connaître l'Indochine: Essai d'une bibliographie," in *Revue Indochinoise*, 36 (1922): 399-490; 38 (1924): 135-45, 273-94, 431-50; 2e Sem. 1924: 137-60, 309-35, 479-511; 1e Sem. 1925: 187-206, 354-67, 513-30; 2e Sem. 1925: 163-84, 345-64, 488-508.

3042. The PHONG, *The Vietnamese Literary Scene from 1900 to 1956*. Translated by Dam Xuan Can (Saigon: Dai Nam Van Hien Books, 1970).

3043. Edwin O. REISCHAUER and John K. FAIRBANK, *East Asia: The Great Tradition*. A History of East Asian Civilization: Volume One (Boston: Houghton Mifflin, [c 1960]), Chapter Three, "Classic China: The Golden Age of Chinese Thought," 62-84.

3044. Franz SCHURMANN and Orville SCHELL, *Imperial China: The Decline of the Last Dynasty and the Origins of Modern China. The 18th and 19th Centuries*. The China Reader. Edited, annotated, and with introductions by... A Vintage Book, V-375 (New York: Vintage Books, [c 1967]).

3045. L. SLUIMERS, review of *A Bibliography of North Vietnamese Publications in the Cornell University Library* by J.G. Keyes, in *BTLV*, 119 (1963).4: 448.

3046. Thanh-SON, "Les prédictions de Maître Trang-Trinh, le nostradamus Viêtnamien," in *Sud-Est: Périodique Mensuel* (Saigon), 1 (1949).1: 10-5.

3047. *Nguyễn-hữu-TẤN, "La femme vietnamienne d'autrefois à travers les chansons populaires," in *BSEI*, Nouvelle Série, XLV (1970).1: 1-113. Exhaustive study of the rôle of women as reflected in folksong.

3048. Nguyen-minh-THAN, *Voprosy socialističeskogo realizma i sovremennaja vjetnamskaja literatura*. Doctoral dissertation, Institut Mirovoj Literatury imeni A.M. Gorjkogo, Akademii Nauk SSSR, Moskva, 1965.

3049. Pham-Huy-THONG, "Vietnamese Literature Since 1939," in *Asian Horizon*, I (1948).1: 57-64.

3050. Do-manh-TRI, *La signification morale des contes et des romans nôm*. Doctoral dissertation, Université de Paris, 1966. Study of "traditional" Vietnamese mentality through examination of *nôm* literature.

3051. Dao-dang-VY, "Le roman vietnamien contemporain (I)," in *FA*, III (1948).27: 732-9.

3052. Arthur WALEY, *The Analects of Confucius*. Translated and annotated by... Modern Library Paperbacks, P-66 (New York: Random House, [c 1938]).

3053. Peter WEISS, *Notes on the Cultural Life of the Democratic Republic of Vietnam*. Translated from the German. A Seymour Lawrence Book. An Original Delta Book: Delta... (New York: Dell, [c 1970]), "Beginnings of a Modern Literature" (44-54), "Conversations with Authors" (55-73), "Tradition, Ceremonials, Poetics" (74-84), "Literature in South Vietnam" (85-94).

FOLK LITERATURE

3054. Anonymous, *Come to the Fields, Buffalo: Vietnamese Folk Songs*

(Hanoi: Foreign Languages Publishing House, 1958).

3055. Anonymous, *The First Mosquito, and other stories* (Hanoi: Foreign Languages Publishing House, 1958).

3056. Anonymous, "Riddles," in *A/AQCS*, III (1954).12: 573-5. Vietnamese text with English translation.

3057. *(Mrs)* L.T. BACH-LAN, *Vietnamese Legends* (Saigon: privately printed, 1958).

3058. *Dam BO [= Jacques Dournes], *Les populations montagnardes du Sud Indochinois (Pémsiens)*. Numéro spécial de *FA*, V (1950).49-50: 1046-68, 1099-1121. Valuable literary background.

3059. *Jean BOULBET, "Trois légendes maa," [traduction de]..., in *FA*, XIV (1957).138-139: 399-402.

3060. Jean BOULBET, "Quelques aspects du coutumier (*N'dri*) des Cau Maa," in *BSEI*, Nouvelle Série, XXXII (1957).2: 113-78. On Srê customary law, including numerous texts with translation and commentary.

3061. Nam CAO, *Chi Pheo, and Other Stories* (Hanoi: Foreign Languages Publishing House, 1961).

3062. Cl. CHIVAS-BARON, *Stories and Legends of Annam*. Translated from the French *Contes et légendes de l'Annam* by E.M. Smith-Dampier (London and New York: Andrew Melrose, 1920). Contains 31 tales.

3063. Le-Hong-CHUONG, "Students and Girls of Viet-Nam Seen Through Popular Songs," in *A/AQCS*, II (1952).6: 243-9.

3064. Jean-Yves CLAEYS, "Len Dong (conte ethnographique viêtnamien)," in *FA*, XIII (1957).128: 505-17.

3065. *H. DEYDIER, "A propos d'un conte muờng," in *BSEI*, Nouvelle Série, XXIV (1949).1: 47-53. Translation and analysis of the tale of "Ta-keo-Rauh and the Tree of Immortality."

3066. *J. DOURNES, "Chants de la Montagne: La Tradition des Montagnards du Haut-Donnaï, recueillie avec le concours de Jean Seo et traduites par...," in *BSEI*, Nouvelle Série, XXIII (1948).3-4: 9-111. Numerous myths, legends and tales, with notes and vocabulary.

3067. *Jacques DOURNES, *Nri: Recueil des coutumes srê du Haut-Donnai*, recueillies, traduites et annotées par... (Saigon: Editions France-Asie, [c 1951]). Valuable codification of Srê customary law, with text and translation.

3068. Jean DOURNES, "Pages Montagnardes," in *FA*, IV (1948).33: 401-3.

3069. M.B. EMENEAU and Archer TAYLOR, "Annamese, Arabic, and Panjabi
       Riddles," in *JAF*, 58.227 (January-March 1945): 12-20.

3070. Truc-GIANG, "La naissance d'un saint," in *FA*, III (1948).26: 611-
       8.

3071. Marylin B. GREGERSON, "Rengao Myths: A Window on the Culture,"
       in *Practical Anthropology*, 16 (1969): 216-27.

3072. Le-huy-HAP, *Vietnamese Legends*. Revised edition, with annota-
       tions (Saigon: Khai Tri, [c 1963]).

3073. Nguyen Dinh HOA, "Double Puns in Vietnamese: A Case of 'Linguis-
       tic Play'," in *Word*, 11 (August 1955): 237-44.

3074. Nguyen Dinh HOA, "Vietnamese Riddles," in *Asian Culture*, 2
       (January-March 1960): 107-27.

3075. Tô HOAI, *Récits du pays thai*. Traduits par G. Boudard. 2e édition,
       revue et corrigée (Hanoi: Editions en Langues Etrangères, 1961).

3076. Nguyen-chong-HUAN, "Le crapaud est l'Oncle du dieu du Ciel," in
       FA/A, Nouvelle Série, XVII (1961).170: 2610-2.

3077. Nguyễn Văn HUYÊN, *Les chants alternés des garçons et des filles
       en Annam* (Paris: Paul Geuthner, 1934).

3078. *Le D*ʳ B.Y. JOUIN, "Les traditions des Rhadé," in *BSEI*, Nouvelle
       Série, XXV (1950).4: 357-400. Origin myths and various legends.

3079. *Le D*ʳ B.Y. JOUIN, "Légende du Sadet du Feu," in *BSEI*, Nouvelle
       Série, XXVI (1951).1: 73-84.

3080. *Le D*ʳ B.Y. JOUIN, "Deux contes Rhadés," in *BSEI*, Nouvelle Série,
       XXVI (1951).1: 89-95.

3081. Pham-Duy-KHIEM, "Legends of the Peaceful Lands," in *A/AQCS*, 1
       (1951).3: 387-93.

3082. Pham Duy KHIEM, "The Mandarin and the Flower Festival," transla-
       ted by K. Filshie, in Wigmore [item 3300], 90-4.

3083. *Pham Duy KHIÊM, *Légendes des terres sereines* (Paris: Mercure de
       France, 1959).

3084. Pham-van-KY, "Celui qui règnera," in *FA*, V (1949).41: 35-56; 42:
       162-81.

3085. A. LANDES, "Histoire de Con Tấm et de Con Cấm," in Leclère,
       "Contes" [item 895], 91-8. A Vietnamese version of the Cinderel-
       la tale, preceded by its Khmer analogue (70-90). See item 3109.

3086. Maïté LAVEISSIÈRE, *Contes du Viêt-Nam*. Illustrations de l'auteur (Coubron: Pierru, [c 1968]).

3087. Georges LEBRUN, "Grand Frère Tigre (légende cochinchinoise)," in *FA*, IV (1948).33: 399-400.

3088. Nguyen Dang LIEM, "Vietnamese Folk Songs," in *Hemisphere*, 12 (1968).7: 32-4.

3089. Nguyễn Ðang LIÊM, *Four-syllable Idiomatic Expressions in Vietnamese*. Paper presented to the Asian Studies on the Pacific Coast Conference, 1969, Seattle, Washington.

3090. Hoa MAI, *The Peasant, the Buffalo and the Tiger: Vietnamese Legends* (Hanoi: Foreign Languages Publishing House, n.d.)

3091. *Albert MAURICE et Georges Marie PROUX, "Prières, avec leur traduction juxtalinéaire," appendix (223-58) to their "L'âme du riz," in *BSEI*, Nouvelle Série, XXXIX (1954).2-3: 123-258. Rhadé agricultural litanies. *Cf.* Sandin, "Simpulang or Pulang Gana" [item 2485].

3092. Glenn W. MONIGOLD, *Folk Tales from Vietnam*. Compiled by... With illustrations by Jeanyee Wong. A Peter Pauper Press Book (Mount Vernon, New York: The Peter Pauper Press, [c 1964]).

3093. *Professor Dr* Hans NEVERMANN, *Die Reiskugel: Sagen und Göttergeschichten, Märchen, Fabeln und Schwänke aus Vietnam*. Aus dem Vietnamesischen übersetzt und herausgegeben von... (Eisenach: Imerich Röth, [c 1952]).

3094. Tuyêt-NGA, "Histoire de Chu-Dong-Tu," in *FA*, IV (1949).40: 1255-8.

3095. *Nha-Trang Công-Huyên-Tôn-Nữ, *Vietnamese Folklore: An Introductory and Annotated Bibliography*. Occasional Paper No. 7 (Berkeley: Center for South and Southeast Asia Studies, University of California, 1970).

3096. Y-Blul NIE-BLO et F.P. ANTOINE, "L'origine des Rhadé," légende rhadé, in *FA*, X (1954).97: 763-6.

3097. Kay NIELSEN, *The Wishing Pearl, and other tales of Vietnam*, [retold] by Jon and Kay Nielsen. Translation by Lam Chan Quan (Irvington-on-Hudson, N.Y.: Harvey House, [c 1969]).

3098. Le-van-PHAT, "Le lièvre, l'oiseau et le moustique," in *FA*, IV (1948).31: 63-4.

3099. Ho-PHU, "Sagesse populaire du Viet-Nam," in *FA*, III (1948).22: 183-5; 23: 298-9; 25: 518-9; 26: 619-21; 27: 740-2.

3100. Chi Qua Ho-PHU, "Sagesse populaire de France et du Vietnam," in
       FA, XIV (1957).138-139: 383-9. French proverbs with analogues in
       Vietnamese and French translation.

3101. R. ROBERT, *Notes sur les Tay Dèng de Lang Chảnh (Thanh-hoả - An-
       nam)*. Institut Indochinois pour l'Etude de l'Homme, Mémoire Nº 1
       (Hanoi: Imprimerie d'Extrême-Orient, 1941). Contains "L'invita-
       tion à la jarre" (97-100), "Chants alternés" (100-2), "Souhaits
       de bienvenue" (102-3), "Chanson pour une fête de charité" (103-5),
       "Chansons d'amour" (105-10), "Proverbes, brocards et dictons"
       (110-8).

3102. *Léopold SABATIER, *La chanson de Damsan: Légende radé du XVIᵉ siè-
       cle*... Transmise par la tradition orale, recueillie et transcrite
       en français par M. ... Préfaces de MM. Pasquier et Roland Dorge-
       lès. Compositions de Maurice de Becque (Paris: Leblanc et Traut-
       mann, n.d. [*ca* 1928]). Rhadé epic in French translation.

3103. *L. SABATIER, "La chanson de Damson," in *BEFEO*, 33 (1933).1: 143-
       302.

3104. *L. SABATIER, *Recueil des coutumes rhadées du Darlac*... Recueillies
       par... Traduites et annotées par D. Antomarchi. Collection de
       Textes et Documents sur l'Indochine, IV. Ecole Française d'Extrême-
       Orient (Hanoi: Imprimerie d'Extrême-Orient, 1940). Detailed codi-
       fication of Rhadé customary law with valuable commentary.

3105. George F. SCHULTZ, *Vietnamese Legends*. Adapted from the Vietnamese
       by... (Rutland & Tokyo: Charles F. Tuttle, 1965).

3106. Ruth Q. SUN, *Land of Seagull and Fox: Folk Tales of Vietnam*. Col-
       lected and retold by... Illustrations by Ho Thanh Duc. A Weather-
       mark Edition (Rutland: Charles E. Tuttle, 1967).

3107. Nguyễn Hữu TẤN, "La femme vietnamienne d'autrefois à travers les
       chansons populaires" [item 3047].

3108. Huynh Dinh TÊ, *Vietnamese Cultural Patterns and Values as Expres-
       sed in Proverbs*. Doctoral dissertation, Columbia University, 1962.

3109. ĐÕ THẬN, "Une version annamite du conte de Cendrillon," in *BEFEO*,
       VII (1907).1-2: 101-7. See item 3085.

3110. Jerry TINKER, "Voices of Vietnam," in *Weekend Review* (New Delhi),
       II.24 (18 May 1968): 31-3. Contains lyrics to five songs on theme
       of hope and agony by South Vietnamese folk-singer Pham Duy, trans-
       lated by Pham Duy and Steve Addis, from Pham Duy, *Dan Ca (Folk
       Songs)*, Saigon, 1966: "The Rain on the Leaves" (31b), "Day of
       Homecoming" (31c-32a), "Recommendations" (32ab), "The Mother of
       Gia Linh" (32bc), "The Wounded Soldier" (32c-33ab).

3111. Truong-Vinh-TONG, "Vietnamian Folklore: Love Songs and Riddles," collected by..., in *A/AQCS*, I (1951).2: 275-9.

3112. Thach XUYEN, "The Bonze and the Cobbler," in *A/AQCS*, III (1953). 11: 401-5.

PRE-MODERN PROSE AND POETRY

3113. AI MY, "Une grande poétesse: Ho Xuang Huong," in *FA*, VIII (1952). 78: 941-50.

3114. Ngo-AN [19th century], "The Nothingness Mind," in Raffel [item 3167], 64.

3115. *Anonymous, *Anthologie de la poésie vietnamienne* (Paris: Les Editeurs Français Réunis, [c 1969]).

3116. Anonymous, "Vietnamese Literature in 'Chu Nom': *Kim-Van-Kieu*, By Nguyen-Du (1765-1820)," in *Vietnam Bulletin*, V.5 (1 February 1971): 3-5.

3117. Anonymous, "Vietnamese Poetry: Tran Quang Khai (1241-1294)," in *Vietnam Bulletin*, II (1968).4: 68.

3118. Anonymous [18th century], "West Lake, Late Afternoon," in Raffel [item 3167], 45.

3119. Anonymous [18th century], "A Woodcutter on His Way Home," in Raffel [item 3167], 45.

3120. *Jacques BARUCH, *Notes sur le poème viêtnamien* Kim-Vân-Kiêu *de Nguyên-Du* (Casteau: [Thanh-Long], 1961).

3121. *M. J. BARUCH, "Le *Kim-Van-Kiêu*, poème national viêtnamien de Nguyên-Du," in *Revue du Sud-est asiatique*, 1963.3: 185-213.

3122. *Nguyen Ngoc BICH, "War Poems from the Vietnamese," in *The Hudson Review*, XX (1967).3: 361-8. Detailed study of the theme of war in poetry of the modern as well as the classical period.

3123. Tran-Cuu-CHAN, "La satire dans le *Kim-Van-Kiêu*," in *FA*, III (1948).25: 502-7.

3124. Tran-Cuu-CHAN, "Analyse du *Luc-Van-Tien*, poème populaire du Sud-Vietnam," in *FA*, IV (1948).31: 59-62.

3125. Cuu-CHI [19th century], "Truth Is One," in Raffel [item 3167], 66.

3126. Nguyen Huu CHINH [d. 1787], "Firecracker," in Raffel [item 3167], 46.

3127. *Đặng Trần CÔN, "Chin-Phu (ngâm-khúc) / Femme de guerrir (élégie)," Traduit en français par Huỳnh Khắc Dụng, in BSEI, Nouvelle Série, XXX (1955).3: 215-327. Text, translation, notes on 18th-century classic poem. See items 3128-3131 and 3139.

3128. Dang Tran CON, "Lament of a Warrior's Wife," translated [from the Sino-Vietnamese] into Vietnamese by Phan Huy Ich, translated [from Vietnamese into English] by Burton Raffel and Nguyen Ngoc Bich, in Chuồng Việt, XVI (1965).144.

3129. Dang Tran CON, "Lament of a Warrior's Wife," in The Texas Quarterly, Summer 1966: 101-11. Reprint of item 3128.

3130. Dang Trần CÔN et Phan Huy ÍCH, Chant de la femme du combattant [Titre original: Chinh phu ngâm]. Traduction et notes de Lê Thành Khôi (Paris: Gallimard, [c 1967]).

3131. Doan-thi-DIEM [= Dang Tran Con], "Truong," translated by Nguyên Son from her Chinh Phu Ngam, in A/AQCS, II (1952).7: 454-7.

3132. Nguyen DU [1765-1820], "At Tu Fu's Tomb," in Raffel [item 3167], 35.

3133. Nguyen DU, "Calling the Lost Souls," in Raffel [item 3167], 35-41.

3134. *Nguyên-DU, Vaste recueil de légendes merveilleuses [Titre original: Truyện ky man luc]. Traduit du vietnamien par Nguyen-Tran-Huan. Collection UNESCO d'œuvres représentatives, série vietnam-ienne. Collection "Connaissance d'Orient," 15 (Paris: Gallimard, [c 1962]). Classic collection of literary tales of mystery.

3135. *Nguyen DU, Kim Van Kieu. Traduit en français par Xuan Phuc et Zuan Viet (Paris: Gallimard, 1961).

3136. Nguyên-DU, Kim-Van-Kiêu. English translation, Footnotes, and Commentaries by Le-Xuan-Thuy (Saigon: Khai Tri, 1963).

3137. *Nguyên-DU, Kim Vân Kiều (Truyện Thủy Kiều): The Story of Lady Kiều... Translated from the Vietnamese into English, with Notes and Commentary, by William Negherbon. Best translation available; typescript, 96 + 155 pages.

3138. Dang DUNG [18th century], "Regrets," in Raffel [item 3167], 42.

3139. *Maurice DURAND, "La Complainte de l'Epouse du guerrier de Đặng Tran-Côn," in BSEI, Nouvelle Série, XXVIII (1953).2: 101-81. Text, translation, notes of outstanding quality. See items 3127-31.

3140. *Maurice DURAND, *L'oeuvre de la poétesse viêtnamienne Ho-Xuan-Huong*. Textes, traduction et notes par... Collection de Textes et Documents sur l'Indochine, IX (Paris: Ecole Française d'Extrême-Orient, 1968).

3141. *Emile GASPARDONE, "L'inscription du Ma-nhai," in *BSEI*, Nouvelle Série, XLVI (1971).1: 71-88. Text and translation of a Sino-Vietnamese inscription of 1337 A.D. found on the Laos frontier.

3142. Man GIAĆ [19th century], "Rebirth," in Raffel [item 3167], 61.

3143. Van-HANH, "Man's Body," in Raffel [item 3167], 59.

3144. *On-Nhu HAU, *Cung Oan Ngam Khuc: The Complaints of an Odalisque*. Translated into English Poem [*sic*] by Vu-Trung-Lap. Vietnamese Old Literature (Saigon: Viet-Tien Translation and Publishing House, n.d. [*ca* 1967]). See item 3168.

3145. Vien HOC [12th century], "Awakening," in Raffel [item 3167], 23.

3146. Ho Xuan-HUONG [late 18th century], "Three Exchanges with Chieu Ho," in Raffel [item 3167], 33-4.

3147. Tran-Quang KHAI [1241-1294], "Homecoming," in Raffel [item 3167], 25-6.

3148. Tran Quang KHAI, "The Phuc-Hung Garden," in Raffel [item 3167], 25.

3149. Doan Van-KHAM [19th century], "In Memoriam Priest Quang-Tri," in Raffel [item 3167], 65.

3150. Nguyen Binh KHIEM [1491-1585], "Ironic Apology," translated by Nguyen Ngoc Bich and Robin Morgan, in Bich [item 3122], 361.

3151. Nguyen Binh KHIEM, "Everyone can't be Buddha," in Raffel [item 3167], 32.

3152. Phung Khac KHOAN [16th century], "On War," translated by Nguyen Ngoc Bich and W.S. Merwin, in Bich [item 3122], 362.

3153. Nguyen KHUYEN [1835-1909], "Going on the Wagon," in Raffel [item 3167], 49.

3154. Nguyen KHUYEN, "To a Stone," in Raffel [item 3167], 49.

3155. Nguyen KHUYEN, "The Sky Speaks: No. 1," in Raffel [item 3167], 50.

3156. Nguyen KHUYEN, "The Sky Speaks: No. 2," in Raffel [item 3167], 50.

3157. Nguyen KHUYEN, "To a Terracotta Figure," in Raffel [item 3167], 51.

3158. Nguyen KHUYEN, "Mourning Duong Khue," in Raffel [item 3167], 51-2.

3159. Thai-Van-KHIEM, "A Literary, Philosophic and Scientific Study of the *Kim-Van-Kiêu*," in *A/AQCS*, I (1951).3: 403-14; I (1952).4: 560-5; II (1952).6: 250-60.

3160. Thai-Van-KHIEM, "A Great Vietnamien Poet: Han-Mac-Tu," in *A/AQCS*, IV (1955).16: 549-65.

3161. Ngo Chi LAN [19th century], "The Four Seasons," in Raffel [item 3167], 67.

3162. Khong LO [*d.* 1119], "The Ideal Retreat," in Raffel [item 3167], 22.

3163. Ngo Chan LUU [19th century], "To the Chinese Ambassador, at his Departure," in Raffel [item 3167], 62.

3164. Ngo Chan LUU, "Fire in the Wood," in Raffel [item 3167], 62.

3165. Cung-giu-NGUYEN, "Nguyên-Du's Poetical Drama," in *A/AQCS*, IV (1954).13: 73-80.

3166. Trang QUYNH [18th century], "Pho Hien," in Raffel [item 3167], 43.

3167. *Burton RAFFEL, *From the Vietnamese: Ten Centuries of Poetry*. Translated and with an Introduction by... OH 21 (New York: October House, [c 1968]). Valuable anthology of representative works.

3168. *George F. SCHULTZ, "The Plaints of An Odalisque. An adaptation of Nguyên Gia-Thiêu's *Cung-oán Ngâm-Khúc*," in *Việt-Mỹ*, VI (1961).1: 3-17. See item 3144.

3169. *George F. SCHULTZ, "Tran Hung Dao's Proclamation to His Officers," Translated and adapted by..., in *Vietnam Bulletin*, V.5 (1 February 1971): 8-10. Good specimen of hortatory genre.

3170. Hue-SINH [19th century], "The Law," in Raffel [item 3167], 63.

3171. Ly Dao TAI [1254-1334], "Pity for Prisoners," translated by Nguyen Ngoc Bich and Burton Raffel, in Bich [item 3122], 361.

3172. Ly Dao TAI, "Chrysanthemums," in Raffel [item 3167], 29-30.

3173. Ly Dao TAI, "Mountain House," in Raffel [item 3167], 29.

3174. Ly Dao TAI, "The Toad," in Raffel [item 3167], 30.

3175. Nguyen Quy TAN [18th century], "Pigeon," in Raffel [item 3167], 44.

3176. Võ Long-TÊ, "Contribution à l'étude d'un des premiers poèmes narratifs d'inspiration catholique en langue vietnamienne romanisée: Inê Tử-Đạo vãn ou le martyre d'Agnès," in *BSEI*, Nouvelle Série, XLII (1967).4: 305-36. Includes partial translation.

3177. Dang Tran THUONG [1759-1813], "Borrowing Money," in Raffel [item 3167], 48.

3178. Ban-TINH [19th century], "Transcendence," in Raffel [item 3167], 60.

3179. Ly Thai TONG [999-1054], "The Essence of Buddhism," in Raffel [item 3167], 21.

3180. Tran Nhan-TONG [1258-1308], "Autumn Evening," in Raffel [item 3167], 27.

3181. Tran Nhan-TONG, "On a Visit to Thai-Tong's Mausoleum," in Raffel [item 3167], 27.

3182. Tran Nhan-TONG, "Spring Dawn," in Raffel [item 3167], 28.

3183. Tran Nhan-TONG, "Spring View," in Raffel [item 3167], 28.

3184. Tran Thanh-TONG [1240-1290], "The Grottoes," in Raffel [item 3167], 24.

3185. Tran Thanh-TONG, "In Memoriam," in Raffel [item 3167], 24.

3186. Nguyen TRAI [1380-1442], "I'm still not a Duke," in Raffel [item 3167], 31.

3187. Nguyen TRAI, "Stolen from Nature," in Raffel [item 3167], 31.

3188. Nguyen Cong TRU [1773-1858], "Fleeting Life," in Raffel [item 3167], 47.

3189. *Ly-Chanh-TRUNG, *Introduction to Vietnamese Poetry*. Translated by Kenneth Filshire. Vietnam Culture Series, No. 3 (Saigon: Department of National Education, 1961).

3190. Tran Van TUNG, *L'Annam, pays du rêve et de la poésie* (Paris: J. Susse, 1945). Contains specimens of traditional poetry.

3191. *Tran Van TUNG, *Deux mille ans de poésie viêtnamienne* (Paris: Serge, 1965). Excellent anthology of representative works.

3192. V.-L., "Vietnamian Poetry in the 15th Century," in *A/AQCS*, II (1952).7: 442-8.

3193. V.-L., "Vietnamien [*sic*] Poetry in the 16th Century," in *A/AQCS*, IV (1955).16: 566-74.

3194. Tran Te XUONG [1869-1907], "Drumbeats," in Raffel [item 3167], 53.

3195. Tran Te XUONG, "Graduation," in Raffel [item 3167], 55.

3196. Tran Te XUONG, "Me," in Raffel [item 3167], 53.

3197. Tran Te XUONG, "New Year's and Its Poetasters," in Raffel [item 3167], 54.

3198. Tran Te XUONG, "Night Sadness," in Raffel [item 3167], 55.

3199. Tran Te XUONG, "Picking Heaven's Leavings," in Raffel [item 3167], 57.

3200. Tran Te XUONG, "Sub-Professor Nhu," in Raffel [item 3167], 56.

3201. Tran Te XUONG, "To an Official," in Raffel [item 3167], 56.

3202. Tran Te XUONG, "Women," in Raffel [item 3167], 54.

3203. Tran Te XUAN, "Sudden Reflections," in Raffel [item 3167], 57-8.

MODERN PROSE

3204. *Phan DU, "The Two Pots of Orchids," in José [item 3297], 289-98.

3205. *Phan DU, "The Two Pots of Orchids," in *Of Love and Hope* [item 3291], 148-59.

3206. Nguyen Cong HOAN, *Canton Chief Ba Loses His Slippers: Selected Short Stories* (Hanoi: Foreign Languages Publishing House, 1960).

3207. Nguyen Cong HOAN, *Impasse* (Hanoi: Foreign Languages Publishing House, 1963). Translation of 1938 novel *Buoc Duong Cung* describing peasant life in Tonkin.

3208. Nguyen-Tien-LANG, "I Chose Love (The Story of a Vietnamien Resistant)," in *A/AQCS*, I (1952).4: 542-8; II (1952).6: 223-37; II (1952).7: 421-36; II (1952).8: 622-35; III (1953).9: 58-67; III (1953).10: 203-15; III (1953).11: 383-94.

3209. Nhât LINH, "The Edge of Life," translated by Stephen O'Harrow
from his "Chết Do," from the collection *Thế Rồi Một Buổi Chiều*
(1937). Typescript.

3210. Huu MAI et al., *The Beacon Banner: Short Stories About the War of
Resistance in Vietnam* (Hanoi: Foreign Languages Publishing House,
1964).

3211. Ho-chi-MINH, *Prison Diary*. Translated by Aileen Palmer. 4th Edition (Hanoi: Foreign Languages Publishing House, 1967).

3212. Pham Nhu OANH, *When the Light Is Out*. Translated by Ngo Tat To
(Hanoi: Foreign Languages Publishing House, 1960). Translation of
novel *Tat Den*.

3213. Nguyen-SANG, *Le cabaret au patron muet (nouvelles)* (Sud Vietnam
[*sic*]: Giai Phong, 1969).

3214. THEPONG [= The Pong], "From a Writer's Diary," translated by Dam
Xuan Can, in *Tenggara*, II (1968).2: 52-7.

MODERN POETRY

3215. Nguyen Ngoc BICH, "War Poems from the Vietnamese" [item 3122].

3216. Huy CAN, "The Long River," translated by Nguyen Ngoc Bich, in
Chapbook of Contemporary Asian Poetry [item 3289], 62.

3217. Huy CAN, "The Long River," in Raffel [item 3167], 74.

3218. Huy CAN, "Peasants Funeral Song," in Raffel [item 3167], 75.

3219. Huy CAN, "Peasants Conjuring Song," in Raffel [item 3167], 75.

3220. Hoang Thoai CHAU, "Love of the Land," translated by Bang Ba Lan,
in his "Some Remarks on Contemporary Vietnamese Poetry" [item
3239].

3221. Ha Huyen CHI, "In the Sky of North Vietnam," translated by Bang
Ba Lan, in his "Some Remarks on Contemporary Vietnamese Poetry"
[item 3239].

3222. Ha Huyen CHI, "Mother Country," translated by Bang Ba Lan, in his
"Some Remarks on Contemporary Vietnamese Poetry" [item 3239].

3223. Hoang Vu DUC, "War," translated by Bang Ba Lan, in his "Some Remarks on Contemporary Vietnamese Poetry" [item 3239].

3224. Tran Van DUC, "Nostalgia," translated by Bang Ba Lan, in his "Some Remarks on Contemporary Vietnamese Poetry" [item 3239].

3225. Mireille GANSEL, "Etude: Poésie et résistance au Vietnam du Sud. Une parole reprise de bouche en bouche," in *Le Monde*, 29.8422, Vendredi 11 Février 1972: 16-7.

3226. Te HANH, "Home," translated by Nguyen Ngoc Bich, in Bich [item 3122], 367.

3227. Te HANH, "The River Back Home," translated by Nguyen Ngoc Bich, in Bich [item 3122], 367-8.

3228. Ngo Xuan HAU [= Xuan Dieu], "Hue Now," translated by Bang Ba Lan, in his "Some Remarks on Contemporary Vietnamese Poetry" [item 3239].

3229. Bùi HIỀN, "The Hunger Strike," translated by Harrison L. Shaffer, Jr., in *Việt-Mỹ*, IX (1964).1: 2-15.

3230. Nhu HIEN, "Separation," translated by Bang Ba Lan, in his "Some Remarks on Contemporary Vietnamese Poetry" [item 3239].

3231. Nguyen HOE, "Native Land," translated by Bang Ba Lan, in his "Some Remarks on Contemporary Vietnamese Poetry" [item 3239].

3232. Y HUONG, "A sad rhyme," translated by Bang Ba Lan, in his "Some Remarks on Contemporary Vietnamese Poetry" [item 3239].

3233. To HUU [*b*. 1920], "Road Sabotage," translated by Nguyen Ngoc Bich and Robin Morgan, in Bich [item 3122], 362-3.

3234. Tố HỮU, *Depuis, poèmes* (Hanoi: Editions en Langues Etrangères, 1968).

3235. To HUU, "Le Sud," traduit par Mireille Gansel, in her "Poésie et résistance au Vietnam du Sud" [item 3225].

3236. *Neil L. JAMIESON, *A Cycle of Poetry in North Vietnam*. Typescript, February 1972. Best available exposition of the development of modern poetry.

3237. Truong Quoc KHANH, "Serment," traduit par Mireille Gansel, in her "Poésie et résistance au Vietnam du Sud" [item 3225].

3238. Bằng Bá LÂN, "Some Remarks on Contemporary Vietnamese Poetry," in *Việt-Mỹ*, XV (1970).1: 78-135.

3239. Bang Ba LAN, "Some Remarks on Contemporary Vietnamese Poetry," lecture delivered at the Vietnamese American Association, Saigon, on March 13, 1970, in *Vietnam Bulletin*, V.13 (29 March 1971): 2-13.

3240. Nguyen LANG, "Sadness," translated by Bang Ba Lan, in his "Some Remarks on Contemporary Vietnamese Poetry" [item 3239].

3241. Du Tu LE, "Oh! This is nothing," translated [from Vietnamese] into French by Lê Hao and from French by Chan Soo Ping, in *Tenggara*, 4 (1969): 39.

3242, Du Tu LE, "When one dies young," translated [from Vietnamese] into French by Du Tu Le and from French by Chan Soo Ping, in *Tenggara*, 4 (1969): 39.

3243. Tuong LINH, "Hau Giang Mother," translated by Bang Ba Lan, in his "Some Remarks on Contemporary Vietnamese Poetry" [item 3239].

3244. Hoang LOC, "My new verses," translated by Bang Ba Lan, in his "Some Remarks on Contemporary Vietnamese Poetry" [item 3239].

3245. Nguyen Tan LOC, "The Frontier Zone," translated by Bang Ba Lan, in his "Some Remarks on Contemporary Vietnamese Poetry" [item 3239].

3246. *The LU [= Nguyen Thu Le, *b*. 1906], "Green Nostalgia (Soliloquy of a Tiger in the Zoo," translated by Nguyen Ngoc Bich and Oliver Rice, in *Chapbook of Contemporary Asian Poetry* [item 3289], 63-4.

3247. *The LU, "Green Nostalgia: Soliloquy of a Tiger in the Zoo / *Nho Rung*," in Raffel [item 3167], 68-9.

3248. Ho Chi MINH, "Eleven Prison Poems," in Raffel [item 3167], 70-3.

3249. Giang NAM, "La première pierre," traduit par Mireille Gansel, in her "Poésie et résistance au Vietnam du Sud" [item 3225].

3250. Nguyen Kim NGAN, "Une mère de Ban-Co," traduit par Mireille Gansel, in her "Poésie et résistance au Vietnam du Sud" [item 3225].

3251. Cao Hoang NHAN, "Travelling on a long river," translated by Bang Ba Lan, in his "Some Remarks on Contemporary Vietnamese Poetry" [item 3239].

3252. Giang NINH, "Two Colors," translated by Bang Ba Lan, in his "Some Remarks on Contemporary Vietnamese Poetry" [item 3239].

3253. Hoang Khoi PHONG, "This is for my son not yet born and named," translated [from Vietnamese] into French by Hoang Khoi Phong and from French by Chan Soo Ping, in *Tenggara*, 4 (1969): 40-1.

3254. Hoang Khoi PHONG, "City of Lights," translated by Bang Ba Lan, in his "Some Remarks on Contemporary Vietnamese Poetry" [item 3239].

3255. Phan Kim PHUNG, "Misunderstanding," translated by Bang Ba Lan, in his "Some Remarks on Contemporary Vietnamese Poetry" [item 3239].

3256. *Burton RAFFEL, *From the Vietnamese: Ten Centuries of Poetry* [item 3167].

3257. Nguyen Quoc THAI, "My Country and Points for Questioning," translated [from Vietnamese] into French by Nguyen Ngoc Lan and from French by Chan Soo Ping, in *Tenggara*, 4 (1969): 37.

3258. Mien Duc THANG, "Un peuple ne cesse pas de grandir," traduit par Mireille Gansel, in her "Poésie et résistance au Vietnam du Sud" [item 3225].

3259. Dieu-THANH, "Forest on fire," translated by Bang Ba Lan, in his "Some Remarks on Contemporary Vietnamese Poetry" [item 3239].

3260. Dieu-THANH, "Protesting against life," translated by Bang Ba Lan, in his "Some Remarks on Contemporary Vietnamese Poetry" [item 3239].

3261. Dieu-THANH, "Struggling," translated by Bang Ba Lan, in his "Some Remarks on Contemporary Vietnamese Poetry" [item 3239].

3262. Dieu-THANH, "When I am a devil," translated by Bang Ba Lan, in his "Some Remarks on Contemporary Vietnamese Poetry" [item 3239].

3263. THEPONG, "Kennedy," translated by X.H., in *Tenggara*, II (1968).1: 5-8.

3264. THEPONG, "Asian Morning, Western Music," translated by X.H., in *Tenggara*, II (1968).1: 9-12.

3265. Thanh TON, "Perfume of Fields and Meadows," translated by Bang Ba Lan, in his "Some Remarks on Contemporary Vietnamese Poetry" [item 3239].

3266. Phan-Chau-TRINH, "Poems," in *A/AQCS*, IV (1954).15: 403-5. Vietnamese text with translation.

3267. Tra Quang TRUNG, "Wild Grass," translated [from Vietnamese] into French by Lê Hao and from French by Chan Soo Ping, in *Tenggara*, 4 (1969): 38.

3268. Tran Mong TUONG, "Heritage," translated by Bang Ba Lan, in his "Some Remarks on Contemporary Vietnamese Poetry" [item 3239].

3269. Tu Ke TUONG, "That Painter in the City," translated by Nguyen Ngoc Bich and Robin Morgan, in Bich [item 3122], 363-4.

3270. Pham Nha UYEN, "The Universe," translated by Nguyen Ngoc Bich, in

Bich [item 3122], 366-7.

3271.   Tru VI, "The Statue of the Century," translated by Nguyen Ngoc
        Bich and Robin Morgan, in Bich [item 3122], 364.

3272.   Che Lan VIEN, "Etre mère au Vietnam," traduit par Mireille Gansel,
        in her "Poésie et résistance au Vietnam du Sud" [item 3225].

3273.   Trieu VU, "First Tragedy," translated by Nguyen Ngoc Bich, in
        Bich [item 3122], 365.

3274.   Đào Đang VỸ, "A Modern Vietnamese Poet: Thê-Lũ," Adapted by the
        editors from the article by..., in Việt-Mỹ, I (1956).1: 36-8.

3275.   Le Anh XUAN, "Chant pour Nguyen Van Troi," traduit par Mireille
        Gansel, in her "Poésie et résistance au Vietnam du Sud" [item
        3225].

3276.   Ly Thuy Y, "Because," translated by Bang Ba Lan, in his "Some Re-
        marks on Contemporary Vietnamese Poetry" [item 3239].

3277.   Ly Thuy Y, "War and a twenty-year-old boy," translated by Bang Ba
        Lan, in his "Some Remarks on Contemporary Vietnamese Poetry"
        [item 3239].

3278.   Y YEN, "After the battle...," translated by Bang Ba Lan, in his
        "Some Remarks on Contemporary Vietnamese Poetry" [item 3239].

                                    DRAMA

3279.   Anonymous, *Les cigales: pièce en 5 actes*. Traduit par Henri Lau-
        monier (Hanoi: Imprimerie de l'Avenir du Tonkin, n.d.).

3280.   Anonymous, "Le marchand de porc: comédie bouffante en un acte,"
        in *BSEI*, 9-10 (1915).

3281.   Anonymous, *La tasse de poison: Chen Thuoc Doc*. Comédie annamite
        en trois actes en prose. Traduite par Georges Cordier (Hanoi:
        Tan-Dan-Thu-Quan, 1927).

3282.   Anonymous, *La terre du dragon*. Deuxième Edition, augmentée de *La
        tortue: comédie annamite*. Traduction de Jean Ricquebourg (Saigon:
        Aspar, 1936).

3283.   Anonymous, *Théâtre annamite:* Tien-Buu, *ou La jeune batelière, co-
        médie*. Traduction de Paul Viator (Saigon: Claude, 1897).

3284.   *Claude BOURRIN, *Le vieux Tonkin: le théâtre - le sport - la vie*

mondaine, [Volume I] de 1884 à 1889, [Volume II] de 1890 à 1894.
Deuxième édition (Hanoi: Imprimerie d'Extrême-Orient, 1941). Rich
in information on the theater and theatrical activities in late
19th century.

3285.   J. MARQUET et Jean NOREL, "Le drama tonkinois (deuxième étude
d'après des documents inédits)," in *BSEI,* 5 (1937): 5-199.

3286.   Doan-Quan-TAN, "Le théâtre annamite: Le chemin de Hué-Dung (tra-
gédie sino-annamite)," in *FA,* 11 (Février 1947): 50-62 and 12
(Mars 1947): 192-205.

3287.   Nguyen-Phuoc-THIEN, "Cai-Luong and the Vietnamese Theatre," in
Việt-Mỹ, 8 (1963).4: 2-10.

3288.   Duc-TRUNG, *The Legend of the Wait: A Drama in Ten Scenes.* Translated by Duane Hauch. Typescript.

X. REGIONAL AND GENERAL WORKS

ANTHOLOGIES

3289. Anonymous, *A Chapbook of Contemporary Asian Poetry*. Published as *The Beloit Poetry Journal*, 13.2 (Winter 1962-63).

3290. Anonymous, *Loneliness and Agony in World Poetry* (Honolulu: The East-West Center, 1966). Mimeographed collection compiled by East-West Center grantees and consisting of three sections, one of which comprises English translations of poems from eight Asian languages.

3291. Anonymous, *Of Love and Hope: Fourteen Stories from Africa and Asia* (Lahore: The Afro-Asian Book Club, 1966).

3292. Harold COURLANDER, *Ride With the Sun: An Anthology of Folk Tales and Stories from the United Nations*. Edited by... for the United Nations Women's Guild. Illustrated by Roger Duvoisin (New York / Toronto / London: McGraw-Hill, [c 1955]).

3293. Harold COURLANDER, *The Tiger's Whisker, and Other Tales and Legends from Asia and the Pacific*. Illustrated by Enrico Arno (New York: Harcourt, Brace & World, [c 1959]).

3294. Wilma Leslie GARNETT, Betsy FLEET, and Jane MAHIN, *Literature of Other Lands: Asia*. Compiled and edited by... (New York: Harper & Row, [c 1965]).

3295. *Gene Z. HANRAHAN, *50 Great Oriental Stories*. Edited by... A Bantam Classic, NC266 (New York: Bantam Books, [c 1965]). Excellent selection including Southeast Asian short stories and tales.

3296. Arthur T. HATTO, *Eos: An Enquiry into the Theme of Lovers' Meetings and Partings at Dawn in Poetry* (London / Paris: Mouton, 1965). Contains numerous specimens of the Southeast Asia *alba* or dawn song.

3297. *F. Sionil JOSÉ, *Asian PEN Anthology*. Edited by... and with an Introduction by Norman Cousins (New York: Taplinger, [c 1966]). One of most valuable collections available.

3298. *Daniel L. MILTON and William CLIFFORD, *A Treasury of Modern Asian Stories*. Edited by... A Mentor Book, MD 329 (New York: The New American Library, [c 1961]). Overconcentrated on South and East Asia.

3299. *Dorothy Blair SHIMER, *The Mentor Book of Modern Asian Literature, from the Khyber Pass to Fuji.* Edited by... With an introduction, critical commentary, and biographical notes. A Mentor Book, MW961 (New York: The New American Library, 1969). Eminently valuable collection, tastefully conceived, with useful editorial aids.

3300. *Lionel WIGMORE, *Span: An Adventure in Asian and Australian Writing.* Edited for the Canberra Fellowship of Australian Writers (Melbourne: F.W. Cheshire, 1958). Well organized selection of recent prose and poetry, flawed only by its title.

3301. *John D. YOHANNAN, *A Treasury of Asian Literature.* Edited with an Introduction and Commentaries by... A Mentor Book, MT340 (New York: The New American Library, 1961). Too sweeping in time and space to be more than a useful miscellany.

FOLK LITERATURE

3302. *Antti AARNE, *The Types of the Folk-tale: A Classification and Bibliography.* Translated and Enlarged by Stith Thompson. FF Communications No. 74 (Helsinki: Academia Scientiarum Fennica, 1928). The classic work on tale-type classification.

3303. William R. BASCOM, "Folklore and Anthropology," in Dundes [item 3317], 25-33. Reprinted from *JAF*, 66 (1953): 283-90.

3304. *William R. BASCOM, "Four Functions of Folklore," in Dundes [item 3317], 279-98. Reprinted from *JAF*, 67 (1954): 333-49.

3305. Ernest W. BAUGHMAN, *Type and Motif Index of the Folktales of England and North America.* Indiana University Folklore Series No. 20 (The Hague: Mouton, 1966). Valuable supplement to items 3302 and 3322, especially helpful in discovery of analogues of Southeast Asian tale-types and motifs.

3306. *C. Tj. BERTLING, "Notes on Myth and Ritual in Southeast Asia" [item 1079].

3307. *Joseph CAMPBELL, *The Hero with a Thousand Faces.* Meridian Books M22 (Cleveland and New York: World, 1967). Eloquent and well-reasoned analysis of the essential ingredients of myth, epic and romance, directly applicable to Southeast Asian literatures.

3308. *Joseph CAMPBELL, *The Flight of the Wild Gander: Explorations in the Mythological Dimension* (New York: Viking, [c 1969]).

3309. *Joseph CAMPBELL, *The Masks of God: Primitive Mythology.* A Viking

Compass Book, C298 (New York: The Viking Press, 1970).

3310. *Joseph CAMPBELL, *The Masks of God: Oriental Mythology*. A Viking Compass Book, C299. Second Printing (New York: The Viking Press, 1971).

3311. *Joseph CAMPBELL, *The Masks of God: Occidental Mythology*. A Viking Compass Book, C300. Third Printing (New York: The Viking Press, 1971).

3312. *Joseph CAMPBELL, *The Masks of God: Creative Mythology*. A Viking Compass Book, C301. Second Printing (New York: The Viking Press, 1971).

3313. Kenneth and Mary CLARKE, *A Concise Dictionary of Folklore*. Kentucky Folklore Series No. 1 (Bowling Green, Kentucky: Kentucky Folklore Record, n.d. [1965]).

3314. *Tom Peete CROSS, *Motif-Index of Early Irish Literature*. Indiana University Publications, Folklore Series No. 7 (Bloomington: Indiana University, 1952). Helpful in discovery of analogues of Southeast Asian motifs.

3315. Isaac d'ISRAELI, "The Philosophy of Proverbs," in his *Curiosities of Literature*. Selected, edited and introduced by Everett Bleiler (New York: Dover, [c 1964]), 254–84. Classic essay on proverb literature by father of Benjamin Disraeli (1804-1881).

3316. Richard M. DORSON, "The Eclipse of Solar Mythology," in Dundes [item 3317], 57-83. Reprinted from *JAF*, 68 (1955): 393-416.

3317. *Alan DUNDES, *The Study of Folklore* (Englewood Cliffs, N.J.: Prentice-Hall, [c 1965]). Carefully selected essays representing the anthropological approach to folklore.

3318. *Mircea ELIADE, *Cosmos and History: The Myth of the Eternal Return*. Translated from the French by Willard R. Trask. Harper Torchbooks, TB50 (New York: Harper, [c 1959]).

3319. *Mircea ELIADE, *Myth and Reality*. Translated from the French by Willard R. Trask. World Perspectives, Volume 31 (New York: Harper & Row, [c 1963]).

3320. M.B. EMENEAU, "Oral Poets of South India: the Todas," in *JAF*, 71. 281 (July-September 1958): 312-24.

3321. H.J. FLEURE, "Folk-lore and Culture-Contacts," in *BJRL*, 23 (1939). 2: 403-16.

3322. *Hiroko IKEDA, *A Type and Motif Index of Japanese Folk Literature*. FF Communications 209 (Helsinki: Suomalainen tiedeakatemia, 1971).

Pre-eminently useful in discovery of analogues in Southeast Asian literatures.

3323. Wm. Hugh JANSEN, "The Esoteric-Exoteric Factor in Folklore," in Dundes [item 3317], 43-51. Reprinted from *Fabula: Journal of Folktale Studies*, 2 (1959): 205-11.

3324. *Bacil F. KIRTLEY, *A Motif-Index of Traditional Polynesian Narratives* (Honolulu: University of Hawaii Press, 1971). Expansion of first section of 1955 doctoral dissertation on Polynesian, Micronesian and Melanesian tales; especially useful in discovery of analogues in Southeast Asian literatures.

3325. Orrin E. KLAPP, "The Clever Hero," in *JAF*, 67.263 (January-March 1954): 21-34.

3326. *Clyde KLUCKHORN, "Recurrent Themes in Myths and Mythmaking," in Dundes [item 3317], 158-68. Reprinted from *Daedalus: Journal of the American Academy of Arts and Sciences*, 88 (1959): 268-79.

3327. *Claude LÉVI-STRAUSS, *Mythologiques: Le cru et le cuit* (Paris: Plon, [c 1964]). Representing the structuralist approach to myth and literature; see item 3328.

3328. *Claude LÉVI-STRAUSS, *The Raw and the Cooked*. Introduction to a Science of Mythology, I. Translated from the French by John and Doreen Weightman. Harper Torchbooks, TB/1487 (New York and Evanston: Harper & Row, 1970).

3329. G.W. LOCHEN, "Myth in a Changing World," in *BTLV*, 112 (1956).2: 169-92.

3330. John C. MESSENGER, *Jr.*, "The Role of Proverbs in a Nigerian Judicial System," in Dundes [item 3317], 299-307. Reprinted from *Southwestern Journal of Anthropology*, 15 (1959): 64-73.

3331. *Axel OLRIK, "Epic Laws of Folk Narrative," in Dundes [item 3317]. Free translation by Jeanne P. Steager of his "Epische Gesetze der Volksdichtung," in *Zeitschrift für Deutsches Altertum und Deutsche Literatur*, 51 (1909): 1-12. Classic statement on some essential attributes of the folktale.

3332. *Lord RAGLAN, "The Hero of Tradition," in Dundes [item 3317], 142-57. Reprinted from *Folklore*, 45 (1934): 212-31.

3333. P.R. SUBRAMANIAN, *A Myth: Its Development and Treatment*. Conference-Seminar of Tamil Studies, IATR (Kuala Lumpur: International Association of Tamil Research, 1966), Section A6. Mimeographed.

3334. Archer TAYLOR, "Problems in the Study of Proverbs," in *JAF*, 47. 183 (January-March 1934): 1-21.

3335. *Archer TAYLOR, "Folklore and the Student of Literature," in Dundes [item 3317], 34-42. Reprinted from *The Pacific Spectator*, 2 (1948): 216-23.

3336. *Stith THOMPSON, *The Folktale* (New York: Holt, Rinehart and Winston, [c 1946]). Exhaustive introduction to the nature of the oral tale, its relationship to the literary tale, its structural types, its component motifs, and its classification, with background on the development of folklore studies and techniques of collection. Representative of the Finnish approach to folk literature as opposed to the anthropological [items 3317, 3327-8], the philosophical [items 3318-9], the psychoanalytical [items 3307-12], and the ritualist (e.g., Gaster) approaches.

3337. *Stith THOMPSON, *The Folktale* (New York: The Dryden Press, 1946).

3338. *Stith THOMPSON, *The Folktale*. Second Printing (New York: The Dryden Press, 1951).

3339. *Stith THOMPSON, *Narrative Motif-Analysis as a Folklore Method*. FF Communications, No. 161 (Helsinki: Suomalainen tiedeakatemia, 1955). Seven-page statement on folk literature and the motif index, valuable as introduction to folklore.

3340. *Stith THOMPSON, *Motif-Index of Folk-Literature*. A Classification of Narrative Elements in Folktales, Ballads, Myths, Fables, Mediæval Romances, Exempla, Fabliaux, Jest-Books and Local Legends [in six volumes]. Revised and enlarged edition (Bloomington: Indiana University Press, 1955-58). At once the great achievement of the Finnish school of folklore and an indispensable tool for the classification of minimal recurrent themes in folk literature.

3341. *Stith THOMPSON and Jonas BALYS, *The Oral Tales of India*. Indiana University Publications, Folklore Series No. 10 (Bloomington: Indiana University Press, 1958). Motif index of Indian folktales, of special value in classifying materials from Southeast Asia.

3342. *Stith THOMPSON and Warren E. ROBERTS, *Types of Indic Oral Tales: India, Pakistan, and Ceylon*. FF Communications No. 180 (Helsinki: Suomalainen tiedeakatemia, 1960). Classification of tale-types, directly applicable to Southeast Asia.

3343. William THOMS, "Folklore," in Dundes [item 3317], 4-6. Reprinted from *The Athenaeum*, No. 982 (22 August 1846 [*sic*]): 862-3.

3344. Francis Lee UTLEY, "Folk Literature: An Operational Definition," in Dundes [item 3317], 7-24. Reprinted from *JAF*, 74 (1961): 193-206.

3345. *C.W. von SYDOW, "Folktale Studies and Philology: Some Points of

View," in Dundes [item 3317], 219-42. Reprinted from his *Selected Papers on Folklore*, edited by Laurits Bødker (Copenhagen: Rosenkilde og Baggers, 1948), 189-219.

LITERARY BACKGROUND

3346. M.H. ABRAMS, *A Glossary of Literary Terms*, Based on an earlier book by Dan. S. Norton and Peters Rushton. Revised Edition (New York: Holt, Rinehart and Winston, [c 1957]).

3347. A. Owen ALDRIDGE, *Comparative Literature: Matter and Method* (Urbana: The University of Illinois Press, 1969).

3348. R.S. CONWAY, "The Architecture of the Epic," in *BJRL*, 9 (1925).2: 481-500.

3349. James P. DEGNAN and William HEFFERNAN, *Writing Analyses of Literature* (New York: Holt, Rinehart and Winston, [c 1969]). Helpful in analysis of folktales.

3350. *William H. GASS, "The Concept of Character in Fiction," in *New American Review, Number 7*. A Signet Book, Y3953 (New York: The New American Library, 1969), 128-44. Penetrating essay on the philosophy and psychology of character portrayal in modern fiction, useful as a critical tool applicable to contemporary Southeast Asian literatures.

3351. Wilfred L. GUERIN, Earle G. LABOR, Lee MORGAN, John R. WILLINGHAM, *A Handbook of Critical Approaches to Literature* (New York and London: Harper & Row, [c 1966]).

3352. *O.B. HARDISON, "The Rhetoric of Hitchcock's Thrillers," in *Man and the Movies*, edited by W.R. Robinson with assistance from George Garrett. Pelican Books, A1061 (Baltimore: Penguin Books, 1969), 137-52. Brilliant essay indirectly relevant to an understanding of the Southeast Asian romance.

3353. *W.T.H. JACKSON, *Medieval Literature: A History and a Guide*. Collier Books 05229 (New York: Collier Books / London: Collier-Macmillan, 1967). Excellent introduction to European epics, romances, and other works of the period, valuable in discovery of parallels with Southeast Asia.

3354. James William JOHNSON, *Concepts of Literature* (Englewood Cliffs, N.J.: Prentice-Hall, [c 1970]).

3355. Richard A. LANHAM, *A Handlist of Rhetorical Terms: A Guide for Students of English Literature* Berkeley and Los Angeles: University of California Press, 1969).

3356. Burton RAFFEL, "How to Read a Translation: Poetry," in *BA*, 41 (1967).3: 279–85.

3357. Wilbur S. SCOTT, *Five Approaches of Literary Criticism: An Arrangement of Contemporary Critical Essays*. Collier Books, 05368 (London: Collier-Macmillan, 1970).

3358. A.J. SMITH, "Theory and Practice in Renaissance Poetry: Two Kinds of Imitation," in *BJRL*, 47 (1964).1: 212–43. Helpful in understanding the non-uniqueness of Southeast Asian metrical works.

3359. *Rabindranath TAGORE, "The Nature of Literature," in *VBQ*, 24 (1959).4: 307–14.

3360. *J. Chesley TAYLOR, "The Short Story as a Literary Type," in his *The Short Story: Fiction in Transition* (New York: Charles Scribner's Sons, [c 1969]), 1–7. Directly applicable to the contemporary Southeast Asian short story.

3361. William Flint THRALL and Addison HIBBARD, *A Handbook to Literature*. Revised and Enlarged by C. Hugh Holman (New York: The Odyssey Press, [c 1960]).

3362. *E. VINAVER, "Epic to Romance," in *BJRL*, 45–46 (1964): 476–503. Masterly statement of main features of epic and romance and of differences between the two, easily applicable to Southeast Asian literatures.

3363. *Sir* Richard WINSTEDT, "Notes. I: A Literary Device Common to Homer and the East," in *JSS*, XXXVII (1948).1: 47–50.

3364. Heinrich ZIMMER, *The King and the Corpse: Tales of the Soul's Conquest of Evil*. Edited by Joseph Campbell (New York: Pantheon, 1948). Especially useful in illustrating the psychoanalytical approach to myth and folktale.

REGIONAL BACKGROUND

3365. Paul K. BENEDICT, "Languages and Literatures of Indochina," in *FEQ*, VI (1947).4: 379–89.

3366. *Robbins BURLING, *Hill Farms and Padi Fields: Life in Mainland Southeast Asia*. A Spectrum Book, S-110 (Englewood Cliffs, N.J.: Prentice-Hall, [c 1965]). Scholarly essays on the main features of the area, remarkably straightforward and lucid.

3367. Ai-Li S. CHIN, "Family Relations in Modern Chinese Fiction," in
       Family and Kinship in Chinese Society, edited by Maurice Freed-
       man (Stanford: Stanford University Press, 1970), 87-120.

3368. P.E. de JOSSELIN de JONG, review of *Prehistory and Religion in
       South-East Asia* by H.G. Quaritch Wales, in *BTLV*, 117 (1961).2:
       291-4.

3369. *John F. EMBREE and Lillian Ota DOTSON, *Bibliography of the Peo-
       ples and Cultures of Mainland Southeast Asia* (New Haven: South-
       east Asia Studies, Yale University, 1950). Despite its age, still
       the best such work available; rich sections on folklore, litera-
       ture, and language.

3370. Rupert EMERSON, "An Analysis of Nationalism in Southeast Asia,"
       in *FEQ*, V (1946).2: 208-15.

3371. N.V.M. GONZALEZ, "The Artist in Southeast Asia," in *BA*, 30 (1956).
       4: 388-91.

3372. A. GOODWIN, "The Social Origins and Privileged Status of the
       French Eighteenth-Century Nobility," in *BJRL*, 47 (1965).2: 382-
       403. Numerous useful parallels with Southeast Asia having rele-
       vance to literature.

3373. Frédéric JOÜON des LONGRAIS, *L'Est et l'Ouest: institutions du
       Japon et de l'Occident comparées (Six études de sociologie juri-
       dique)* (Tokyo: Maison Franco-Japonaise, 1958). Helpful model in
       bringing Southeast Asian institutions and norms into sharper focus.

3374. Jan KNAPPERT, review of *Literacy in Traditional Societies*, edited
       by Jack Goody, in *BTLV*, 126 (1970).4: 466-8.

3375. Frank M. LEBAR, Gerald C. HICKEY, John K. MUSGRAVE, *Ethnic Groups
       of Mainland Southeast Asia* (New Haven: Human Relations Area Files
       Press, [c 1964]).

3376. *Ivan MORRIS, *The World of the Shining Prince: Court Life in An-
       cient Japan*. Peregrine Books, Y83 (Harmondsworth, Middlesex: Pen-
       guin Books, 1969). Of uncommon interest in describing the impact
       of an older upon a younger civilization and in suggesting paral-
       lels with Vietnam and other parts of Southeast Asia; Chapters III
       to VII are especially germane to esthetics and literature.

3377. Thomas A. SEBEOK, "The Languages of Southeastern Asia," in *FEQ*,
       II (1943).4: 349-56.

3378. Lauriston SHARP, "Cultural Continuities and Discontinuities in
       Southeast Asia," in *JAS*, XXII (1962).1: 3-11.

3379. Amry VANDENBOSCH, "Regionalism in Southeast Asia," in *FEQ*, V

(1946).4: 427-38.

3380. C.E.L. WICKREMISINGHE, *The Press in Asia*. Magnetic tape recording
       (27 minutes). Asia Society Presents series.

LOCAL VALUES AND COGNITIVE PATTERNS

3381. Göran AIJMER, "A Structural Approach to Chinese Ancestor Worship,"
       in *BTLV*, 124 (1968).1: 91-8.

3382. Anonymous, *The Kamthieng House: an Introduction* (Bangkok: The Siam
       Society, 1966).

3383. A.L. BASHAM, *The Wonder That Was India*... Evergreen Encyclopedia
       Volume 1, E-145 (New York: Grove Press, 1959), Appendix I, "Cosmo-
       logy and Geography" (488-9) and Appendix II, "Astronomy" (489-91).

3384. C. Tj. BERTLING, "Vierzahl, Kreuz und Maṇḍala in Asien," in *BTLV*,
       110 (1954).2: 93-115.

3385. Asutosh BHATTACHARYA, "The Serpent as a Folk-Deity in Bengal," in
       AFS, XXIV (1965).1: 1-10.

3386. S.G.F. BRANDON, "The Personification of Death in Some Ancient Re-
       ligions," in *BJRL*, 43 (1961).2: 317-35.

3387. A.K. COOMARASWAMY, *Elements of Buddhist Iconography* (Cambridge:
       Harvard University Press, 1935). Useful for an understanding of
       Southeast Asian esthetics and symbolism, especially *mudrā*.

3388. Jeanne CUISINIER, "The Gestures in the Cambodian Ballet: Their
       Traditional and Symbolic Significance," translated from the auth-
       or's French MS., in *IAL*, New Series, I (1927).2: 93-103. On the
       mudrā in Cambodia.

3389. Clark E. CUNNINGHAM, "Order in the Atoni House," in *BTLV*, 120
       (1964).1: 34-68.

3390. Tyra de KLEEN, *Mudrās, the Ritual Hand-poses of the Buddha Priests
       and the Shiva Priests of Bali*. With an introduction by A.J.D. Camp-
       bell (London: Kegan Paul, Trench, Trubner, 1924).

3391. E.-M. DURAND, "Notes sur les Chams. VIII. -La chronique de Pō Na-
       gar" [item 1019]. Some striking references to directionality.

3392. Louis FINOT, "Dharmaçālās au Cambodge," in *BEFEO*, XXV (1925).3-4:
       417-22 + plates.

3393. T. FISH, "Some Ancient Mesopotamian Traditions Concerning Men and Society," in *BJRL*, 30 (1946).1: 41-56.

3394. James F. FOX, "Bad Death and the Left Hand," in Needham [item 3413].

3395. *Bernard FRANK, "Kata-imi et kata-tagae: étude sur les interdits de direction à l'époque Heian," published as *Bulletin de la Maison Franco-Japonaise*, Nouvelle Série, V (1958).2-4. Detailed study of directionality in early Japan, of unusual interest because of partial applicability to Southeast Asia.

3396. Maurice FREEDMAN, "Ancestor Worship: Two Facets of the Chinese Case," in his *Social Organization: Essays Presented to Raymond Firth*, edited by... (London: Frank Cass / Chicago: Aldine, 1967), 85-103.

3397. *Numa Dénis FUSTEL de COULANGES, *La Cité antique* (Paris: Hachette, 1952). Classic study of religion in Greece and Rome, with numerous references to India and general relevance to the ancestor cult of Southeast Asia. See item 3414.

3398. *Numa Denis FUSTEL de COULANGES, *The Ancient City: A Study on the Religion, Laws, and Institutions of Greece and Rome*. A Doubleday Anchor Book, A 76 (Garden City, N.Y.: Doubleday, 1956).

3399. Eugène Félicien Albert *Comte* GOBLET d'ALVIELLA, *The Migration of Symbols*. With an Introduction by Sir George Birdwood (New York: University Books, [c 1956]).

3400. E. Kathleen GOUGH, "Cults of the Dead Among the Nāyars," in *JAF*, 71.281 (July-September 1958): 446-78.

3401. Erik HAARH, "Contributions to the Study of Maṇḍala and Mudrā," in *AO*, XXIII (1959).1-2: 59-91.

3402. *E.S. Craighill HANDY, *Polynesian Religion*. Bernice P. Bishop Museum Bulletin 34 (Honolulu: Bernice P. Bishop Museum, 1927). Synthetic description of beliefs and practices in Polynesia, of great value in investigation of indigenous Southeast Asian cultures.

3403. *Lafcadio HEARN, *Japan: An Interpretation* (New York: Grosset & Dunlap, 1904). Inimitable description of ancestor cult of Japan, exemplifying relevance of Fustel de Coulanges [item 3397] to Asian religion, readily adaptable to Southeast Asia.

3404. *Robert HEINE-GELDERN, "Conceptions of State and Kingship in Southeast Asia," in *FEQ*, II (1942).1: 15-30. Classic statement on certain cosmological and derivative assumptions common to Southeast Asia, of special value to students of literature. See items 3405 and 3420.

3405. *Robert HEINE-GELDERN, *Conceptions of State and Kingship in South-
       east Asia*. Data Paper No. 18 (Ithaca, N.Y.: Southeast Asia Pro-
       gram, Department of Far Eastern Studies, Cornell University,
       1956). Revised version of item 3404.

3406. William HOWELLS, *The Heathens: Primitive Man and His Religions*.
       The American Museum of Natural History. The Natural History Lib-
       rary, N19. A Doubleday Anchor Book (Garden City, N.Y.: Doubleday,
       1962). Useful as introduction to indigenous Southeast Asian reli-
       gious features.

3407. *Dr* Alb. C. KRUYT, "Rechts en links bij de bewonders van Midden-
       Celebes," in *BTLVNI*, 100 (1941): 339-55.

3408. Claude LÉVI-STRAUSS, *The Savage Mind*. The Nature of Human Society
       Series. A Phoenix Book, P325 (Chicago: The University of Chicago
       Press, [c 1966]). Translation of his *La pensée sauvage*.

3409. *Saveros LEWITZ, "Recherches sur le vocabulaire cambodgien (VI):
       Les noms des points cardinaux en khmer," in *JA*, 1970: 131-41.
       Unique contribution to the study of directionality in Southeast
       Asia.

3410. Donald Alexander MACKENZIE, *The Migration of Symbols and Their
       Relation to Beliefs and Customs* (Detroit: Gale Research Co.,
       1968).

3411. William MADSEN, "Hot and Cold in the Universe of San Francisco
       Tecospa, Valley of Mexico," in *JAF*, 68.268 (April-June 1955):
       123-39. Contains useful parallels with Southeast Asia.

3412. Edward S. MORSE, *Japanese Homes and Their Surroundings*. With il-
       lustrations by the author. With a New Introduction by Clay Lan-
       caster. Dover Books, T746 (New York: Dover, [c 1961]). Contains
       much useful information on housetypes and orientation applicable,
       with due caution, to Southeast Asia.

3413. R. NEEDHAM, *The Right and the Left Hand*. Edited by... (Chicago:
       University of Chicago Press, 1972). Essays on concepts of right
       and left; in press as of mid-1972.

3414. Marcel NER, "Caractères généraux de l'œuvre de Fustel," in *BSEI*,
       Nouvelle Série, V (1930).3: 187-215. Lecture on relevance of
       Fustel de Coulanges [item 3397] to understanding of Southeast
       Asian cultures by officer of Ecole Française d'Extrême-Orient.

3415. P. PARIS, "L'importance rituelle du Nord-Est et ses applications
       en Indochine," in *BEFEO*, XLI (1942).2: 303-33.

3416. W.H.R. RIVERS, "Dreams and Primitive Culture," in *BJRL*, 4 (1918).
       3-4: 387-410.

3417. Ernest Dale SAUNDERS, *Mudrā: a Study of Symbolic Gestures in
       Japanese Buddhist Sculpture*. Bollingen Series, 58 (New York: Pan-
       theon, [c 1960]).

3418. G. Elliot SMITH, "Dragons and Rain Gods," in *BJRL*, 5 (1919).3-4:
       317-80.

3419. D. Howard SMITH, "Religious Developments in China Prior to Con-
       fucius," in *BJRL*, 44 (1962).2: 432-54.

3420. Robert L. SOLOMON, "Aspects of State, Kingship and Succession in
       Southeast Asia." The RAND Corporation, Santa Monica, California.
       Undated (*ca* 1968) research paper expanding upon ideas of Heine-
       Geldern [item 3404].

3421. Norman J. SPARNON, *Japanese Flower Arrangement, Classical and
       Modern* (Tokyo: Tuttle, [c 1960]), 40-4. Exemplifying application
       of *yin-yang* conception to art.

3422. M.M. SUKARTO K. ATMODJO, "Preliminary Report on the Copper-plate
       Inscription of Asahduren" [item 2040]. Useful references to cos-
       mological ideas.

3423. Han SUYIN, "Onward and Upward with the Arts: The Harmonies of
       Heaven," in *The New Yorker*, XXXIX.45 (28 December 1963): 38-51.
       On astrology in Southeast Asia.

3424. J.L. SWELLENGREBEL, "Three Patterns of the Cosmic Order," in In-
       troduction to *Bali: Studies in Life, Thought, and Ritual*. Selec-
       ted Studies on Indonesia, By Dutch Scholars. Volume Five (The
       Hague and Bandung: W. van Hoeve, 1960), 36-53.

3425. J.H. TELFORD, "Animism in Kengtung State," in *JBRS*, 27 (1937).2:
       85-238.

3426. H. WIESCHOFF, "Concepts of Right and Left in African Cultures,"
       in *JAOS*, 58 (1938).1: 202-17.

3427. W.C. WILLOUGHBY, *The Soul of the Bantu: A Sympathetic Study of
       the Magico-Religious Practices and Beliefs of the Bantu Tribes of
       Africa* (Garden City, N.Y.: Doubleday, Doran, 1928). Contains much
       information of concepts of right and left, orientation, and the
       like providing parallels with Southeast Asia.

THE HINDU-BUDDHIST TRADITION

3428. Anonymous, "The Ramayana, ancient epic remains a living part of popular culture in Southeast Asia," in *AM*, 6.30 (24 July 1966): 4-9.

3429. R.E. ASHER, review of *A History of Tamil Literature* by J.M. Somasundaram Pillai, in *JAS*, XXVIII (1969).3: 634-5.

3430. H.W. BAILEY, "Rāma," in *BSOAS*, X (1940-2).2: 365-76; 3: 559-98. On the Khotanese version of the *Rāmāyaṇa*.

3431. A.L. BASHAM, *The Wonder That Was India* [item 3383], Chapter IX, "Languages and Literature" (386-487).

3432. *Dr F.D.K. BOSCH, "The Problem of the Hindu colonisation of Indonesia," in his *Selected Studies in Indonesian Archaeology*. Koninklijk Instituut voor Taal-, Land- en Volkenkunde, Translation Series 5 (The Hague: Martinus Nijhoff, 1961), 1-22. Applicable to the entire Indianized zone of Southeast Asia.

3433. *Harry M. BUCK, "An Introduction to the Study of the *Ramayana* in South and South-East Asia," in *Proceedings of the First International Conference Seminar of Tamil Studies, Kuala Lumpur - Malaysia*, April 1966 (Kuala Lumpur: International Association of Tamil Research, 1966), I: 72-88.

3434. Joseph CAMPBELL, *Masks of God, East and West*. Magnetic tape recording (27 minutes). Asia Society Presents series.

3435. Joseph CAMPBELL, *Indian Art and Religion*. Magnetic tape recording (27 minutes). Asia Society Presents series.

3436. Krishna CHAITANYA, *A New History of Sanskrit Literature* (Bombay: Asia Publishing House, [c 1962]).

3437. N.P. CHAKRAVARTI, "Indian Dance Forms in South-East Asia," in *FA/A*, XVII (1960).164: 1494-8.

3438. *Lord CHALMERS, *Buddha's Teachings, being the* Sutta-Nipāta *or Discourse-Collection*. Edited in the original Pali text with an English version facing it... Harvard Oriental Series, Volume 37 (Cambridge: Harvard University Press, 1932).

3439. Edward CONZE, *Buddhism: Its Essence and Development*. With a preface by Arthur Waley. Harper Torchbooks, TB 58 (New York: Harper, 1959).

3440. *Ananda K. COOMARASWAMY, *Hinduism and Buddhism* (New York: Philosophical Library, n.d.).

3441. *E.B. COWELL, *The Jātaka, or Stories of the Buddha's Former Births.*
Translated from the Pāli by various hands under the Editorship of
Professor... Published for the Pali Text Society (London: Luzac,
1957). Full translation of the canonical *jātaka*, with copious
notes and indexing; indispensable in the study of Southeast Asian
tale-types.

3442. S.N. DASGUPTA, *A History of Sanskrit Literature: Classical Period.* Volume I. Second Edition (Calcutta: University of Calcutta,
1962).

3443. T.W. Rhys DAVIDS, "The Early History of the Buddhists," Chapter
VII in Rapson [item 3468], 171-97.

3444. Har DAYAL, *The Bodhisattva Doctrine in Buddhiot Sanskrit Literature* (London: Kegan Paul, Trench, Trubner, 1932).

3445. *René de BERVAL, *Présence du Bouddhisme,* sous la direction de...
Numéro spécial de *FA*, XVI.153-157 (1959). Eminently useful source
for history and doctrine in Southeast Asia.

3446. Mahendra V. DESAI, "Literatures of India," in *BA*, 28 (1954).3:
261-80.

3447. Mark J. DRESDEN, *The Jātakastava or "Praise of the Buddha's Former
Births".* Indo-Scythian (Khotanese) Text, English Translation, Gram-
matical Notes, and Glossaries. Published as *Transactions of the
American Philosophical Society,* New Series, 45.5 (Philadelphia: The
American Philosophical Society, 1955).

3448. Sukumar DUTT, *Early Buddhist Monachism: 600 B.C. - 100 B.C.* Trubner's Oriental Series (London: Kegan Paul, Trench, Trubner, 1924).

3449. *Franklin EDGERTON, *The Panchatantra Reconstructed...* Text, Critical Apparatus, Introduction, Translation by... [in two volumes].
American Oriental Series, Volumes 2 and 3 (New Haven: American
Oriental Society, 1924). Indispensable in discovery of analogues
of Southeast Asian tale-types and motifs.

3450. H. Julius EGGELING, John ALLAN, and John Evelyn Bury GRAY, "Sanskrit Literature," in *EB (1969),* 19: 1027a-35b.

3451. Léon FEER, "Etudes bouddhiques: Les Jātakas," in *JA*, 7ᵉ Série,
Mai-Juin 1875 and Août-Septembre 1875.

3452. Léon FEER, *A Study of the Jātakas,* Analytical and Critical. Translated by G.M. Foulkes from the French article in the *Journal Asiatique* (Calcutta: Susil Gupta, 1963).

3453. Jean FILLIOZAT, "Agastya et la propagation du brahmanisme au Sud-
Est asiatique," in *ALB* (Dr V. Raghavan Felicitation Volume), 31-

32 (1967-68): 442-9.

3454. William GEMMELL, *The Diamond Sutra* (Chin-Kang-Ching) *or Prajna-Paramita*. Translated from the Chinese with an Introduction and Notes by... (London: Kegan Paul, Trench, Trübner, 1912).

3455. T.E. GNANAMOORTHY, *Theory of the Tamil Epic*. Conference-Seminar of Tamil Studies (Kuala Lumpur: International Association of Tamil Research, 1966), Section A3. Mimeograped.

3456. *Sir* George A. GRIERSON, "On the *Adbhuta-Rāmāyaṇa*," in *BSOAS*, IV (1926-28).1: 11-27.

3457. *Sir* George A. GRIERSON, "Sītā Forlorn, a Specimen of the Kāshmīrī Rāmāyaṇa. Edited and translated by...," in *BSOAS*, V (1928-30).2: 285-301.

3458. *Professor* E. Washburn HOPKINS, "The Period of the Sūtras, Epics, and Law-Books," Chapter IX in Rapson [item 3468], 220-6.

3459. *Professor* E. Washburn HOPKINS, "Family Life and Social Customs As They Appear in the Sūtras," Chapter X in Rapson [item 3468], 227-50.

3460. *Professor* E. Washburn HOPKINS, "The Princes and Peoples of the Epic Poems," Chapter XI in Rapson [item 3468], 251-76.

3461. *Professor* A. Berriedale KEITH, "The Age of the Rigveda," Chapter IV in Rapson [item 3468], 77-113.

3462. *Professor* A. Berriedale KEITH, "The Period of the Later Saṃhitās, the Brahmaṇas, the Āraṇyakas, and the Upanishads," Chapter V in Rapson [item 3468], 114-49.

3463. A. Berriedale KEITH, *Buddhist Philosophy in India and Ceylon* (Oxford: at the Clarendon Press, 1923).

3464. P. LAL, *The Dhammapada*. Translated from the Pali by... Noonday, N348 (New York: Farrar, Straus and Giroux, 1970).

3465. *N.M. PENZER, *The Ocean of Story: Being C.H. Tawney's Translation of Somadeva's* Kathā Sarit Sāgara *(or Ocean of Streams of Story)*, now edited with introduction, fresh explanatory notes and terminal essay by... In ten volumes. UNESCO Collection of Representative Works - Indian Series (Delhi / Patna / Varanasi: Motilal Banarsidass, 1968). Fully indexed; invaluable in discovery of Southeast Asian analogues.

3466. *Maurice PERCHERON, *Buddha and Buddhism*. Translated by Edmund Stapleton. Men of Wisdom Books, MW3 (London: Longmans, Green /

New York: Harper, [c 1957]). One of best introductions to Buddhist doctrine and history.

3467.   David C. PIERCE, "The Middle Way of the Jātaka Tales," in *JAF*, 82. 325 (July-September 1969): 245-54.

3468.   *E.J. RAPSON, *The Cambridge History of India*. Volume I: *Ancient India*. Edited by... (New York: Macmillan, 1922).

3469.   *Professor* E.J. RAPSON, "The Purāṇas," Chapter XIII in Rapson [item 3468], 296-318.

3470.   Louis RENOU, *Indian Literature*. Translated from the French by Patrick Evans. A Sun Book, SB-27 (New York: Walker, [c 1964]).

3471.   Reinhold ROST and anonymous, "Tamils," in *EB (1962)*, 21: 772b-4a.

3472.   *S. SINGARAVELU, "A Comparative Study of the Story of Rama in South India and South-east Asia," in *Proceedings of the First International Conference Seminar of Tamil Studies, Kuala Lumpur - Malaysia*, April 1966 (Kuala Lumpur: International Association of Tamil Research, 1966), I: 89-140.

3473.   Milton SINGER, *Krishna: Myths, Rites, and Attitudes.* Edited by... with a Foreword by Daniel H.H. Ingalls. A Phoenix Book, P329 (Chicago and London: The University of Chicago Press, 1968). Eight essays on the Kṛṣṇa legend.

3474.   K. SIVATHAMBY, *The Ritualistic Origins of Tamil Drama*. Conference-Seminar of Tamil Studies (Kuala Lumpur: International Association of Tamil Research, 1966). Mimeographed.

3475.   C.H. TAWNEY, *The Ocean of Story*. See item 3465.

3476.   Xavier S. THANI NAYAGAM, "Tamil Cultural Influences in South East Asia," in *Tamil Culture*, IV (1955).3: 203-20.

3477.   E.J. THOMAS, *Early Buddhist Scriptures*. A Selection translated and edited by... (London: Kegan Paul, Trench, Trubner, 1935).

3478.   *Dr* F.W. THOMAS, "Political and Social Organisation of the Maurya Empire," Chapter XIX in Rapson [item 3468], 474-94.

3479.   F.N. TRAGER, "Reflections on Buddhism and the Social Order in Southern Asia," in *Burma Research Society Fiftieth Anniversary Publication Nº 1:* Some of the Papers read at the Fiftieth Anniversary Conference (Rangoon: Burma Research Society, 1961), 529-43.

3480.   Hans [= J.A.B.] van BUITENEN, "The Indian Hero as a Vidyādhara," in *JAF*, 71.281 (July-September 1958): 305-11.

3481. *J.A.B. van BUITENEN, *Tales of Ancient India*. Translated from the Sanskrit by... A Bantam Classic, FC60 (New York: Bantam Books, 1961). A good, readable selection of tales from the classical period.

3482. A. VENKATASUBBIAH, *"Pañcatantra* Studies," in *AMaj*, III (1926): 307-20.

3483. A. VENKATASUBBIAH, "A Tamil Version of the *Pañcatantra*," in *ALB*, XXIX (1965).1-4: 74-143.

3484. *Henry Clarke WARREN, *Buddhism in Translations*. Passages Selected from the Buddhist Sacred Books and Translated from the Original Pali into English by... Harvard Oriental Series, Volume 3 (Cambridge: Harvard University Press, 1947). Excellent anthology of Theravāda writings.

3485. *M. WINTERNITZ, *A History of Indian Literature*. Translated from the Original German by Mrs S. Ketkar and Revised by the Author (Calcutta: University of Calcutta, 1962).

3486. *Heinrich ZIMMER, *The King and the Corpse* [item 3364]. Part II contains "Four Episodes from the Romance of the Goddess" (239-306), incorporating the first European translation of the *Kālikāpurāṇa*, of special interest insofar as it reveals the subtle humor underlying much of the *purāṇa, upaniṣad* and kindred literature.

3487. *Heinrich ZIMMER, *The Art of Indian Asia, Its Mythology and Transformations*. Completed and Edited by Joseph Campbell. Second Edition (New York: Pantheon Books, [c 1960]). Synthesis of Indian art and literature, important for appreciation both of Indian literature and of Indian impact on Southeast Asia; a work of literature in its own right.

ADDENDA

I. BURMA

FOLK LITERATURE

3488. Anonymous, "The Four Young Men," in Courlander, *Ride With the Sun* [item 3292], 42-5.

3489. Anonymous, "The Hidden Treature of Khin," in Courlander, *The Tiger's Whisker* [item 3293], 29-32.

3490. Anonymous, "The King Who Ate Chaff," in Courlander, *The Tiger's Whisker* [item 3293], 33-4.

3491. Anonymous, "The Musician of Tagaung," in Courlander, *The Tiger's Whisker* [item 3293], 35-7.

3492. Anonymous, "The Tiger's Minister of State," in Courlander, *The Tiger's Whisker* [item 3293], 20-3.

3493. Anonymous, "The Trial of the Stone," in Courlander, *The Tiger's Whisker* [item 3293], 24-8. Shan tale.

3494. Herbert GO SUAN NANG, "Mandawng and Her Seven Brothers," a Chin legend, very much abridged, in *G*, VIII (1961).4: 50-1.

3495. *Maung* HTIN AUNG, *Burmese Monk's Tales*. Collected, Translated, and Introduced by... (New York and London: Columbia University Press, 1966). Modern didactic tales, witty for the most part and forming a new sub-genre of Burmese oral literature.

3496. Jean PERRIN, "Chants du pays khamti," in *Langues et Techniques, Nature et Société*. Editée par Jacqueline M.C. Thomas [et] Lucien Bernot. Publié avec le concours du CNRS. Tome I: Approche linguistique (Paris: Klincksieck, [c 1972]), 371-84.

PRE-MODERN POETRY

3497. *The Most Rev* Friedrich V. LUSTIG, *Burmese Classical Poems*, Selected and translated by... (Rangoon: U Khin Pe Gyi, Rangoon Gazette,

n.d. [*ca* 1966]). Bilingual text. The translator is Buddhist Arch-
bishop of Latvia.

3498. *The Most Rev* Friedrich V. LUSTIG, *Burmese Poems Through the Ages:
A Selection* translated by... (Rangoon: printed at Rangoon Gazette,
Ltd., 1969). Bilingual text.

3499. Friedrich V. LUSTIG, "Some Thoughts About Burmese Poetry," reprint
from *The Aryan Path*, September 1971. Penetrating comments useful
as introduction to best pre-modern works.

3500. ANANTASURIYA [12th century], "The Nature of Things (Release from
Anger)," translated by Friedrich V. Lustig in his *Burmese Classical
Poems* [item 3497], 36.

3501. Anonymous, "The City of Shwebo," translated by Friedrich V. Lustig
in his *Burmese Poems* [item 3498], 40.

3502. Anonymous, "Dearly Loved Son," translated by Friedrich V. Lustig
in his *Burmese Classical Poems* [item 3497], 16.

3503. Anonymous, "Dear Warrior," translated by Friedrich V. Lustig in
his *Burmese Poems* [item 3498], 39.

3504. Anonymous, "Lu-ga-lay," a lullaby, translated by Friedrich V. Lustig in his *Burmese Classical Poems* [item 3497], 2.

3505. Anonymous, "The Month of *Tabaung*," translated by Friedrich V. Lustig in his *Burmese Classical Poems* [item 3497], 4. Ode to February-
March.

3506. Anonymous, "Mountains and Forests," translated by Friedrich V.
Lustig in his *Burmese Classical Poems* [item 3497], 3.

3507. Anonymous, "Paddy Planting Song," translated by Friedrich V. Lustig in his *Burmese Classical Poems* [item 3497], 24.

3508. CHATURINGA BALA [14th century] and *Nemyo* MIN TIN KYAW KHAUNG [19th
century], "Noble Wisdom," translated by Friedrich V. Lustig in his
Burmese Classical Poems [item 3497], 29. Composed as a Pāli *lokanīti*, later translated into Burmese.

3509. *Princess* HLAING-HTEIK-KHAUNG-TIN [1833-1875], "Don't Soothe Me,"
translated by Friedrich V. Lustig in his *Burmese Poems* [item
3498], 33.

3510. *Princess* HLAING-HTEIK-KHAUNG-TIN, "I Am Longing," part of a long
song translated by Friedrich V. Lustig in his *Burmese Classical
Poems* [item 3497], 25-6.

3511. *Princess* HLAING-HTEIK-KHAUNG-TIN, "Oh To Dwell In a Forest," translated by Friedrich V. Lustig in his *Burmese Poems* [item 3498], 34.

3512. *Princess* HLAING-HTEIK-KHAUNG-TIN, "Song of the Forest," translated by Friedrich V. Lustig in his *Burmese Classical Poems* [item 3497], 8.

3513. *U* KHAING, "Remorse," translated by Friedrich V. Lustig in his *Burmese Classical Poems* [item 3497], 33.

3514. KHIN SONE [1788-1858], "Please Tell It Into Both My Ears," translated by Friedrich V. Lustig in his *Burmese Poems* [item 3498], 30.

3515. *U* KU [1827-1895], "Golden Capital City," translated by Friedrich V. Lustig in his *Burmese Poems* [item 3498], 38.

3516. *U* KYAW [1839-1888], "Bastard Teak," translated by Friedrich V. Lustig in his *Burmese Poems* [item 3498], 32.

3517. *U* KYAW, "Forest Flowers," translated by Friedrich V. Lustig in his *Burmese Classical Poems* [item 3497], 15.

3518. *U* KYAW, "The Golden-yellow *Padauk*," translated by Friedrich V. Lustig in his *Burmese Classical Poems* [item 3497], 5. Ode to *Pterocarpus macrocarpus* (!)

3519. *U* KYAW, "The Royal *Kason*," translated by Friedrich V. Lustig in his *Burmese Classical Poems* [item 3497], 10. Ode to May.

3520. *U* KYAW THAMEE [19th century], "No Cooling of Anguish," translated by Friedrich V. Lustig in his *Burmese Classical Poems* [item 3497], 35.

3521. *U* KYAW THAMEE, "Painful As It Is," translated by Friedrich V. Lustig in his *Burmese Classical Poems* [item 3497], 34.

3522. *U* KYI [1838-1888], "Come To Our Village," translated by Friedrich V. Lustig in his *Burmese Poems* [item 3498], 31.

3523. *U* KYI, "I Would Smile," translated by Friedrich V. Lustig in his *Burmese Classical Poems* [item 3497], 28.

3524. KYIGAN KOSHINGYI [1757-1813], "Mother's Love," a *yadu*, excerpted from his *Kyigan Shingyi Myittaza* and translated by Friedrich V. Lustig in his *Burmese Poems* [item 3498], 18-21.

3525. *U* KYIN U [*fl.* 1819-1853], "In the Forest Valley," translated by Friedrich V. Lustig in his *Burmese Poems* [item 3498], 29.

3526. *U* KYIN U, "Inconsolable," translated by Friedrich V. Lustig in his *Burmese Poems* [item 3498], 28.

3527. *U* KYIN U, "Military March," translated by Friedrich V. Lustig in his *Burmese Classical Poems* [item 3497], 14.

3528. *U* KYIN U, "Sea Snails," translated by Friedrich V. Lustig in his *Burmese Classical Poems* [item 3497], 9.

3529. MAE KHWE [18th century], "Present of a Cheroot," translated by Friedrich V. Lustig in his *Burmese Classical Poems* [item 3497], 22.

3530. MAE KHWE, "Short Pipe," translated by Friedrich V. Lustig in his *Burmese Classical Poems* [item 3497], 1.

3531. *Shin* MAHARATTATHARA, "Deliverance Cannot Be Far Distant," translated by Friedrich V. Lustig in his *Burmese Classical Poems* [item 3497], 12-3.

3532. *Taungdwin Shin* NYEIN MAI [first half of 18th century], "Village Vicinity," translated by Friedrich V. Lustig in his *Burmese Poems* [item 3498], 15.

3533. *Taungdwin Shin* NYEIN MAI, "My Worry," translated by Friedrich V. Lustig in his *Burmese Poems* [item 3498], 16-7.

3534. *Seintakyawthu U* OW [*b.* 1736], "The Thirteen Ways Wherein One Comes To Harm," excerpt from his *Ow-wa-da-du Pyo*, translated by Friedrich V. Lustig in his *Burmese Poems* [item 3498], 24-5.

3535. *Wungyi* PADETHAYAZA [1672-1752], "A Peasant," translated by Friedrich V. Lustig in his *Burmese Classical Poems* [item 3497], 23.

3536. *Achoketan Saya* PE [1838-1888], "Surpassing the Portrayal," translated by Friedrich V. Lustig in his *Burmese Poems* [item 3498], 36.

3537. *U* PONNYA [1812-1867], "Jasmine," translated by Friedrich V. Lustig in his *Burmese Classical Poems* [item 3497], 11.

3538. *U* PONNYA, "Let Us Both Worship Together," translated by Friedrich V. Lustig in his *Burmese Poems* [item 3498], 35.

3539. *U* PONNYA, "*Mya Man Setkya*," translated by Friedrich V. Lustig in his *Burmese Classical Poems* [item 3497], 21.

3540. *Shin Maha* RAHTATHARA [1468-1529], "Conjugal Life," excerpt from his *Kogan Pyo*, translated by Friedrich V. Lustig in his *Burmese Poems* [item 3498], 11-2.

3541. *Shin Maha* RAHTATHARA, "Real Fools," excerpt from his *Kogan Pyo*, translated by Friedrich V. Lustig in his *Burmese Poems* [item 3498], 7-8.

3542. *Shin Maha* RAHTATHARA, "When One Has Education," excerpt from his

Kogan Pyo, translated by Friedrich V. Lustig in his *Burmese Poems* [item 3498], 5-6.

3543. *Shin Maha* RAHTATHARA, "When One Lacks Education," excerpt from his *Kogan Pyo*, translated by Friedrich V. Lustig in his *Burmese Poems* [item 3498], 4.

3544. *Shin Maha* RAHTATHARA, "Worldly Treasures Versus Transcendental Values," from his *Kogan Pyo*, translated by Friedrich V. Lustig in his *Burmese Poems* [item 3498], 9-10.

3545. *Myawadi Mingyi U* SA [1766-1853], "The Lake With One Embankment," translated by Friedrich V. Lustig in his *Burmese Poems* [item 3498], 22-3.

3546. *Myawadi Mingyi U* SA, "Rain," translated by Friedrich V. Lustig in his *Burmese Classical Poems* [item 3497], 17.

3547. SAHTON *Sayadaw* [probably 18th century], "Take To Heart (A Father's Admonition to His Son)," translated by Friedrich V. Lustig in his *Burmese Classical Poems* [item 3497], 18-20.

3548. *U* SAUNG [*fl.* 1819-1837], "Life in the Village," translated by Friedrich V. Lustig in his *Burmese Poems* [item 3498], 27.

3549. *Shin* TEZOTHARA, "Donations (*Dana*)," translated by Friedrich V. Lustig in his *Burmese Classical Poems* [item 3497], 21-2.

3550. *Sayedawgyi U* THA ZAN, "Please Convey To Her My Message," translated by Friedrich V. Lustig in his *Burmese Poems* [item 3498], 37.

3551. *Maung* THWA [19th century], "Love In Secret Encountered," translated by Friedrich V. Lustig in his *Burmese Classical Poems* [item 3497], 27.

3552. *Shin* UTTAMAGYAW [1453-1542], "The Force of Immeasurable Service," excerpt from his *Shin Uttamagyaw Tawla*, translated by Friedrich V. Lustig in his *Burmese Poems* [item 3498], 1-3.

3553. *U* YA KYAW [19th century], "Carved Bullock-Cart," translated by Friedrich V. Lustig in his *Burmese Classical Poems* [item 3497], 6-7.

MODERN SHORT STORIES

3554. Annemarie ESCHE, *Der Markt von Pagan: Prosa aus Burma*. Herausgegeben und aus dem Burmesischen und Russischen übersetzt von... (Berlin: Volk und Welt, 1968). One of finest collections available, with 20 well-chosen stories.

3555. AUNG SEJA (= Aung Zeya) [*b*. 1926], "Der Realist," in Esche, *Markt von Pagan* [item 3554], 13-25.

3556. DHEJN PE MJIN (= Thein Pe Myint) [*b*. 1914], "Erdöl," in Esche, *Markt von Pagan* [item 3554], 82-91.

3557. DHEJN PE MJIN, "Ngwe Sejns Ruder zerbrach," in Esche, *Markt von Pagan* [item 3554], 132-64.

3558. DHOR TA SWÉ (= Thor Ta Swe) [*b*. 1919], "Wer ist schuldig?," in Esche, *Markt von Pagan* [item 3554], 66-81.

3559. JAN AUNG (= Yan Aung) [*b*. 1904], "Die heiligen Blumen," in Esche, *Markt von Pagan* [item 3554], 92-103.

3560. JAN AUNG, "Ein böser Beamter," in Esche, *Markt von Pagan* [item 3554], 165-72.

3561. KHIN HNIN JU (= Khin Hnin Yu) [*b*. 1925], "Der Opiumraucher Ja Tjan," in Esche, *Markt von Pagan* [item 3554], 182-91.

3562. MA MA LÉ [*b*. 1917], "Verwahtes Gras," in Esche, *Markt von Pagan* [item 3554], 110-31.

3563. MIN DHU WUN (= Min Thu Wun) [*b*. 1909], "Onkel Aung hat betrogen," in Esche, *Markt von Pagan* [item 3554], 236-41.

3564. MIN SCHIN (= Min Shin) [*b*. 1927], "Der Anfänger," in Esche, *Markt von Pagan* [item 3554], 192-7.

3565. MIN SCHIN, "Ein Sohn kommt zurück," in Esche, *Markt von Pagan* [item 3554], 198-209.

3566. MO WE [*b*. 1927], "Das Museum," in Esche, *Markt von Pagan* [item 3554], 43-51.

3567. NJEJN NAING (= Nyein Naing), "Der alte Djor ist wieder froh," in Esche, *Markt von Pagan* [item 3554], 210-9.

3568. *Dagon* SCHWE HMJA (= Dagon Shwe Hmyar) [*b*. 1896], "Echo der Vergangenheit," in Esche, *Markt von Pagan* [item 3554], 26-42.

3569. SEJA (= Zeya) [*b*. 1890], "Der Wanderer," in Esche, *Markt von Pagan* [item 3554], 104-9.

3570. SEJA, "Der Mönch und das Mädchen," in Esche, *Markt von Pagan* [item 3554], 220-5.

3571. SOR DJI (= Zawgyi) [*b*. 1908], "Der Markt von Pagan," in Esche, *Markt von Pagan* [item 3554], 5-12.

3572. SOR DJI, "Seine Frau," in Esche, *Markt von Pagan* [item 3554], 226-35.

3573. *Dagon* TAJA (= Dagon Taya) [*b*. 1919], "Der Kamerad," in Esche, *Markt von Pagan* [item 3554], 52-65.

3574. *Bamor* TIN AUNG (= Bhamo Tin Aung), "Kwé Pju und seine Autos," in Esche, *Markt von Pagan* [item 3554], 173-81.

MODERN POETRY

3575. *Professor U* E MAUNG [*b*. 1905], "Demonstrator of Ethics," translated by Friedrich V. Lustig in his *Burmese Poems* [item 3498], 48-9. Composed in September 1957.

3576. *Professor U* E MAUNG, "The Green Barbet," translated by Friedrich V. Lustig in his *Burmese Poems* [item 3498], 45-7. Composed in February 1934.

3577. *Professor U* E MAUNG, "The *Thazin* Flower," translated by Friedrich V. Lustig in his *Burmese Poems* [item 3498], 43-4. Composed in June 1932.

3578. *Thakin Kodaw* HMAING [1875-1964], "Sayadaw U Ottama," excerpt from *Myauk-tiga*, translated by Friedrich V. Lustig in his *Burmese Poems* [item 3498], 41-2.

3579. *Popa* HNIN-WAY-WAY [*b*. 1941], "*Kyet Mauk Nan*," translated by Friedrich V. Lustig in his *Burmese Poems* [item 3498], 68-9.

3580. *Maung* HTWE AUNG [*b*. 1944], "This Earth This Man," translated by Friedrich V. Lustig in his *Burmese Poems* [item 3498], 70-1.

3581. *The Most Rev* Friedrich V. LUSTIG, *Burmese Poems Through the Ages* [item 3498].

3582. MINTHUWUN [*b*. 1909], "Traveller," translated by Friedrich V. Lustig in his *Burmese Poems* [item 3498], 52.

3583. MINTHUWUN, "*Metta Sutta*," translated by Friedrich V. Lustig in his *Burmese Poems* [item 3498], 55.

3584. MINTHUWUN, "The Violinist," translated by Friedrich V. Lustig in his *Burmese Poems* [item 3498], 53-4.

3585. NGWETAYEE [1925-1958], "Towards a Better Land," translated by Friedrich V. Lustig in his *Burmese Poems* [item 3498], 62-3.

3586. NU YIN [*b*. 1916], "The Cemetery," translated by Friedrich V. Lustig in his *Burmese Poems* [item 3498], 58-9.

3587. NU YIN, "Silvery Beach," translated by Friedrich V. Lustig in his *Burmese Poems* [item 3498], 60-1.

3588. NU YIN, "A Toy To Her Liking," translated by Friedrich V. Lustig in his *Burmese Poems* [item 3498], 56-7.

3589. *Maung* SWAN YI [*b*. 1937], "The Raft of Verse," translated by Friedrich V. Lustig in his *Burmese Poems* [item 3498], 67.

3590. TIN MOE [*b*. 1933], "Lantern," translated by Friedrich V. Lustig in his *Burmese Poems* [item 3498], 64.

3591. TIN MOE, "To Each Thing Its Own Beauty," translated by Friedrich V. Lustig in his *Burmese Poems* [item 3498], 65-6.

3592. ZAW GYI [*b*. 1907], "Our Pagan," translated by Friedrich V. Lustig in his *Burmese Poems* [item 3498], 50-1.

II. CAMBODIA

GENERAL

3593. AU CHHIENG, *Catalogue du fonds khmer*. Bibliothèque Nationale, Département des Manuscrits. Ouvrage publié avec le concours du Centre National de la Recherche Scientifique (Paris: Imprimerie Nationale, 1953). Descriptive bibliography of manuscript holdings in Bibliothèque Nationale.

3594. Pierre BITARD, "Essai sur la satire sociale dans la littérature du Cambodge," in *BSEI*, Nouvelle Série, XXVI (1951).2: 189-218.

3595. George COEDÈS, "Letterature del Cambogia, della Thailandia, del Laos e del Viêt-Nam," estratto da *Le Civiltà dell' Oriente* (Roma: Gherardo Casini, 1957), II.

3596. LY VAN ONG, "Les manuscrits sur feuilles de latanier," in *Annales de l'Université Royale des Beaux Arts*, 1967: 97-108 + 3 plates.

FOLK LITERATURE

3597. *Professor Dr* Hans NEVERMANN, *Die Stadt der tausend Drachen.* Göt-
ter- und Dämonengeschichten, Sagen und Volkserzählungen aus Kam-
bodscha. Übersetzt und herausgegeben von... (Eisenach und Kassel:
Erich Röth, [c 1956]).

3598. *M* Camille NOTTON, *Légendes sur le Siam et le Cambodge.* Traduction
de... (Bangkok: Imprimerie de l'Assomption, 1939).

3599. Eveline PORÉE-MASPERO, "Traditions orales de Pursat et de Kampot,"
in *Felicitation Volume* presented to Professor George Cœdès on the
occasion of his seventy-fifth birthday, published as special number of *AA*, XXIV (1961).3-4: 394-8.

HINDU-BUDDHIST LITERATURE

3600. François MARTINI, "Note sur l'empreinte du bouddhisme dans la version cambodgienne du Rāmāyaṇa," in *JA*, 1952: 67-9.

3601. François MARTINI, "Quelques notes sur le Rāmker," in *Felicitation
Volume* presented to Professor George Cœdès on the occasion of his
seventy-fifth birthday, published as special number of *AA*, XXIV
(1961).3-4: 351-62.

INSCRIPTIONS

3602. David P. CHANDLER, "An Eighteenth Century Inscription from Angkor
Wat," in *JSS*, 59 (1971).2: 151-9.

3603. *Dr* Kalyan Kumar SARKAR, *Opening Formula in Some Cambodian Inscriptions.* Vishveshvaranand Indological Paper Series - 224 (Hoshiarpur:
Vishveshvaranand Institute of Sanskrit and Indological Studies,
Panjab University, 1969). Reprinted from *Vishveshvaranand Indological Journal*, VI (1968).

CHRONICLES

3604. E. AYMONIER, "Chronique des anciens rois du Cambodge," Traduite et
commentée par..., in *ER*, 1880: 149-85.

3605.   Camille NOTTON, *Légende d'Angkor et chronique du Bouddha de cristal* (Limoges: Rougerie, 1960).

III.   CHAMPA

FOLK LITERATURE

3606.   A. LANDES, *Contes tjames*, traduits et annotés par... (Saigon: Imprimerie Coloniale, 1887). Contents same as item 999.

IV.   INDONESIA

GENERAL

3607.   Raymond KENNEDY, *Bibliography of Indonesian Peoples and Cultures*. Revised and edited by Thomas W. Maretzki and H.Th. Fischer. 2d revised edition. Behavior Science Bibliographies (New Haven: Yale University, Southeast Asia Studies, by arrangement with HRAF, 1962).

FOLK LITERATURE

3608.   N. ADRIANI, "De schoone slaapster in 't bosch, en een gelijkluidend verhaal in Midden-Celebes," extract from *Verslagen en Mededeelingen der Koninklijke Akademie van Wetenschappen, Amsterdam*, V (1917).2: 171-86.

3609.   Anonymous, "Guno and Koyo and the Kris," in Courlander, *The Tiger's Whisker* [item 3293], 118-21. Javanese tale.

3610.   Anonymous, "Kantchil's Lime Pit," in Courlander, *Ride With the Sun* [item 3292], 28-31.

3611.   Anonymous, "The Learned Men," in Courlander, *The Tiger's Whisker* [item 3293], 122-6. Javanese tale.

3612. Anonymous, "The Well Diggers," in Courlander, *The Tiger's Whisker*
       [item 3293], 115-7. Javanese tale.

3613. Harold COURLANDER, *Kantchil's Lime Pit, and Other Stories from
       Indonesia.* With illustrations by Robert W. Kane (New York: Har-
       court, Brace, [c 1950]).

3614. Jan de VRIES, *Volksverhalen uit Oost-Indië (sprookjes en fabels),*
       verzameld door dr... Met illustraties van G.J. van Overbeek [in
       two volumes] (Zutphen: W.J. Thieme, 1925 and 1928). Pioneer work
       on Indonesian folklore.

3615. W. DUNNEBIER, "Een Mongondowsch verhaal met vertaling en aanteeke-
       ningen," Land- en Volkenkunde van Nederlandsch Oost-Indië, offprint
       from *Mededeelingen van Wege het Nederlandsche Zendelinggenootschap,*
       55 (1910).2: 95-120.

3616. W. DUNNEBIER, *Bolaang Mongonowse Teksten.* Koninklijk Instituut voor
       Taal-, Land- en Volkenkunde ('s-Gravenhage: Martinus Nijhoff,
       1953). 81 tales, with text and translation in parallel columns.

3617. Paul HAMBRUCH, *Malaiische Märchen aus Madagaskar und Insulinde,*
       Herausgegeben von... Die Märchen der Weltliteratur, herausgegeben
       von Friedrich von den Leyen und Paul Zaunert (Jena: Eugen Diede-
       richs, 1922). 10 tales from Madagascar, 51 from Indonesia.

3618. M.A. JASPAN, *Folk Literature of South Sumatra: Redjang Ka-Ga-Nga
       Texts* (Canberra: The Australian National University, 1964).

3619. *Dr* Hans KÄHLER, *Die Insel der schönen Si Melu: Indonesische Dämo-
       nengeschichten, Märchen und Sagen aus Simalur.* Auf einer Forschungs-
       reise aufgenommen und in Auswahl herausgegeben von... "Das Gesicht
       der Völker": Der malaiische Kulturkreis, Indonesische Dichtung
       (Eisenach: Erich Röth, [c 1952]). 52 tales from Simalur, off north
       Sumatra.

3620. Edwin LOEB, "Mentawei Myths," extract from *BTLVNI*, 85 (1929).1:
       66-244. 16 myths, legends, and folktales.

3621. Jan ten HOVE, "Een Minahassisch verhaal met aanteekeningen," ex-
       tract from *BTLVNI*, LVI (1904): 497-507.

3622. Jac. WOENSDREGT, "Mythen en Sagen der Berg-Toradja's van Midden-
       Selebes," vertaald en van aanteekeningen voorzien door..., pub-
       lished as *Verhandelingen van het Koninklijk Bataviaasch Genootschap
       van Kunsten en Wetenschappen,* LXV (1925).3: v + 1-179.

INSCRIPTIONS

3623. G. COEDÈS, "A Possible Interpretation of the Inscription at Kĕdu-
       kan Bukit (Palembang)," in *Malayan and Indonesian Studies: Essays
       presented to Sir Richard Winstedt on his eighty-fifth birthday*,
       Edited by John Bastin and R. Roolvink (Oxford: at the Clarendon
       Press, 1964), 24-32. On earliest dated (683 A.D.) inscription
       from Śrī Vijaya, with implications for early Indonesian relations
       with Cambodia.

CHRONICLES

3624. L. Marcel DEVIC, *Légendes et traditions historiques de l'archipel
       indien (Sedjarat malayou)*, traduit pour la première fois du malais
       en français et accompagné de notes par... Bibliothèque Orientale
       Elzévirienne, XXII (Paris: Ernest Leroux, 1878).

PRE-MODERN PROSE AND POETRY

3625. Anthony H. JOHNS, *Rantjak diLabueh* [sic]: *A Minangkabau Kaba*. A
       Specimen of the Traditional Literature of Central Sumatra, based
       on the version of Datuk Paduko Alam and Sutan Pamuntjak, as reprin-
       ted by Firma Soeleiman, Bukit Tinggi, 1951. Edited, translated, and
       with an introduction by... Data Paper No. 32 (Ithaca, New York:
       Southeast Asia Program, Department of Far Eastern Studies, Cornell
       University, 1958).

MODERN PROSE

3626. Mochtar LUBIS, *A Road With No End*. Translated from the Indonesian
       and edited by Anthony H. Johns (Chicago: H. Regnery, 1970).

3627. Mochtar LUBIS, *Twilight in Djakarta*. Translated from the Indonesian
       by Claire Holt. New Voices in Translation (New York: Vanguard,
       1964).

3628. Mochtar LUBIS, *Twilight in Djakarta*. Translated from the Indonesian
       by Claire Holt. New Voices in Translation (London: Hutchinson,
       1964).

DRAMA

3629. Utuy SONTANI, "Si Kabayan," translated by Adibah Amin, in *Three South East Asian Plays*: supplement to *Tenggara*, 4 (1969): 1-24.

V. LAOS

GENERAL

3630. Solange BERNARD-THIERRY, "Littérature laotienne," in *Histoires des Littératures* (Paris: Gallimard, 1955), I: 1342-52.

3631. George COEDÈS, "Letterature del Cambogia, della Thailandia, del Laos e del Viêt-Nam" [item 3595], II.

HINDU-BUDDHIST LITERATURE

3632. G. TERRAL-MARTINI, "Velāmajātaka," in *BEFEO*, XLIX (1959).2: 609-16 + plate. Analysis of one tale from the Lao recension of the *Paññāsajātaka*.

CHRONICLES

3633. Charles ARCHAIMBAULT, "Les annales de l'ancien royaume de S'ieng Khwang," in *BEFEO*, LIII (1967).2: 557-673 + 6 plates and 3 folding maps and 4 genealogical tables.

VI.   MALAYSIA AND SINGAPORE

GENERAL

3634.   Joseph MINATTUR, "Dravidian Elements in Malay Culture," in *Proceedings of the First International Conference Seminar of Tamil Studies, Kuala Lumpur - Malaysia,* April 1966 (Kuala Lumpur: International Association of Tamil Research, 1966), I: 261-6.

3635.   R.O. WINSTEDT, "Kingship and Enthronement in Malaya," in *JRAS,* October 1945: 134-45.

CHRONICLES

3636.   L. Marcel DEVIC, *Légendes et traditions historiques de l'archipel indien (Sedjarat malayou)* [item 3624].

3637.   R.O. WINSTEDT, "The Chronicles of Pasai," in *JMBRAS,* XVI (1938).2: 24-30. Commentary on oldest Malay chronicles.

3638.   R.O. WINSTEDT, "The Kedah Annals," in *JMBRAS,* XVI (1938).2: 31-5. Commentary, with synopsis of text.

PRE-MODERN PROSE AND POETRY

3639.   R.O. WINSTEDT, "The Date, Authorship, Contents and Some New MSS. of the Malay Romance of Alexander the Great," in *JMBRAS,* XVI (1938). 2: 1-23.

VII.   PHILIPPINES

FOLK LITERATURE

3640.   F. Landa JOCANO, *Hinilawod: An Epic from Panay Island, Central*

Philippines. Transcription, translation, and analysis in preparation; over 53,000 lines in iambic hexameter.

3641. Monina A. MERCADO, "Filipino Folk Epics," in *SEATO Record,* XI (1972).1: 36-40. Good introduction to Philippine epic literature.

VIII. THAILAND

GENERAL

3642. J.J. BOELES, "A Note on Tamil Relations with South Thailand and the Identification of Tacola," in *Proceedings of the First International Conference Seminar of Tamil Studies, Kuala Lumpur - Malaysia,* April 1966 (Kuala Lumpur: International Association of Tamil Research, 1966), I: 53-7.

3643. George COEDÈS, "Letterature del Cambogia, della Thailandia, del Laos e del Viêt-Nam" [item 3595].

3644. E.H.S. SIMMONDS, "Tai Literatures: a bibliography of works in foreign languages," in *Bulletin of the Association of British Orientalists,* New Series, 3 (1965).1-2: 5-60. Contains 589 items, with author index.

FOLK LITERATURE

3645. Annick LÉVY, "Phādeen et Nāṅ Ai," in *Langues et Techniques, Nature et Société.* Editée par Jacqueline M.C. Thomas [et] Lucien Bernot. Publié avec le concours du CNRS. Tome II: Approche ethnologique, approche naturaliste (Paris: Klincksieck, [c 1972]), 63-5. Translation of legend collected in Northeast Thailand in 1968, showing close analogies with the *Nang* Oua *Nang* Malong cycle [item 2888].

3646. M Camille NOTTON, *Légendes sur le Siam et le Cambodge* [item 3598].

3647. Klaus WENK, *Die Ruderlieder* - kāp hē rǖö - *in der Literatur Thailands.* Abhandlungen für die Kunde des Morgenlandes..., Band XXXVII, 4 (Wiesbaden: Deutsche Morgenländische Gesellschaft / Franz Steiner, 1968).

INSCRIPTIONS

3648. G. COEDÈS, *Recueil des Inscriptions du Siam.* Deuxième Partie: In-
       scriptions de Dvāravatī, de Çrīvijaya et de Lavo, éditées et tra-
       duites par... Deuxième édition, revue et mise à jour. [No publi-
       cation data.] v + (iv) + 66 pages Thai text + XVIII plates, (iv)
       + 40 pages French text.

3649. A.B. GRISWOLD and Prasert ṇa NAGARA, "An Inscription in Old Mon
       from Wieng Manó in Chieng Mai Province. Epigraphic and Historical
       Studies No. 6," in *JSS*, 59 (1971).1: 153-6 + plate.

3650. A.B. GRISWOLD and Prasert ṇa NAGARA, "The Inscription of King Rāma
       Gaṃhèṅ of Sukhodaya (1292 A.D.). Epigraphic and Historical Studies
       No. 9," in *JSS*, 59 (1971).2: 179-228 + 18 plates.

CHRONICLES

3651. David K. WYATT, *The Nan Chronicle.* Translated by Prasoet Churatana.
       Edited by... Data Paper No. 59 (Ithaca, New York: Southeast Asia
       Program, Department of Asian Studies, Cornell University, 1966).

PRE-MODERN METRICAL WORKS

3652. Søren EGEROD, *Phayaphrom: The Poem in Four Songs.* A Northern Thai
       Tetralogy. Transcription, English translation, and Vocabulary by
       ... Scandinavian Institute of Asian Studies Monograph Series No. 7
       (Lund: Studentlitteratur, [c 1971]). Only available translation of
       work by Phayaphrom, 1802-1887.

3653. Ginette MARTINI, "Pañcabuddhabyākaraṇa," in *BEFEO*, LV (1969): 125-
       44 + 3 plates. Translation of text from Thai recension of *Paññāsa-
       jātaka*, with commentary.

3654. Camille NOTTON, *The Chronicle of the Emerald Buddha.* Translated
       by... (Bangkok: printed at The Bangkok Times Press, 1932). Trans-
       lation of palm-leaf manuscript in Pāli and Chiang Mai Thai.

3655. Thong-in SOONSAWAD, *The Thai Poets*, Written and translated by...
       A Guide to the Collected Poetry of Thailand and the Works of the
       Major Thai Poets (Bangkok: Poetry Society of Thailand & Office of

Panorama of Thailand, 1968). Bilingual text; curious example of
bad translation.

3656. Dr Christian VELDER, *Der Kampf der Götter und Dämonen*. Aus dem
thailändischen Ramakien übertragen und mit einem Nachwort versehen
von... (Schweinfurt: Neues Forum, 1962).

IX. VIETNAM

GENERAL

3657. George COEDÈS, "Letterature del Cambogia, della Thailandia, del
Laos e del Viêt-Nam" [item 3595].

3658. G. CORDIER, *Littérature annamite: morceaux choisis* (Hanoi, 1914).

3659. G. CORDIER, "Essai sur la littérature annamite," in *Revue indochinoise*, 1919.

3660. Nguyên Đinh HOA, review of *Introduction à la littérature viêtnamienne* by Maurice Durand and Nguyên Trân Huân [item 3023], in
JAOS, 92 (1972).2: 364-8. Valuable critique of valuable work.

FOLK LITERATURE

3661. Dominique ANTOMARCHI, "Le chant épique de Kdam Yi: *Klei Khan Kdam
Yi*," recueilli et traduit par..., in *BEFEO*, XLVII (1955).2: 547-
615 + 4 plates. Rhadé epic.

3662. J. BOULBET, *Dialogue lyrique des Cau Maa'* (Tam pöt maa'), présenté
par... Publications de l'Ecole Française d'Extrême-Orient, Volume
LXXXV (Paris: Ecole Française d'Extrême-Orient, 1972). Detailed
study of Maa' song and poetry, with Maa' texts and translations.

3663. Georges CONDOMINAS, "Chansons Mnong Gar," in *FA*, 87 (Août 1953):
648-56.

3664. Vo-DINH, *The Toad Is the Emperor's Uncle: Animal Folktales from
Viet-Nam*, told and illustrated by... (Garden City, New York:
Doubleday, [c 1970]).

3665. Paul GUILLEMINET, *Coutumier de la tribu bahnar, des Sedang et des Jarai de la province de Kontum* selon la coutume appliquée dans les tribunaux de cette province de 1908 à 1939 [in two volumes]. Publications de l'Ecole Française d'Extrême-Orient, XXXII. Ouvrage honoré d'une souscription du Cabinet de S.M. Bao-Dai (Paris: E. de Boccard / Hanoi: Ecole Française d'Extrême-Orient, 1952). Compendium of oral law among three highland peoples of Central Vietnam.

3666. Roger LEGAY et Trần-văn-TỐT, "Essai de bibliographie pratique sur les populations montagnardes du Sud-Vietnam (1935-1966)," in *BSEI*, Nouvelle Série, XLII (1967).3: 257-99. Folklore studies, mostly in Vietnamese, 293-5.

X.   REGIONAL AND GENERAL WORKS

GENERAL

3667. Alessandro BAUSANI, *Le letterature del sud-est asiatico: birmana, siamese, laotiana, cambogiana, viètnamita, giavanese, malese-indonesiana, filippina.* Le letterature del mondo, 37 (Firenze: Sansoni / Milano: Accademia, [c 1970]). Only existing survey of Southeast Asian literatures, of high order of competence considering problems involved; contains numerous extract translations, many from secondary sources.

FOLK LITERATURE

3668. David BIDNEY, "The Concept of Myth," in Clarke, *Folklore Reader* [item 3671], 89-100. Excerpted from his *Theoretical Anthropology* (New York: Columbia University Press, [c 1953]), Chapter 10: 293-7, 300-1, 322-6.

3669. Franz BOAS, "Literature, Music, and Dance," in Clarke, *Folklore Reader* [item 3671], 65-77. Reprinted from his *General Anthropology*, edited by Franz Boas (New York: D.C. Heath, 1938).

3670. Rhys CARPENTER, "Literature Without Letters," in Clarke, *Folklore Reader* [item 3671], 17-22. Reprinted from his *Folktale, Fiction, and Saga in Homeric Epics* (Berkeley and Los Angeles: University of California Press, [c 1946]).

3671. Kenneth and Mary CLARKE, *A Folklore Reader* (New York: A.S. Barnes
       / London: Thomas Yoseloff, [c 1965]).

3672. Theodor H. GASTER, *Thespis: Ritual, Myth and Drama in the Ancient
       Near East*. Foreword by Gilbert Murray. The Academy Library. Harper
       Torchbooks, TB 1281 (New York: Harper & Row, 1966). Represents the
       ritualist approach to myth and folk literature, emphasizing devel-
       opment of drama out of seasonal rites.

3673. J.A. HADFIELD, "Dreams as Archetypal," in Clarke, *Folklore Reader*
       [item 3671], 78-83. Excerpted from his *Dreams and Nightmares*. A
       Pelican Book (Harmondsworth, Middlesex: Penguin Books, [c 1954]),
       Chapter 3: 42-3, 44, 46-8.

3674. Edwin Sidney HARTLAND, "The Art of Story-Telling," in his *The
       Science of Fairy Tales* [items 3676, 3680], Chapter I (1-21).

3675. Edwin Sidney HARTLAND, "Swan-maidens," in his *The Science of Fairy
       Tales* [items 3676, 3680], Chapters X and XI (255-332).

3676. Edwin Sidney HARTLAND, *The Science of Fairy Tales*. An Inquiry into
       Fairy Mythology (London: Walter Scott, 1891). In most respects
       still sound and useful despite its age.

3677. Edwin Sidney HARTLAND, *Mythology and Folktales: Their Relation and
       Interpretation*. Popular Studies in Mythology, Romance and Folklore,
       No. 7 (London: D. Nutt, 1900).

3678. Edwin Sidney HARTLAND, *Folklore: What is it and what is the good
       of it?* Popular Studies in Mythology, Romance and Folklore, No. 2.
       Second Edition (London: D. Nutt, 1904).

3679. Edwin Sidney HARTLAND, *Mythology and Folktales: Their Relation and
       Interpretation*. Popular Studies in Mythology, Romance and Folklore,
       No. 7. Second Edition (London: D. Nutt, 1914).

3680. Edwin Sidney HARTLAND, *The Science of Fairy Tales*. An Inquiry into
       Fairy Mythology (Detroit: Singing Tree Press, 1968). Reissue of
       1891 edition.

3681. MacEdward LEACH, "Problems of Collecting Oral Literature," in Clarke,
       Folklore Reader [item 3671], 48-61. Reprinted from *PMLA*, LXVII
       (1962).3.

3682. Stith THOMPSON, "Story-Writers and Story-Tellers," in Clarke, *Folk-
       lore Reader* [item 3671], 40-7. Reprinted from Thomas A. Kirkby and
       Henry Bosley, *Philologica:* The Malone Anniversary Studies (Balti-
       more: The Johns Hopkins Press, [c 1949]).

LITERARY BACKGROUND

3683. Robert A. GEORGES, "Silone's Use of Folk Beliefs," in Clarke,
       Folklore Reader [item 3671], 197-206. Reprinted from *Midwest Folk-
       lore*, XII (1962).4.

3684. Francis B. GUMMERE, "The Epic," in Clarke, *Folklore Reader* [item
       3671], 296-307. Reprinted from his *Handbook of Poetics* (Boston:
       Ginn, 1885).

3685. Raphael PATAI, "Jewish Folklore and Jewish Tradition," in Clarke,
       Folklore Reader [item 3671], 217-30. Reprinted from *Studies in
       Biblical and Jewish Folklore*, edited by Raphael Patai, Francis Lee
       Utley, and Dov Noy. Indiana University Folklore Series Vol. 51
       (Bloomington: Indiana University Press, 1960).

REGIONAL BACKGROUND

3686. George COEDÈS, "Religioni dell' Indocina (Birmania, Thailandia,
       Cambogia, Laos e Viêt-Nam)," estratto da *Le Civiltà dell' Oriente*
       (Roma: Gherardo Casini, 1958), III.

3687. Henri CORDIER, *Bibliotheca indosinica:* Dictionnaire bibliographi-
       que des ouvrages relatifs à la péninsule indochinoise. Publica-
       tions de l'Ecole Française d'Extrême-Orient, Volumes XV-XVIII
       (Paris: Imprimerie Nationale / Ernest Leroux, 1912-1915).

3688. *Professor* Gordon H. LUCE, "Rice and Religion: a study of Old Mon-
       Khmer evolution and culture," in *JSS*, LIII (1965).2: 139-52 + 7
       folding charts and 2 tables.

LOCAL VALUES AND COGNITIVE PATTERNS

3689. Michel FERLUS, "La cosmogonie selon la tradition khmou," in *Langues
       et Techniques, Nature et Société*. Editée par Jacqueline M.C. Thomas
       [et] Lucien Bernot. Publié avec le concours du CNRS. Tome I: Ap-
       proche linguistique (Paris: Klincksieck, [c 1972]), 277-82.

3690. *Mme* de VAUX-PHALIPAU, "Les Nagas et les Dragons dans le folklore
       asiatique," in *L'Ethnographie*, Nouvelle Série, 42 (1944): 72-86.

ASIAN STUDIES AT HAWAII

(No. 1) *Bibliography of English Language Sources on Human
         Ecology, Eastern Malaysia and Brunei.* Compiled by
         Conrad P. Cotter with the assistance of Shiro
         Saito. September 1965. Two parts.

No. 2   *Economic Factors in Southeast Asian Social Change.*
         May 1968. Robert Van Niel, editor.

No. 3   *East Asian Occasional Papers (1).* Harry J. Lamley,
         editor. May 1969.

No. 4   *East Asian Occasional Papers (2).* Harry J. Lamley,
         editor. July 1970.

No. 5   *A Survey of Historical Source Materials in Java and
         Manila.* Robert Van Niel. February 1971.

No. 6   *Educational Theory in the People's Republic of
         China: The Report of Ch'ien Chung-Jui.* Translation
         by John N. Hawkins. May 1971.

No. 7   *Hai Jui Dismissed from Office.* Wu Han. Translation
         by C.C. Huang. June 1972.

No. 8   *Aspects of Vietnamese History.* Edited by Walter F.
         Vella. January 1973.